Principles of Computational Biology

Principles of
Computational Biology

Constance Stanton

www.callistoreference.com

Callisto Reference,
118-35 Queens Blvd., Suite 400,
Forest Hills, NY 11375, USA

Visit us on the World Wide Web at:
www.callistoreference.com

ISBN: 978-1-64116-558-7 (Hardback)

Cataloging-in-Publication Data

Principles of computational biology / Constance Stanton.
    p. cm.
Includes bibliographical references and index.
ISBN 978-1-64116-558-7
1. Computational biology. 2. Bioinformatics.
3. Botany--Data processing. I. Stanton, Constance.
QH324.2 .P75 2022
570.285--dc23

TABLE OF CONTENTS

This book is a culmination of my many years of practice in this field. I attribute the success of this book to my support group. I would like to thank my parents who have showered me with unconditional love and support and my peers and professors for their constant guidance.

Computational biology is concerned with the application and development of theoretical and data-analytical methods, computational simulation techniques and mathematical modeling to study behavioral, ecological, biological and social systems. Computational biology is a broad field which uses principles and concepts from computer science, genetics, genomics, biochemistry, biophysics, applied mathematics, molecular biology and statistics. Computational anatomy, computational biomodeling, cancer computational biology, computational pharmacology and computational neuroscience are a few of the important sub-fields of computational biology. It can be used to assist the creation of accurate models of the human brain and in modeling biological systems. Computational biology also helps in sequencing the human genome. This book provides comprehensive insights into the field of computational biology. The various sub-fields within this discipline along with technological progress that have future implications are glanced at in it. This book is appropriate for those seeking detailed information in this area.

The details of chapters are provided below for a progressive learning:

Chapter – What is Computational Biology?

The development and application of data-analytical and theoretical methods, computational simulation techniques and mathematical modeling in order to study the ecological, biological, and social systems is referred to as computational biology. This is an introductory chapter which will briefly introduce all the significant aspects of computational biology.

Chapter – Subfields of Computational Biology

Computational biology is a vast field that can be categorized into computational anatomy, computational genomics, computational neuroscience and computational biomodeling. This chapter has been carefully written to provide an easy understanding of these sub-fields of computational biology.

Chapter – Bioinformatics

The interdisciplinary field which is concerned with the development of methods and software tools used for analyzing and interpreting biological data is known as bioin-formatics. It branches into structural bioinformatics which focuses on the analysis and prediction of the three-dimensional structure of proteins, RNA and DNA. The topics elaborated in this chapter will help in gaining a better perspective about bioinformatics.

Chapter – Phylogenetics Analysis

The application of computational algorithms, methods, and programs to phylogenetic analysis is referred to as computational phylogenetics. The fundamental concepts that come under this field are phylogenetic tree, tree alignment, treefinder, etc. This chapter closely examines these key concepts related to computational phylogenetics to provide an extensive understanding of the subject.

Chapter – Systems Biology: An Integrated Study

The mathematical and computational models that are used for the analysis of complex biological systems are referred to as systems biology. Biochemical systems theory, bio-logical network inference, BioPAX, cellular model and cancer systems biology are a few concepts that come under systems biology. The topics elaborated in this chapter will help in gaining a better perspective about systems biology.

Constance Stanton

What is Computational Biology? 1

The development and application of data-analytical and theoretical methods, computational simulation techniques and mathematical modeling in order to study the ecological, biological, and social systems is referred to as computational biology. This is an introductory chapter which will briefly introduce all the significant aspects of computational biology.

Computational biology is a branch of biology involving the application of computers and computer science to the understanding and modelling of the structures and processes of life. It entails the use of computational methods (e.g., algorithms) for the representation and simulation of biological systems, as well as for the interpretation of experimental data, often on a very large scale.

The beginnings of computational biology essentially date to the origins of computer science. British mathematician and logician Alan Turing often called the father of computing, used early computers to implement a model of biological morphogenesis (the development of pattern and form in living organisms) in the early 1950s, shortly before his death. At about the same time, a computer called MANIAC, built at the Los Alamos National Laboratory in New Mexico for weapons research, was applied to such purposes as modelling hypothesized genetic codes. Pioneering computers had been used even earlier in the 1950s for numeric calculations in population genetics, but the first instances of authentic computational modelling in biology were the work by Turing and by the group at Los Alamos.

By the 1960s, computers had been applied to deal with much more varied sets of analyses, namely those examining protein structure. These developments marked the rise of computational biology as a field and they originated from studies centred on protein crystallography, in which scientists found computers indispensable for carrying out laborious Fourier analyses to determine the three-dimensional structure of proteins.

Starting in the 1950s, taxonomists began to incorporate computers into their work, using the machines to assist in the classification of organisms by clustering them based on similarities of sets of traits. Such taxonomies have been useful particularly for phylogenetics (the study of evolutionary relationships). In the 1960s, when existing techniques were extended to the level of DNA sequences and amino acid sequences of proteins and combined with a burgeoning knowledge of cellular processes and protein structures, a whole new set of computational methods was developed in support of molecular phylogenetics. These computational methods entailed the creation of increasingly sophisticated techniques for the comparison of strings of symbols that benefited from the formal study of algorithms and the study of dynamic programming in particular. Indeed, efficient algorithms always have been of primary concern in computational biology, given the scale of data available, and biology has in turn provided examples that have driven much advanced research in computer science. Examples include graph algorithms for genome mapping (the process of locating fragments of DNA on chromosomes) and for certain types of DNA and peptide sequencing methods, clustering algorithms for gene expression analysis and phylogenetic reconstruction, and pattern matching for various sequence search problems.

Beginning in the 1980s, computational biology drew on further developments in computer science, including a number of aspects of artificial intelligence (AI). Among these were knowledge representation, which contributed to the development of ontologies (the representation of concepts and their relationships) that codify biological knowledge in "computer-readable" form, and natural-language processing, which provided a technological means for mining information from text in the scientific literature. Perhaps most significantly, the subfield of machine learning found wide use in biology, from modelling sequences for purposes of pattern recognition to the analysis of high-dimensional (complex) data from large-scale gene-expression studies.

Applications of Computational Biology

Initially, computational biology focused on the study of the sequence and structure of biological molecules, often in an evolutionary context. Beginning in the 1990s, however, it extended increasingly to the analysis of function. Functional prediction involves assessing the sequence and structural similarity between an unknown and a known protein and analyzing the proteins' interactions with other molecules. Such analyses may be extensive, and thus computational biology has become closely aligned with systems biology, which attempts to analyze the workings of large interacting networks of biological components, especially biological pathways.

Biochemical, regulatory, and genetic pathways are highly branched and interleaved, as well as dynamic, calling for sophisticated computational tools for their modelling and analysis. Moreover, modern technology platforms for the rapid, automated (high-throughput) generation of biological data have allowed for an extension from traditional hypothesis-driven experimentation to data-driven analysis, by which computational experiments can be performed on genome-wide databases of unprecedented scale. As a result, many aspects of the study of biology have become unthinkable without the power of computers and the methodologies of computer science.

Distinctions Among Related Fields

How best to distinguish computational biology from the related field of bioinformatics, and to a lesser extent from the fields of mathematical and theoretical biology, has long been a matter of debate. The terms bioinformatics and computational biology are often used interchangeably, even by experts, and many feel that the distinctions are not useful. Both fields fundamentally are computational approaches to biology. However, whereas bioinformatics tends to refer to data management and analysis using tools that are aids to biological experimentation and to the interpretation of laboratory results, computational biology typically is thought of as a branch of biology, in the same sense that computational physics is a branch of physics. In particular, computational biology is a branch of biology that is uniquely enabled by computation. In other words, its formation was not defined by a need to deal with scale; rather, it was defined by virtue of the techniques that computer science brought to the formulation and solving of challenging problems, to the representation and examination of domain knowledge, and ultimately to the generation and testing of scientific hypotheses.

Computational biology is more easily distinguished from mathematical biology, though there are overlaps. The older discipline of mathematical biology was concerned primarily with applications of numerical analysis, especially differential equations, to topics such as population dynamics and enzyme kinetics. It later expanded to include the application of advanced mathematical approaches in genetics, evolution, and spatial modelling. Such mathematical analyses inevitably benefited from computers, especially in instances involving systems of differential equations that required simulation for their solution. The use of automated calculation does not in itself qualify such activities as computational biology. However, mathematical modelling of biological systems does overlap with computational biology, particularly where simulation for purposes of prediction or hypothesis generation is a key element of the model. A useful distinction in this regard is that between numerical analysis and discrete mathematics; the latter, which is concerned with symbolic rather than numeric manipulations, is considered foundational to computer science, and in general its applications to biology may be considered aspects of computational biology.

Computational biology can also be distinguished from theoretical biology (which itself is sometimes grouped with mathematical biology), though again there are significant relationships. Theoretical biology often focuses on mathematical abstractions and speculative interpretations of biological systems that may or may not be of practical use in analysis or amenable to computational implementation. Computational biology generally is associated with practical application, and indeed journals and annual meetings in the field often actively encourage the presentation of biological analyses using real data along with theory. On the other hand, important contributions to computational biology have arisen through aspects of theoretical biology derived from information theory, network theory, and nonlinear dynamical systems (among other areas). As an example, advances in the mathematical study of complex networks have increased scientists' understanding of naturally occurring interactions among genes and gene products, providing insight into how characteristic network architectures may have arisen in the course of evolution and why they tend to be robust in the face of perturbations such as mutations.

Challenges in Computational Biology

While all science proceeds mostly by evolution and not revolution, the imagination of the public at large, not to mention that of the scientific community itself, is often caught by a few widely publicized events that are seen as landmarks in the evolution of a subject. In the area of biology, the mapping of the human genome, announced simultaneously by two different groups in February 2001, was one such event. The mapping of the human genome is a perfect illustration of both the increased speed and decreased cost of biological experimentation. Originally conceived as a ten-year program, the mapping of the human genome was in fact completed in just over two years. This was followed in quick succession by the mapping of the mouse genome and the mosquito genome. These advanced led the public at large to fantasize about designer drugs, personalized medicine, and other such futuristic scenarios.

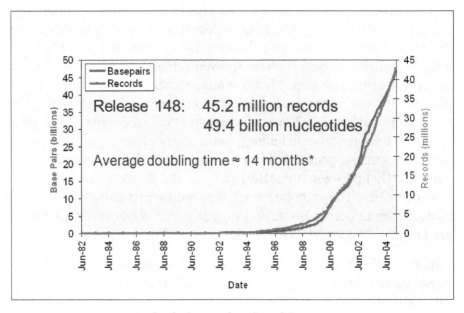

Genbank size as a function of time.

However, the genome of any organism is just "raw data". In order to be useful, this data needs to be turned into "information". This is the aim of a discipline known earlier as "computational biology," and more recently as "bioinformatics".

The mathematical and computational problems associated with biology have attracted the attention of some top-notch mathematicians for several decades now. Perhaps one of the best examples is S. Karlin, whose book "Stochastic Processes" published in the 1960's already refers to the relationships between Markov chains and biological problems. Karlin is also a co-inventor of a widely used probabilistic method known as BLAST (Basic Linear Alignment Search Technique) for aligning two strings defined over a common alphabet. Thus, while there has been a long-standing tradition of studying biological problems using mathematical approaches, the recent excitement about advances in experimental biology has substantially enhanced the interest of the mathematical and computer community in the subject of computational biology. It is by now realized that, unless some significant advances are made in this area, much of the promise of biology will remain unrealized. This is exemplified by the fact that, whereas earlier biology was considered to be almost exclusively an experimental science, nowadays it is thought of as both an experimental as well as an information-based science.

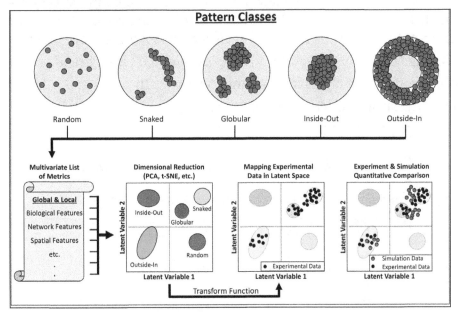

Protein database size as a function of time.

String Alignment

Problem Formulation and Current Status From the preceding discussion, it is clear that a central problem in computational biology is string alignment. This problem arises in at least two contexts: (i) Matching an RNA fragment with another that is known to be a gene, to determine the similarity if any. (ii) Matching an amino acid sequence with another whose 3-D structure is known to determine the similarity if any. While biologically the two problems are quite distinct, from a computational standpoint both problems are quite similar. A general problem formulation that encompasses both can be stated as follows:

Suppose A is the alphabet of interest (either the four-symbol nucleotide alphabet or the twenty-symbol amino acid alphabet), and suppose u, v are two strings over A. Suppose to be specific that u is shorter than v. It is straight-forward to determine whether u is a perfect substring of v. For this purpose, one can set up a finite state machine with input that stops if and only if it encounters the input stream u. Text editors do this kind of thing routinely. A slight variation of this approach can be used to determine the longest substring of u that is a perfect substring of v.

However, in biological applications it will rarely happen that one string will be a perfect substring of another. Rather, it is often necessary to introduce "gaps" in one string or the other in order to get a good match. Moreover, one often has to settle for "matches" of one symbol in one string against a different (i.e., not identical) symbol in the other string. The figure below shows an example of gapped alignment. In this figure, by introducing gaps in the two sequences to be aligned, we can ensure that there are only two genuine mismatches, namely of two C symbols in u against G symbols in v. To formulate this problem precisely, define a "scoring" matrix $w : A \times A \to \Re$. Thus if a symbol $x \in A$ in one string is aligned against a symbol $y \in A$ in the other string, the weight assigned to the match is $w(x, y)$. Typically $w(x, x)$ is large and positive, while $w(x, y)$ is negative (and either large or small) if $x \neq y$. In case a gap is introduced in one or the other string, one can assign a gap penalty γ.

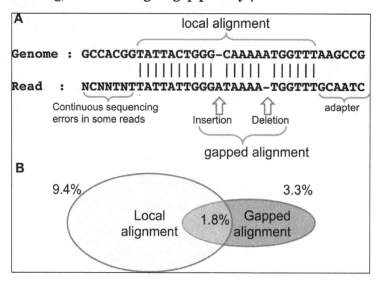

Example of gapped alignment.

Note that it makes no sense to place gaps in both strings, one against the other. Thus if a gap is introduced in one string and then extended, the weight can be twice the gap penalty; alternatively, the penalty for introducing a gap can be larger than the incremental penalty for extending a gap. In any case, the sum of all the weights from one end to the other is the total score of the alignment. The optimal gapped alignment is one that minimizes the total weight. Note that, in any gapped alignment (optimal or otherwise) the total length of the gapped strings is always equal, whether or not the original strings are of equal length.

The optimal gapped alignment problem can be readily solved using dynamic programming, for the simple reason that an optimal gapped alignment satisfies the principle of optimality, that is: a sub-alignment of an optimal alignment is itself optimal. Let $B(i, j)$ denote the optimal score when string u is matched up to the i-th location against string v up to the j-th location. At this stage, there are only three possibilities, namely: (*i*) Rhe $(i + 1)$-st symbol of u can be matched against the $(j + 1$-st symbol of v. (ii) A gap can be introduced in string u. (iii) A gap can be introduced in string v. We choose the best of these three options. Thus the optimal score satisfies the recursion

$$B(i+1, j+1) = \max \begin{cases} B(i, j) + w(i + 1, j + 1) \\ B(i + 1, j) - \gamma \\ B(i, j + 1) - \gamma \end{cases}$$

Thus, starting with $B(0, 0) = 0$, one can fill up the entire $n \times m$ matrix of optimal values $B(i, j)$, where n and m are respectively the lengths of the strings u and v. Then one can trace the optimal path from the corner $(0, 0)$ to the corner $n \times m$.

A dynamic programming solution to the optimal gapped alignment problem is called the Needleman Wunsch algorithm. It is clear that the computational complexity of this algorithm is O(nm). By a slight modification, the dynamic programming approach can also be used to find an optimal gapped alignment between substrings of u and v. This is called the SmithWaterman algorithm.

Challenges

There are several interesting problems in string alignment that deserve the attention of the research community.

- The dynamic programming approach gives an exact optimal alignment. On the other hand, in biology it is really not necessary to find an optimal alignment. It is necessary only to determine whether or not two strings can be made to resemble each other after the insertion of gaps in both strings. For this purpose, a near optimal alignment would be good enough. Thus it would be worthwhile to find some alignment algorithms that are suboptimal but in a guaranteed sense, i.e., that the score so generated is guaranteed to be within some percentage of the optimal value.

- As of now, the use of parallel computation for string alignment is in its infancy. the insistence on exact optimality is at the heart of the difficulty. If one is willing to settle for guaranteed near-optimality, then some kind of parallelization might be possible.

- In the same way, it appears that the use of randomized algorithms for alignment should be explored.

- The computational complexity of the dynamic programming is quadratic in the length of the strings being aligned (if their lengths are comparable). However, if one wishes to align more than two strings, then the complexity is exponential in terms of the number of strings. Thus adding one more string doubles the complexity. Since in biology, it is quite common to attempt the alignment of dozens of strings, it is essential to find efficient algorithms for this purpose.

Neural Networks for Protein Structure Prediction

Problem Formulation and Current Status

The problem of predicting protein structure starting directly with the primary structure (or amino acid sequence) is called ab initio prediction. It is one of the most challenging problems in computational biology for this purpose. Because it is too difficult to predict the tertiary structure directly, most researchers tackle the problem of predicting the secondary structure.

Recall that the secondary structure of a protein is a kind of simplified description, in which there are only three types of description, namely: (i) α helix, (ii) β strand (or sheet) and (iii) δ coil. Thus the objective is to map the primary structure (which is a string over the twenty symbol alphabet of amino acids) into the secondary structure (which is a string over the three symbol alphabet $\{\alpha, \beta, \delta\}$. One of the complicating factors is that there is no obvious relationship between the length of the primary structure and the length of the secondary structure, other than the rather obvious one that if a protein has a very long primary structure sequence, it will in general also have a very long secondary structure sequence. However, the relationship is by no means monotonic.

Figure shows a feedforward neural network used to predict secondary structure. Out of the roughly 100,000 known proteins, the 3-D structure of about 19,000 proteins has been determined. This 3-D structure is then simplified into a secondary structure description. Some sample of these 19,000 proteins are chosen to "train" a neural network. The input to the neural network consists of a string of amino acid symbols, while the output consists of three real numbers between 0 and 1, corresponding to the likelihood that locally the structure is as an α helix, a β strand, or a coil. Clearly some kind of further processing (e.g., majority polling) is required to process these three numbers and come up with an actual prediction. The input to the neural network consists of anywhere between 13 to 15 amino acid symbols. For example, suppose the window is 13 acids long. Then for a protein with known structure, the substring of the amino acid sequence consisting of symbols 1 through 13 are fed into the network, while the "desired" output is taken as (1, 0, 0) if the local structure is an α helix, and so on. Then the substring consisting of symbols 2 through 14 are fed into the network, then symbols 3 through 15, and so on.

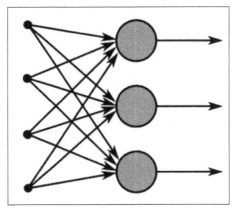

Feedforward neural network for protein structure prediction.

Clearly, if a protein has N amino acids and the window has size r, then it generates $N - r$ + 1 training inputs. With these training inputs (or some subset thereof), the weights of the network are adjusted to match the desired outputs to the training inputs as closely as possible. Given that there are about 19,000 proteins with known structure, if we take 500 to be the average length of a protein sequence, then the number of training inputs is roughly 10^7. However, in practice far fewer inputs are used, as there is a great deal of similarity between many of these training inputs.

One of the major drawbacks of the network architecture used in figure is that it is position-independent. Thus the same string of 13 to 15 symbols produces exactly the same prediction, whether the string occurs near the beginning of the primary structure, the middle, or near the end. However, from a biological standpoint, this is not realistic. To address this issue, some researchers use a recurrent neural network of the type shown in figure.

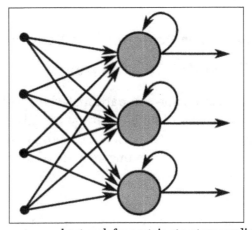

Recurrent neural network for protein structure prediction.

Challenges

One of the characteristic features of the neural network approach is the large number of weights used. This problem persists whether one uses feedforward networks or recurrent networks. In this approach, one is attempting to represent a symbolic map (from the 20-symbol alphabet of amino acids to {α, β, δ} using numerical methods. As a first approximation, it can be said that there is no natural similarity or difference between any of the twenty amino acids.2 Hence if we simply number the 20 acids as 1 through 20, then we run the risk of artificially imposing a metric structure (i.e., acid 1 is "closer" to acid 2 than to acid 8) where none exists in reality. To avoid this difficulty, the research community adopts a "unary representation" of the proteins, whereby

$$\text{Acid No. 1} \leftrightarrow \begin{bmatrix} 1 & 0 & \dots & 0 \end{bmatrix}, \text{Acid No. 2} \leftrightarrow \begin{bmatrix} 0 & 1 & \dots & 0 \end{bmatrix}, \dots \text{Acid No. 20} \leftrightarrow$$

The advantage of this approach is that it is permutation invariant. Because the vectors above are at a pairwise Hamming distance of two, even if we shuffle the labels around, the resulting training inputs and their labels will get shuffled commensurately. The main disadvantage is the huge size of the input vectors. Since each amino acid is represented by a 20-dimensional vector, if the window of the neural network consists of 13 acids, then the input vector has dimension 260. It is easy to see that, even with a relatively modest-sized neural network, the number of adjustable parameters is in the hundreds of thousands if not in the millions. We have seen that, even if every known protein is used as a training input, the total number of training inputs is about 10^7. Clearly it is not reasonable to expect to train a network with 10^6 parameters using 10^7 inputs. One runs into the problem of simply "memorizing" the data, which is a phenomenon well known to the neural network community when the network has too many parameters and too little data. Thus one of the challenges in this area is to come up with an architecture for representing symbolic maps that is permutation invariant, and yet does not use huge-sized input vectors.

Hidden Markov Models for Protein Classification

Problem Formulation and Current Status

In this section we briefly review some standard material on Markov chains. Then the discussion is extended to so-called hidden Markov models (HMM's). Markov models are discussed in many standard texts, such as and so on. Hidden Markov models (HMM's) are used to separate the coding regions of a Prokaryote gene from the non-coding regions, and also to classify a protein into one of a small number of previously classified protein families.

Suppose $X := \{s_1,...,s_n\}$ is a finite set. A stochastic process $\{X_t\} t \geq 0$ assuming values in X is said to be a Markov chain if

$$\Pr\{X_t \mid X_{t-1}, X_{t-2},...\} = \Pr\{X_t \mid X_{t-1}\}$$

The Markov chain is said to be stationary if the above conditional probability is independent of t. The temporal evolution of a Markov chain is captured by an $n \times n$ matrix of transition probabilities, defined as follows:

$$a_{ij} := \Pr\{\mathcal{X}_t = s_j \mid \mathcal{X}_{t-1 = si}\}, \ A = [a_{ij}].$$

Thus a_{ij} is the probability that the Markov chain is in state s_j at the next time instant, given that it is in the state s_i at the current time instant. Obviously the matrix A is column-stochastic; that is,

$$a_{ij} \geq 0 \ \forall i, j, \text{ and } \sum_{j=1}^{n} a_{ij} = 1 \forall i$$

One of the main motivations for studying Markov chains is that in some sense they have a finite description. The Markov property says that the latest measurement $\mathcal{X}_{t-1}$ contains all the information contained in all the past measurements. Thus, once the observer measures $\mathcal{X}_{t-1}$, he can throw all past measurements without any loss of information. Now what happens if a stochastic process is not Markovian? Hidden Markov models (HMM's) are somewhat more general models for stochastic processes that still retain the "finite memory" feature of Markov chains.

Suppose we now have two sets $X := \{s_1, ..., s_n\}$ called the state space, and $Y := \{r_1, ..., r_m\}$ called the output space. Suppose $\{\mathcal{X}_t\}$ is a Markov chain. At each time t, the state $\mathcal{X}_t$ induces a probability distribution on the output space Y, as follows:

$$\Pr\{\mathcal{Y}_t = r_k \mid \mathcal{X}_t = s_j\} = b_{jk}, \ \forall j, k.$$

The stochastic process $\{Y_t\}$ is said to obey a hidden Markov model (HMM). Thus a HMM is described by an $n \times n$ matrix A of state transition probabilities, and another n $\times$ m matrix B of readout probabilities.

Suppose we know the matrices A, B, and we have a single sample path $\{y_t\}_{t \geq 0}^{T}$ of observations of the stochastic process $\{\mathcal{Y}_t\}$. At this point, one can ask three distinct questions.

- Given the matrices A, B, what is the likelihood of this particular sample path? This is called the "likelihood question" and requires us to compute the quantity
  $$\Pr\{\mathcal{Y}_{t=yt} \ \forall t\}, \text{ given } A, B.$$

- What is the most likely sequence of states $\{x_t\}_{t \geq 0}^{T}$? This is called the "decoding question".
- Assuming that we know only the integer n but not the entries in the matrices A and B, can we iteratively compute these entries based on an observation of a sample path $\{y_t\}_{t \geq 0}^{T}$? This is called the "learning question".

Answers to these questions have been known for many years.

At each step along the aligned sequences (which are now viewed as evolving in time, rather than along spatial ordering), one computes the frequency of each of the three events occuring, namely: deletion of an acid, insertion of an acid, or mutation of one acid into another. In each of these states, the 21-dimensional probability vector corresponding to each of the 21 possible outputs is computed as just the actual frequency of occurence of these 21 outputs in the observed sequences. This completes the specification of the HMM for a particular family. Similar constructions are done for each of the small number of protein families.

To classify a new protein sequence, one first does a multiple gapped alignment with all the proteins within each family. This generates a sample path corresponding to each of the three or four HMM's. Then the likelihood of the sample path is computed for each HMM. The HMM for which the sample path likelihood is maximum is declared as the winner, i.e., the new protein sequence is classified as belonging to that particular family.

Challenges

The above method has a number of drawbacks. For one thing, the underlying Markov chain is reducible. This is because there is no path from a state at time i to a state at time $j < i$. In reality, this reducibility comes about because the HMM is actually trying to simulate a nonstationary stochastic process as a stationary process. The second thing to notice about the HMM is that it has a huge number of parameters to be estimated. Suppose the length of the various proteins after gapped alignment is N. Then the total number of states in the Markov chain is $3N+2$. For each of these states (except the start and the end states), we need to compute a 21-dimensional probability vector that the 20 amino acid symbols or the gap symbol is the output. Thus the total number of parameters to be estimated is $21 \times 3N = 63N$. Taking $N = 300$ as a typical value, the total number of parameters to be estimated is 69, 000. At each state, we need to estimate a 21-dimensional probability vector. However, the number of proteins in each family is typically of the order of 100. Clearly it is not meaningful to try and estimate a 21-dimensional probability vector on the basis of 100 sample points.

the reducibility of the Markov chain comes about because one is attempting to model a nonstationary stochastic process using a very large stationary Markov chain. It would be desirable to tackle this problem directly. Also, it would be desirable to determine the number of states of a HMM based on the data, rather than on the basis of ad hoc methods. The paper makes a beginning in this direction, though it does not provide a complete solution.

Subfields of Computational Biology 2

- **Computational Anatomy**
- **Computational Genomics**
- **Computational Neuroscience**
- **Computational Biomodelling**

Computational biology is a vast field that can be categorized into computational anatomy, computational genomics, computational neuroscience and computational biomodeling. This chapter has been carefully written to provide an easy understanding of these sub-fields of computational biology.

Computational Anatomy

Computational anatomy (CA) is the mathematical study of anatomy $I \in \mathscr{I} = I_a \circ \mathscr{G}$, an orbit under groups of diffeomorphisms (i.e., smooth invertible mappings) $g \in \mathscr{G}$ of anatomical exemplars $I_a \in \mathscr{I}$. The observable images are the output of medical imaging devices. There are three components that CA examines: (i) constructions of the anatomical submanifolds, (ii) comparison of the anatomical manifolds via estimation of the underlying diffeomorphisms $g \in \mathscr{G}$ defining the shape or geometry of the anatomical manifolds, and (iii) generation of probability laws of anatomical variation $P(\cdot)$ on the images $\mathscr{I}$ for inference and disease testing within anatomical models.

Group Actions in Computational Anatomy

Group actions are central to Riemannian geometry and defining orbits (control theory). The orbits of computational anatomy consist of anatomical shapes and medical images; the anatomical shapes are submanifolds of differential geometry consisting of points, curves, surfaces and subvolumes,. This generalized the ideas of the more familiar orbits of linear algebra which are linear vector spaces. Medical images are scalar and tensor images from medical imaging. The group actions are used to define models of human shape which accommodate variation. These orbits are deformable templates as originally formulated more abstractly in pattern theory.

The Orbit Model of Computational Anatomy

The central model of human anatomy in computational anatomy is a Groups and group action, a classic formulation from differential geometry. The orbit is called the space of shapes and forms. The space of shapes are denoted $m \in \mathcal{M}$, , with the group $(\mathcal{G}, \circ)$ with law of composition $\circ$; the action of the group on shapes is denoted $g \cdot m$, where the action of the group $g \cdot m \in \mathcal{M}, m \in \mathcal{M}$ is defined to satisfy:

$$(g \circ g') \cdot m = g \cdot (g' \cdot m) \in \mathcal{M}.$$

The orbit M of the template becomes the space of all shapes:

$$\mathcal{M} \doteq \{m = g \cdot m_{\text{temp}}, g \in \mathcal{G}\}.$$

Several Group Actions in Computational Anatomy

The central group in CA defined on volumes in $\mathcal{G} \doteq \text{Diff}$ are the diffeomorphism group which are mappings with 3-components $\circ$, law of composition of functions $(g \circ g') \cdot m = g \cdot (g' \cdot m) \in \mathcal{M}.$, with inverse $\mathcal{M} \doteq \{m = g \cdot m_{\text{temp}}, g \in \mathcal{G}\}$.

Submanifolds: Organs, Subcortical Structures, Charts and Immersions

For sub-manifolds $X \subset \mathbb{R}^3 \in \mathcal{M}$, parametrized by a chart or immersion $m(u), u \in U$, the diffeomorphic action the flow of the position:

$$\phi \cdot m(u) \doteq \phi \circ m(u), u \in U.$$

Scalar Images such as MRI, CT, PET

Most popular are scalar images, $I(x), x \in \mathbb{R}^3$, with action on the right via the inverse:

$$\phi \cdot I(x) = I \circ \phi^{-1}(x), x \in \mathbb{R}^3.$$

Oriented Tangents on Curves, Eigenvectors of Tensor Matrices

Many different imaging modalities are being used with various actions. For images such that $I(x)$ is a three-dimensional vector then:

$$\varphi \cdot I = ((D\varphi)I) \circ \varphi^{-1},$$

$$\varphi \star I = ((D\varphi^T)^{-1}I) \circ \varphi^{-1}.$$

Tensor Matrices

Researchers examined actions for mapping MRI images measured via diffusion tensor imaging and represented via there principle eigenvector. For tensor fields a positively oriented orthonormal basis $I(x) = (I_1(x), I_2(x), I_3(x))$ of $\mathbb{R}^3$, termed frames, vector cross product denoted $I_1 \times I_2$ then:

$$\varphi \cdot I = \left(\frac{D\varphi I_1}{\| D\varphi I_1 \|}, \frac{(D\varphi^T)^{-1} I_3 \times D\varphi I_1}{\| (D\varphi^T)^{-1} I_3 \times D\varphi I_1 \|}, \frac{(D\varphi^T)^{-1} I_3}{\setminus (D\varphi^T)^{-1} I_3 \|} \right) \circ \varphi^{-1},$$

The Fr\'enet frame of three orthonormal vectors, I_1 deforms as a tangent, I_3 deforms like a normal to the plane generated by $I_1 \times I_2$,, and I_3. H is uniquely constrained by the basis being positive and orthonormal. For 3×3 non-negative symmetric matrices, an action would become $\varphi \cdot I = (D\varphi I D\varphi^T) \circ \varphi^{-1}$.

For mapping MRI DTI images (tensors), then eigenvalues are preserved with the diffeomorphism rotating eigenvectors and preserves the eigenvalues. Given eigenelements $\{\lambda_i, e_i, i = 1, 2, 3\}$, then the action becomes:

$$\varphi \cdot I \doteq (\lambda_1 \hat{e}_1 \hat{e}_1^T + \lambda_2 \hat{e}_2 \hat{e}_2^T + \lambda_3 \hat{e}_3 \hat{e}_3^T) \circ \varphi^{-1}$$

$$\hat{e}_1 = \frac{D\varphi e_1}{\| D\varphi e_1 \|}, \hat{e}_2 = \frac{D\varphi e_2 - \langle \hat{e}_1, (D\varphi e_2) \rangle \hat{e}_1}{\| D\varphi e_2 - \langle \hat{e}_1, (D\varphi e_2) \rangle \hat{e}_1 \|}, \hat{e}_3 \doteq \hat{e}_1 \times \hat{e}_2.$$

Orientation Distribution Function and High Angular Resolution HARDI

Orientation distribution function (ODF) characterizes the angular profile of the diffusion probability density function of water molecules and can be reconstructed from High Angular Resolution Diffusion Imaging (HARDI). The ODF is a probability density function defined on a unit sphere, $\mathbb{S}^2$. In the field of information geometry, the space of ODF forms a Riemannian manifold with the Fisher rao metric. For the purpose of LDDMM ODF mapping, the square-root representation is chosen because it is one of the most efficient representations found to date as the various Riemannian operations, such as geodesics, exponential maps, and logarithm maps, are available in closed form.

In the following, denote square-root ODF ($\sqrt{\text{ODF}}$)) as $\psi(\mathbf{s})$, where $\psi(\mathbf{s})$ is non-negative to ensure uniqueness and $\int_{\mathbf{s} \in \mathbb{S}^2} \psi^2(\mathbf{s}) d\mathbf{s} = 1$.

Denote diffeomorphic transformation as ϕ. Group action of diffeomorphism on $\psi(\mathbf{s}), \phi \cdot \psi$, needs to guarantee the non-negativity and $\int_{\mathbf{s} \in \mathbb{S}^2} \phi \cdot \psi^2(\mathbf{s}) d\mathbf{s} = 1$. Based on the derivation in, this group action is defined as:

$$(D\phi) \psi \circ \phi^{-1}(x) = \sqrt{\frac{\det(D_{\phi^{-1}} \phi)^{-1}}{\left\| (D_{\phi^{-1}} \phi)^{-1} \mathbf{s} \right\|^3}} \; \psi \left(\frac{(D_{\phi^{-1}} \phi)^{-1} \mathbf{s}}{\| (D_{\phi^{-1}} \phi)^{-1} \mathbf{s} \|}, \phi^{-1}(x) \right),$$

where $(D\phi)$ is the Jacobian of ϕ.

Diffeomorphometry

Diffeomorphometry is the metric study of imagery, shape and form in the discipline of computational anatomy (CA) in medical imaging. The study of images in computational anatomy rely on high-dimensional diffeomorphism groups $\mathcal{I} \doteq \{\varphi \cdot I \mid \varphi \in Diff_V\}$ which generate orbits of the form $I \in \mathcal{I}$, in which images $\mathcal{M} \doteq \{\varphi \cdot M \mid \varphi \in \mathrm{Diff}_V\}$, can be dense scalar magnetic resonance or computed axial tomography images. For deformable shapes these are the collection of manifolds $(\varphi, I) \mapsto \varphi \cdot I$, points, curves and surfaces. The diffeomorphisms move the images and shapes through the orbit according to $\dot{\phi}_t, t \in [0,1], \phi_t \in \mathrm{Diff}_V$ which are defined as the group actions of computational anatomy.

The orbit of shapes and forms is made into a metric space by inducing a metric on the group of diffeomorphisms. The study of metrics on groups of diffeomorphisms and the study of metrics between manifolds and surfaces has been an area of significant investigation. In Computational anatomy, the diffeomorphometry metric measures how close and far two shapes or images are from each other. Informally, the metric is constructed by defining a flow of diffeomorphisms $\varphi, \psi \in \mathrm{Dif}$ which connect the group elements from one to another, so for then $\phi_0 = \varphi, \phi_1 = \psi$. The metric between two coordinate systems or diffeomorphisms is then the shortest length or geodesic flow connecting them. The metric on the space associated with the geodesics is given by $\rho(\varphi, \psi) = \inf_{\phi:\phi_0 = \varphi, \phi_1 = \psi} \int_0^1 \|\dot{\phi}_t\|_{\phi_t} dt$. The metrics on the orbits $\mathcal{I}, \mathcal{M}$ are inherited from the metric induced on the diffeomorphism group.

The group $\varphi \in \mathrm{Diff}_V$ is thusly made into a smooth Riemannian manifold with Riemannian metric $\|\cdot\|_\varphi$ associated with the tangent spaces at all $\varphi \in \mathrm{Diff}_V$. The Riemannian metric satisfies at every point of the manifold $\phi \in \mathrm{Diff}_V$ there is an inner product inducing the norm on the tangent space $\|\dot{\phi}_t\|_{\phi_t}$ that varies smoothly across Diff_V.

Oftentimes, the familiar Euclidean metric is not directly applicable because the patterns of shapes and images don't form a vector space. In the Riemannian orbit model of Computational anatomy, diffeomorphisms acting on the forms $\varphi \cdot I \in \mathcal{I}, \varphi \in \mathrm{Diff}_V, M \in \mathcal{M}$ don't act linearly. There are many ways to define metrics, and for the sets associated with shapes the Hausdorff metric is another. The method used to induce the Riemannian metric is to induce the metric on the orbit of shapes by defining it in terms of the metric length between diffeomorphic coordinate system transformations of the flows. Measuring the lengths of the geodesic flow between coordinates systems in the orbit of shapes is called diffeomorphometry.

The Diffeomorphisms Group Generated as Lagrangian and Eulerian Flows

The diffeomorphisms in computational anatomy are generated to satisfy the Lagrangian and Eulerian specification of the flow fields, $\varphi_t, t \in [0,1]$, generated via the ordinary differential equation:

$$\frac{d}{dt}\varphi_t = v_t \circ \varphi_t, \varphi_0 = \text{id}; \quad \text{(Lagrangian flow)}$$

with the Eulerian vector fields $v \doteq (v_1, v_2, v_3)$ in $\mathbb{R}^3$ for $v_t = \dot{\varphi}_t \circ \varphi_t^{-1}, t \in [0,1]$. The inverse for the flow is given by and the 3×3 Jacobian matrix for flows in $\mathbb{R}^3$ given as:

$$D\varphi \doteq \left(\frac{\partial \varphi_i}{\partial x_j} \right).$$

To ensure smooth flows of diffeomorphisms with inverse, the vector fields $\mathbb{R}^3$ must be at least 1-time continuously differentiable in space which are modelled as elements of the Hilbert space $(V, \|\cdot\|_V)$ using the Sobolev embedding theorems so that each element $v_i \in H_0^3, i = 1, 2, 3,$ has 3-square-integrable derivatives thusly implies $(V, \|\cdot\|_V)$ embeds smoothly in 1-time continuously differentiable functions. The diffeomorphism group are flows with vector fields absolutely integrable in Sobolev norm:

$$\text{Diff}_V \doteq \{\varphi = \varphi_1 : \dot{\varphi}_t = v_t \circ \varphi_t, \varphi_0 = \text{id}, \int_0^1 \| v_t \|_V \, dt < \infty \}. \quad \text{(Diffeomorphism Group)}$$

The Riemannian Orbit Model

Shapes in Computational Anatomy (CA) are studied via the use of diffeomorphic mapping for establishing correspondences between anatomical coordinate systems. In this setting, 3-dimensional medical images are modelled as diffemorphic transformations of some exemplar, termed the template I_{temp}, resulting in the observed images to be elements of the random orbit model of CA. For images these are defined as:

$$I \in \mathcal{I} \doteq \{I = I_{temp} \circ \varphi, \varphi \in Diff_V\},$$

with for charts representing sub-manifolds denoted as:

$$\{\varphi \cdot {}_{temp} : \varphi \in \text{Diff}_V\}$$

The Riemannian Metric

The orbit of shapes and forms in Computational Anatomy are generated by the group action $\mathcal{I} \doteq \{\varphi \cdot I : \varphi \in \text{Diff}_V\}$, $\mathcal{M} \doteq \{\varphi \cdot M : \varphi \in \text{Diff}_V\}$. These are made into a Riemannian orbits by introducing a metric associated with each point and associated tangent space. For this a metric is defined on the group which induces the metric on the orbit.

Take as the metric for Computational anatomy at each element of the tangent space $\varphi \in \mathrm{Diff}_V$ in the group of diffeomorphisms:

$$\| \dot{\varphi} \|_\varphi \doteq \| \dot{\varphi} \circ \varphi^{-1} \|_V = \| v \|_V,$$

with the vector fields modelled to be in a Hilbert space with the norm in the Hilbert space $(V, \|\cdot\|_V)$. We model V as a reproducing kernel Hilbert space (RKHS) defined by a 1-1, differential operator $A : V \to V^*$, where V^* is the dual-space. In general, $\sigma \doteq Av \in V^*$ is a generalized function or distribution, the linear form associated with the inner-product and norm for generalized functions are interpreted by integration by parts according to for $v, w \in V$,

$$\langle v, w \rangle_V \doteq \int_X Av \cdot w \, dx, \ \| v \|_V^2 \doteq \int_X Av \cdot v \, dx, \ v, w \in V .$$

When $Av \doteq \mu dx,$, a vector density, $\int Av \cdot v \, dx \doteq \int \mu \cdot v \, dx = \sum_{i=1}^{3} \mu_i v_i \, dx$.

The differential operator is selected so that the Green's kernel associated with the inverse is sufficiently smooth so that the vector fields support 1-continuous derivative. The Sobolev embedding theorem arguments were made in demonstrating that 1-continuous derivative is required for smooth flows. The Green's operator generated from the Green's function(scalar case) associated with the differential operator smooths.

For proper choice of A then $(V, \|\cdot\|_V)$ is an RKHS with the operator $K = A^{-1} : V^* \to V$. The Green's kernels associated with the differential operator smooths since for controlling enough derivatives in the square-integral sense the kernel $k(\cdot, \cdot)$ is continuously differentiable in both variables implying:

$$KAv(x)_i \doteq \sum_j \int_{\mathbb{R}^3} k_{ij}(x, y) Av_j(y) dy \in V .$$

The Diffeomorphometry of the Space of Shapes and Forms

The Right-invariant Metric on Diffeomorphisms

The metric on the group of diffeomorphisms is defined by the distance as defined on pairs of elements in the group of diffeomorphisms according to:

$$d_{\mathrm{Diff}_V}(\psi, \varphi) = \inf_{v_t} \left(\int_0^1 \int_X Av_t \cdot v_t \, dx dt : \phi_0 = \psi, \phi_1 = \varphi, \dot{\phi}_t = v_t \circ \phi_t \right)^{1/2} \text{ (metric-diffeomorphisms)}$$

This distance provides a right-invariant metric of diffeomorphometry, invariant to reparameterization of space since for all $\phi \in \mathrm{Diff}_V$,

$$d_{\mathrm{Diff}_V}(\psi, \varphi) = d_{\mathrm{Diff}_V}(\psi \circ \phi, \varphi \circ \phi).$$

The Metric on Shapes and Forms

The distance on images, $d_{\mathcal{I}} : \mathcal{I} \times \mathcal{I} \to \mathbb{R}^+$,

$$d_{\mathcal{I}}(I,J) = \inf_{\phi \in Diff_V : \phi \cdot I = J} d_{Diff_V}(id, \phi) \, ; \; \text{(metric-shapes-forms)}$$

The distance on shapes and forms, $d_{\mathcal{M}} : \mathcal{M} \times \mathcal{M} \to \mathbb{R}^+,,$

$$d_{\mathcal{M}}(M,N) = \inf_{\phi \in Diff_V : \phi \cdot M = N} d_{Diff_V}(id, \phi) . \; \text{(metric-shapes-forms)}$$

The Metric on Geodesic Flows of Landmarks, Surfaces and Volumes within the Orbit

For calculating the metric, the geodesics are a dynamical system, the flow of coordinates $t \mapsto \phi_t \in \mathrm{Diff}_V$ and the control the vector field $t \mapsto v_t \in V$ related via $\dot{\phi}_t = v_t \cdot \phi_t, \phi_0 = \mathrm{id}$

The Hamiltonian view reparameterizes the momentum distribution $Av \in V^*$ in terms of the Hamiltonian momentum, a Lagrange multiplier $p : \dot{\phi} \mapsto (p \,|\, \dot{\phi})$ constraining the Lagrangian velocity $\dot{\phi}_t = v_t \circ \phi_t$ accordingly:

$$H(\phi_t, p_t, v_t) = \int_X p_t \cdot (v_t \circ \phi_t) dx - \frac{1}{2} \int_X Av_t \cdot v_t \, dx.$$

The Pontryagin maximum principle gives the Hamiltonian $H(\phi_t, p_t) \doteq \max_v H(\phi_t, p_t, v)$.
The optimizing vector field $v_t \doteq \mathrm{argmax}_v H(\phi_t, p_t, v)$ with dynamics:

$$\dot{\phi}_t = \frac{\partial H(\phi_t, p_t)}{\partial p}, \dot{p}_t = -\frac{\partial H(\phi_t, p_t)}{\partial \phi}$$

Along the geodesic the Hamiltonian is constant: $H(\phi_t, p_t) = H(id, p_0) = \frac{1}{2} \int_X p_0 \cdot v_0 \, dx$.

The metric distance between coordinate systems connected via the geodesic determined by the induced distance between identity and group element:

$$d_{\mathrm{Diff}_V}(\mathrm{id}, \varphi) = \| v_0 \|_V = \sqrt{2H(\mathrm{id}, p_0)}$$

Landmark or Pointset Geodesics

For landmarks, $x_i, i = 1, \ldots, n$, the Hamiltonian momentum:

$$p(i), i = 1, \ldots, n$$

with Hamiltonian dynamics taking the form:

$$H(\phi_t, p_t) = \frac{1}{2} \sum_j \sum_i p_t(i) \cdot K(\phi_t(x_i), \phi_t(x_j)) p_t(j)$$

with

$$\begin{cases} v_t = \sum_i K(\cdot, \phi_t(x_i)) p_t(i), \\ \dot{p}_t(i) = -(Dv_t)^T_{|\phi_t(x_i)} p_t(i), i = 1, 2, \ldots, n \end{cases}$$

The metric between landmarks $d^2 = \sum_i p_0(i) \cdot \sum_j K(x_i, x_j) p_0(j)$.

The dynamics associated with these geodesics is shown in the accompanying figure.

Surface Geodesics

For surfaces, the Hamiltonian momentum is defined across the surface has Hamiltonian:

$$H(\phi_t, p_t) = \frac{1}{2} \int_U \int_U pt(u) \cdot K(\phi_t(m(u)), \phi_t(m(v))) p_t(v) du\, dv$$

and dynamics:

$$\begin{cases} v_t = \int_U K(\cdot, \phi_t(m(u))) p_t(u) du, \\ \dot{p}_t(u) = -(Dv_t)^T_{|\phi_t(m(u))} p_t(u), u \in U \end{cases}$$

The metric between surface coordinates:

$$d^2 = (p_0 \mid v_0) = \int_U p_0(u) \cdot \int_U K(m(u), m(u')) p_0(u') du\, du'$$

Volume Geodesics

For volumes the Hamiltonian:

$$H(\phi_t, p_t) = \frac{1}{2} \int_{\mathbb{R}^3} \int_{\mathbb{R}^3} p_t(x) \cdot K(\phi_t(x), \phi_t(y)) p_t(y) dx\, dy$$

with dynamics:

$$\begin{cases} v_t = \int_X K(\cdot, \phi_t(x)) p_t(x) dx, \\ \dot{p}_t(x) = -(Dv_t)^T_{|\phi_t(x)} p_t(x), x \in \mathbb{R}^3 \end{cases}$$

The metric between volumes $d^2 = (p_0 \mid v_0) = \int_{\mathbb{R}^3} p_0(x) \cdot \int_{\mathbb{R}^3} K.(x, y) p_0(y) dy\, dx$.

Riemannian Metric and Lie Bracket in Computational Anatomy

Computational anatomy (CA) is the study of shape and form in medical imaging. The study of deformable shapes in computational anatomy rely on high-dimensional diffeomorphism groups $\varphi \in \text{Diff}_V$ which generate orbits of the form $\mathcal{M} \doteq \{\varphi \cdot m \mid \varphi \in \text{Diff}_V\}$. In CA, this orbit is in general considered a smooth Riemannian manifold since at every point of the manifold $m \in \mathcal{M}$ there is an inner product inducing the norm $\|\cdot\|_m$ on the tangent space that varies smoothly from point to point in the manifold of shapes $m \in \mathcal{M}$.. This is generated by viewing the group of diffeomorphisms $\varphi \in \text{Diff}_V$ as a Riemannian manifold with $\|\cdot\|_\varphi$, associated with the tangent space at $\varphi \in \text{Diff}_V$. This induces the norm and metric on the orbit $m \in \mathcal{M}$ under the action from the group of diffeomorphisms.

The Diffeomorphisms Group Generated as Lagrangian and Eulerian Flows

The diffeomorphisms in computational anatomy are generated to satisfy the Lagrangian and Eulerian specification of the flow fields, $\varphi_t, t \in [0,1]$, , generated via the ordinary differential equation:

$$\frac{d}{dt}\varphi_t = v_t \circ \varphi_t, \varphi_0 = \text{id}; \quad \text{(Lagrangian Flow)}$$

with the Eulerian vector fields $v \doteq (v_1, v_2, v_3)$ in $\mathbb{R}^3$ for $v_t = \dot{\varphi}_t \circ \varphi_t^{-1}, t \in [0,1]$, , with the inverse for the flow given by:

$$\frac{d}{dt}\varphi_t^{-1} = -(D\varphi_t^{-1})v_t, \varphi_0^{-1} = \text{id}, \quad \text{(Eulerianflow)}$$

and the 3×3 Jacobian matrix for flows in $\mathbb{R}^3$ given as $D\varphi \doteq \left(\dfrac{\partial \varphi_i}{\partial x_j}\right)$.

To ensure smooth flows of diffeomorphisms with inverse, the vector fields $\mathbb{R}^3$ must be at least 1-time continuously differentiable in space which are modelled as elements of the Hilbert space $(V, \|\cdot\|_V)$ using the Sobolev embedding theorems so that each element $v_i \in H_0^3, i = 1,2,3$, has 3-square-integrable derivatives thusly implies $(V, \|\cdot\|_V)$ embeds smoothly in 1-time continuously differentiable functions. The diffeomorphism group are flows with vector fields absolutely integrable in Sobolev norm:

$$\text{Diff}_V \doteq \{\varphi = \varphi_1 : \dot{\varphi}_t = v_t \circ \varphi_t, \varphi_0 = \text{id}, \int_0^1 \|v_t\|_V dt < \infty\}. \text{ (Diffeomorphism Group)}$$

The Riemannian Orbit Model

Shapes in Computational Anatomy (CA) are studied via the use of diffeomorphic mapping for establishing correspondences between anatomical coordinate systems. In this setting, 3-dimensional medical images are modelled as diffemorphic transformations of some exemplar, termed the template I_{temp}, resulting in the observed images to be elements of the random orbit model of CA. For images these are defined as $I \in \mathcal{I} \doteq \{I = I_{temp} \circ \varphi, \varphi \in \text{Diff}_V\}$, with for charts representing sub-manifolds denoted: as $\mathcal{M} \doteq \{\varphi \cdot m_{temp} : \varphi \in \text{Diff}_V\}$.

The Riemannian Metric

The orbit of shapes and forms in Computational Anatomy are generated by the group action $\mathcal{M} \doteq \{\varphi \cdot m : \varphi \in \mathit{Diff}_V\}$. This is made into a Riemannian orbit by introducing a metric associated with each point and associated tangent space. For this a metric is defined on the group which induces the metric on the orbit. Take as the metric for Computational anatomy at each element of the tangent space $\varphi \in \mathrm{Diff}_V$ in the group of diffeomorphisms:

$$\| \dot{\varphi} \|_{\varphi} \doteq \| \dot{\varphi} \circ \varphi^{-1} \|_V = \| v \|_V ,$$

with the vector fields modelled to be in a Hilbert space with the norm in the Hilbert space $(V, \|\cdot\|_V)$. We model $A : V \to V^*$ as a reproducing kernel Hilbert space (RKHS) defined by a 1-1, differential operator. For $\sigma(v) \doteq Av \in V^*$ a distribution or generalized function, the linear form $(\sigma \mid w) \doteq \int_{\mathbb{R}^3} \sum_i w_i(x) \sigma_i(dx)$ determines the norm:and inner product for $v \in V$ according to:

$$\langle v, w \rangle_V \doteq \int_X Av \cdot w \, dx, \| v \|_V^2 \doteq \int_X Av \cdot v \, dx, v, w \in V .$$

where the integral is calculated by integration by parts for $Av \in V^*$ a generalized function the dual-space. The differential operator is selected so that the Green's kernel associated with the inverse is sufficiently smooth so that the vector fields support 1-continuous derivative.

The Right-invariant Metric on Diffeomorphisms

The metric on the group of diffeomorphisms is defined by the distance as defined on pairs of elements in the group of diffeomorphisms according to:

$$d_{\mathit{Diff}_V}(\psi, \varphi) = \inf_{v_t} (\frac{1}{2} \int_0^1 \int_X Av_t \cdot v_t \, dx \, dt : \varphi_0 = \psi, \varphi_1 = \varphi, \dot{\varphi}_t = v_t \circ \varphi_t)^{1/2} .$$

(Metric-diffeomorphisms)

This distance provides a right-invariant metric of diffeomorphometry, invariant to reparameterization of space since for all $\varphi \in \mathrm{Diff}_V$,

$$d_{\mathrm{Diff}_V}(\psi, \varphi) = d_{\mathrm{Diff}_V}(\psi \circ \varphi, \varphi \circ \varphi).$$

The Lie Bracket in the Group of Diffeomorphisms

The Lie bracket gives the adjustment of the velocity term resulting from a perturbation of the motion in the setting of curved spaces. Using Hamilton's principle of least-action derives the optimizing flows as a critical point for the action integral of the integral of the kinetic energy. The Lie bracket for vector fields in Computational Anatomy was first introduced in Miller, Trouve and Younes. The derivation calculates the perturbation δv on the vector fields $v^\varepsilon = v + \varepsilon \delta v$ in terms of the derivative in time of the group perturbation adjusted by the correction of the Lie bracket of vector fields in this function setting involving the Jacobian matrix, unlike the matrix group case:

$$ad_v : V \mapsto V \text{ given by } ad_v(w) \doteq (Dv)w - (Dw)v, v, w \in V. \qquad \text{(adjoint-Lie-bracket)}$$

Proof: Proving Lie bracket of vector fields take a first order perturbation of the flow at point $\varphi \in Diff_V$.

Lie bracket of vector fields.

The Lie bracket gives the first order variation of the vector field with respect to first order variation of the flow:

$$\delta v_t = \frac{d}{dt} w_t - ad_{v_t}(w_t) = \frac{d}{dt} w_t - ((Dv_t)w_t - (Dw_t)v_t).$$

The Generalized Euler–lagrange Equation for the Metric on Diffeomorphic Flows

The Euler–lagrange equation can be used to calculate geodesic flows through the group which form the basis for the metric. The action integral for the Lagrangian of the kinetic energy for Hamilton's principle becomes:

$$J(\varphi) \doteq \frac{1}{2} \int_0^1 \| \dot{\varphi}_t \|_{\varphi_t}^2 \, dt = \frac{1}{2} \int_0^1 \| \dot{\varphi}_t \circ \varphi_t^{-1} \|_V^2 \, dt = \frac{1}{2} \int_0^1 \int_X A(\dot{\varphi}_t \circ \varphi_t^{-1}) \cdot (\dot{\varphi}_t \circ \varphi_t^{-1}) dx \, dt .$$

$$\text{(Hamilton's Action Integral)}$$

The action integral in terms of the vector field corresponds to integrating the kinetic energy:

$$J(v) \doteq \frac{1}{2} \int_0^1 \| v_t \|_V^2 dt = \frac{1}{2} \int_0^1 \int_X A v_t \cdot v_t \, dx \, dt .$$

The shortest paths geodesic connections in the orbit are defined via Hamilton's Principle of least action requires first order variations of the solutions in the orbits of Computational Anatomy which are based on computing critical points on the metric length or energy of the path. The original derivation of the Euler equation associated with the geodesic flow of diffeomorphisms exploits the was a generalized function equation when $Av \in V^*$ is a distribution, or generalized function, take the first order variation of the action integral using the adjoint operator for the Lie bracket (adjoint-Lie-bracket) gives for all smooth $w \in V$.

$$\frac{d}{d\varepsilon} J(\varphi^\varepsilon)|_{\varepsilon=0} = \int_0^1 \int_X Av_t \cdot \delta v_t \, dx dt = \int_0^1 \int_X Av_t \cdot \left(\frac{d}{dt} w_t - \left((Dv_t)w - (Dw)v_t \right) \right) dx dt.$$

Using the bracket $ad_v : w \in V \mapsto V$ and $ad_v^* : V^* \to V^*$ gives:

$$\frac{d}{dt} Av_t + ad_{v_t}^* (Av_t) = 0 \, , t \in [0,1] \, , \quad \text{(EL-General)}$$

meaning for all smooth:

$$\int_X \left(\frac{d}{dt} Av_t + ad_{v_t}^*(Av_t) \right) \cdot w dx = \int_X \frac{d}{dt} Av_t \cdot w dx + \int_X Av_t \cdot ((Dv_t)w - (Dw)v_t) dx = 0.$$

Equation (Euler-general) is the Euler-equation when diffeomorphic shape momentum is a generalized function. This equation has been called EPDiff, Euler–Poincare equation for diffeomorphisms and has been studied in the context of fluid mechanics for incompressible fluids with L^2 metric.

Riemannian Exponential for Positioning

In the random orbit model of Computational anatomy, the entire flow is reduced to the initial condition which forms the coordinates encoding the diffeomorphism, as well as providing the means of positioning information in the orbit. This was first terms of a geodesic positioning system in Miller, Trouve, and Younes. From the initial condition v_0 then geodesic positioning with respect to the Riemannian metric of Computational anatomy solves for the flow of the Euler–Lagrange equation. Solving the geodesic from the initial condition v_0 is termed the Riemannian-exponential, a mapping $\text{Exp}_{id}(\cdot) : V \to \text{Diff}_V$ at identity to the group.

The Riemannian exponential satisfies $\text{Exp}_{id}(v_0) \doteq \varphi_1$ for initial condition $\dot{\varphi}_0 = v_0, ,$ vector field dynamics $\dot{\varphi}_t = v_t{}^\circ \varphi_t, t \in [0,1]$.

- For classical equation on the diffeomorphic shape momentum as a smooth vector $Av_t = \mu_t dx$ with $\int_X \mu_t \cdot w dx$, $w \in V$ the Euler equation exists in the classical sense as first derived for the density:

$$\frac{d}{dt} \mu_t + (Dv_t)^T \mu_t + (D\mu_t)v_t + (\nabla \cdot v)\mu_t = 0 \, , Av_t = \mu_t dx;$$

- For generalized equation, $Av \in V^*$, then:

$$\frac{d}{dt} Av_t + ad_{v_t}^* (Av_t) = 0 \, , t \in [0,1].$$

It is extended to the entire group, $\varphi = \text{Exp}_\varphi(v_0{}^\circ \varphi) \doteq \text{Exp}_{id}(v_0){}^\circ \varphi.$

The Variation Problem for Matching or Registering Coordinate System Information in Computational Anatomy

Matching information across coordinate systems is central to computational anatomy. Adding a matching term $E : \varphi \in \text{Diff}_V \to R^+$ to the action integral of Equation (Hamilton's action integral) which represents the target endpoint:

$$C(\varphi) \doteq \int_0^1 \int_X Av_t \cdot v_t \, dx \, dt + E(\varphi_1).$$

The endpoint term adds a boundary condition for the Euler–Lagrange equation (EL-General) which gives the Euler equation with boundary term. Taking the variation gives.

- Necessary geodesic condition:

$$\begin{cases} \dfrac{d}{dt} Av_t + (Dv_t)^T Av_t + (DAv_t)v_t + (\nabla \cdot v) Av_t = 0 \,; \\[2ex] Av_1 + \dfrac{\partial E(\varphi)}{\partial \varphi_1} = 0 \end{cases}$$

Proof: The Proof via variation calculus uses the perturbations from above and classic calculus of variation arguments.

Proof via calculus of variations with endpoint energy.

Euler–lagrange Geodesic Endpoint Conditions for Image Matching

The earliest large deformation diffeomorphic metric mapping (LDDMM) algorithms solved matching problems associated with images and registered landmarks. are in a vector spaces. The image matching geodesic equation satisfies the classical dynamical equation with endpoint condition. The necessary conditions for the geodesic for image matching takes the form of the classic Equation (EL-Classic) of Euler–Lagrange with boundary condition:

$$\min_{\varphi:\dot{\varphi}=v_t \circ \varphi_t} C(\varphi) \doteq \frac{1}{2} \int_0^1 \int_X Av_t \cdot v_t \, dx \, dt + \frac{1}{2} \int_X |I \circ \varphi_1^{-1}(x) - J(x)|^2 \, dx$$

- Necessary geodesic condition:

$$\begin{cases} \dfrac{d}{dt} Av_t + (Dv_t)^T Av_t + (DAv_t)v_t + (\nabla \cdot v) Av_t = 0 \,; \\[2ex] Av_1 = (I \circ \varphi_1^{-1} - J)\nabla(I \circ \varphi_1^{-1}) \end{cases}$$

Euler–lagrange Geodesic Endpoint Conditions for Landmark Matching

The registered landmark matching problem satisfies the dynamical equation for generalized functions with endpoint condition:

$$\min_{\varphi:\dot{\varphi}=v_t\circ\varphi_t} C(\varphi) \doteq \frac{1}{2}\int_0^1\int_X Av_t\cdot v_t\, dx\, dt + \frac{1}{2}\sum_i (\varphi_1(x_i)-y_i)\cdot(\varphi_1(x_i)-y_i).$$

- Necessary geodesic conditions:

$$\begin{cases} \dfrac{d}{dt}Av_t + ad^*_{v_t}(Av_t) = 0 \,,\, t\in[0,1], \\[2mm] Av_1 = \displaystyle\sum_{i=1}^n \delta_{\varphi_1(x_i)}(y_i - \varphi_1(x_i)) \end{cases}$$

Proof: The variation $\dfrac{\partial}{\partial\varphi}E(\varphi)$ requires variation of the inverse φ^{-1} generalizes the matrix perturbation of the inverse via $(\varphi+\varepsilon\delta\varphi\circ\varphi)\circ(\varphi^{-1}+\varepsilon\delta\varphi^{-1}\circ\varphi^{-1})=id+o(\varepsilon)$ giving $\delta\varphi^{-1}\ \varphi^{-1} = -(\ \varphi^{-1})\delta\varphi$ giving:

$$\frac{d}{d\varepsilon}\frac{1}{2}\int_X |\, I\circ(\varphi^{-1}+\varepsilon\delta\varphi^{-1}\circ\varphi^{-1})-J\,|^2\, dx\,|_{\varepsilon=0}$$

$$= \int_X (I\circ\varphi^{-1}-J)\nabla I\,|_{\varphi^{-1}} (-D\varphi_1^{-1})\delta\varphi\, dx$$

$$= -\int_X (I\circ\varphi_1^{-1}-J)\nabla(I\circ\varphi_1^{-1})\delta\varphi\, dx.$$

Bayesian Model of Computational Anatomy

Computational anatomy (CA) is a discipline within medical imaging focusing on the study of anatomical shape and form at the visible or gross anatomical scale of morphology. The field is broadly defined and includes foundations in anatomy, applied mathematics and pure mathematics, including medical imaging, neuroscience, physics, probability, and statistics. It focuses on the anatomical structures being imaged, rather than the medical imaging devices. The central focus of the sub-field of computational anatomy within medical imaging is mapping information across anatomical coordinate systems most often dense information measured within a magnetic resonance image (MRI). The introduction of flows into CA, which are akin to the equations of motion used in fluid dynamics, exploit the notion that dense coordinates in image analysis follow the Lagrangian and Eulerian equations of motion. In models based on Lagrangian and Eulerian flows of diffeomorphisms, the constraint is associated with topological properties, such as open sets being preserved, coordinates not crossing implying uniqueness and existence of the inverse mapping, and connected sets remaining connected. The use of diffeomorphic methods grew quickly to dominate the field of mapping methods post Christensen's original paper, with fast and symmetric methods becoming available.

The Main Statistical Model

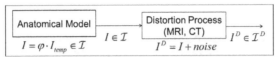

Source-channel model showing the source of images the deformable template
$I \doteq \varphi \cdot I_{\text{temp}} \in \mathcal{I}$ and channel output associated with MRI sensor $I^D \in \mathcal{I}^D$.

The central statistical model of Computational Anatomy in the context of medical imaging has been the source-channel model of Shannon theory; the source is the deformable template of images $I \in \mathcal{I}$, the channel outputs are the imaging sensors with observables $I^D \in \mathcal{I}^D$. The importance of the source-channel model is that the variation in the anatomical configuration are modelled separated from the sensor variations of the Medical imagery. The Bayes theory dictates that the model is characterized by the prior on the source, $\pi_{\mathcal{I}}(\cdot)$ on $I \in \mathcal{I}$,, and the conditional density on the observable

$$p(\cdot | I) \text{ on } I^D \in \mathcal{I}^D$$

conditioned on $I \in \mathcal{I}$.

In deformable template theory, the images are linked to the templates, with the deformations a group which acts on the template; For image action $I(g) \doteq g \cdot I_{\text{temp}}, g \in \mathcal{G}$, then the prior on the group $\pi_{\mathcal{G}}(\cdot)$ induces the prior on images $\pi_{\mathcal{I}}(\cdot)$, written as densities the log-posterior takes the form

$$\log p(I(g) | I^D) \simeq \log p(I^D | I(g)) + \log \pi_{\mathcal{G}}(g).$$

The random orbit model which follows specifies how to generate the group elements and therefore the random spray of objects which form the prior distribution.

The Random Orbit Model of Computational Anatomy

The random orbit model of Computational Anatomy first appeared in modelling the change in coordinates associated with the randomness of the group acting on the templates, which induces the randomness on the source of images in the anatomical orbit of shapes and forms and resulting observations through the medical imaging devices. Such a random orbit model in which randomness on the group induces randomness on the images was examined for the Special Euclidean Group for object recognition in which the group element $g \in \mathcal{G}$ was the special Euclidean group in.

Orbits of brains associated with diffeomorphic group action on templates depicted via smooth flow associated with geodesic flows with random spray associated with random generation of initial tangent space vector field $v_0 \in V$; published in.

For the study of deformable shape in CA, the high-dimensional diffeomorphism groups used in computational anatomy are generated via smooth flows $\varphi_t, t \in [0,1]$ which satisfy the Lagrangian and Eulerian specification of the flow fields satisfying the ordinary differential equation:

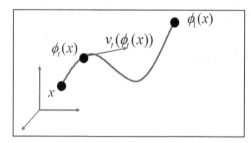

Showing the Lagrangian flow of coordinates $x \in X$ with associated vector fields $v_t, t \in [0,1]$ satisfying ordinary differential equation $\dot{\varphi}_t = v_t(\varphi_t), \varphi_0 = id$.

$$\frac{d}{dt}\varphi_t = v_t \circ \varphi_t, \varphi_0 = id ; \quad \text{(Lagrangian Flow)}$$

with $v \doteq (v_1, v_2, v_3)$ the vector fields on $\mathbb{R}^3$ termed the Eulerian velocity of the particles at position φ of the flow. The vector fields are functions in a function space, modelled as a smooth Hilbert space with the vector fields having 1-continuous derivative. For $v_t = \dot{\varphi}_t \circ \varphi_t^{-1}, t \in [0,1]$, the inverse of the flow is given by:

$$\frac{d}{dt}\varphi_t^{-1} = -(D\varphi_t^{-1})v_t, \varphi_0^{-1} = id, \quad \text{(Eulerianflow)}$$

and the 3×3 Jacobian matrix for flows in $\mathbb{R}^3$ given as $D\varphi \doteq \left(\dfrac{\partial \varphi_i}{\partial x_j} \right)$.

To ensure smooth flows of diffeomorphisms with inverse, the vector fields $\mathbb{R}^3$ must be at least 1-time continuously differentiable in space which are modelled as elements of the Hilbert space $(V, \|\cdot\|_V)$ using the Sobolev embedding theorems so that each element

$v_i \in H_0^3, i = 1, 2, 3$, has 3-square-integrable derivatives. Thus $(V, \|\cdot\|_V)$ embed smoothly in 1-time continuously differentiable functions. The diffeomorphism group are flows with vector fields absolutely integrable in Sobolev norm:

$$Diff_V \doteq \{\varphi = \varphi_1 : \dot{\varphi}_t = v_t \circ \varphi_t, \varphi_0 = id, \int_0^1 \|v_t\|_V \, dt < \infty\}, \quad \text{(Diffeomorphism Group)}$$

where $\|v_t\|_V^2 \doteq \int_X Av_t \cdot v_t dx$ with A a linear operator $A : V \mapsto V^*$ defining the norm of the RKHS. The integral is calculated by integration by parts when Av is a generalized function in the dual space V^*.

Riemannian Exponential

In the random orbit model of computational anatomy, the entire flow is reduced to the initial condition which forms the coordinates encoding the diffeomorphism. From the initial condition v_0 then geodesic positioning with respect to the Riemannian metric of Computational anatomy solves for the flow of the Euler-Lagrange equation. Solving the geodesic from the initial condition v_0 is termed the Riemannian-exponential, a mapping $\text{Exp}_{id}(\cdot) : V \to Diff_V$ at identity to the group.

The Riemannian exponential satisfies $\text{Exp}_{id}(v_0) = \varphi_1$ for initial condition $\dot{\varphi}_0 = v_0, ,$ vector field dynamics $\dot{\varphi}_t = v_t \circ \varphi_t, t \in [0, 1]$,

- for classical equation diffeomorphic shape momentum $\int_X Av_t \cdot w dx, Av \in V$, then

$$\frac{d}{dt} Av_t + (Dv_t)^T Av_t + (DAv_t)v_t + (\nabla \cdot v)Av_t = 0 ;$$

- for generalized equation, then $Av \in V^*, w \in V$,

$$\varphi = \text{Exp}_\varphi(v_0 \circ \varphi) \doteq \text{Exp}_{id}(v_0) \circ \varphi.$$

It is extended to the entire group, $\varphi = \text{Exp}_\varphi(v_0 \circ \varphi) \doteq \text{Exp}_{id}(v_0) \circ \varphi$ Depicted in the accompanying figure is a depiction of the random orbits around each exemplar, $m_0 \in \mathcal{M}$, generated by randomizing the flow by generating the initial tangent space vector field at the identity $v_0 \in V, ,$ and then generating random object $n \doteq \text{Exp}_{id}(v_0) \cdot m_0 \in \mathcal{M}$.

Shown in the figure on the right the cartoon orbit, are a random spray of the sub-cortical manifolds generated by randomizing the vector fields $I \in \mathcal{I}$ supported over the submanifolds. The random orbit model induces the prior on shapes and images conditioned on a particular atlas $I_a \in \mathcal{I}$. For this the generative model generates the mean field I as a random change in coordinates of the template according to $I \doteq \varphi \cdot I_a$, where the diffeomorphic change in coordinates is generated randomly via the geodesic flows.

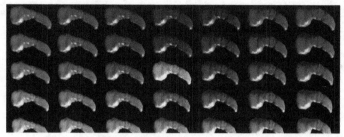

The random spray of synthesized subcortical structures laid out in
the two-dimensional grid representing the variance of the
eigenfunction used for the momentum for synthesis.

MAP Estimation in the Multiple-atlas Orbit Model

The random orbit model induces the prior on shapes and images $I \in \mathcal{I}$ conditioned on a particular atlas $I_a \in \mathcal{I}$. For this the generative model generates the mean field I as a random change in coordinates of the template according to $I \doteq \varphi \cdot I_a$,, where the diffeomorphic change in coordinates is generated randomly via the geodesic flows. The prior on random transformations $\pi_{\mathrm{Diff}}(d\varphi)$ on Diff_V is induced by the flow $\mathrm{Exp}_{id}(v)$, with $v \in V$ constructed as a Gaussian random field prior $\pi_V(dv)$. The density on the random observables at the output of the sensor $I^D \in \mathcal{I}^D$ are given by:

$$p(I^D \mid I_a) = \int_V p(I^D \mid Exp_{id}(v) \cdot I_a) \pi_V(dv).$$

Maximum a posteriori estimation (MAP) estimation is central to modern statistical theory. Parameters of interest $\theta \in \Theta$ take many forms including (i) disease type such as neurodegenerative or neurodevelopmental diseases, (ii) structure type such as cortical or subcortical structures in problems associated with segmentation of images, and (iii) template reconstruction from populations. Given the observed image I^D, MAP estimation maximizes the posterior:

$$\hat{\theta} \doteq \arg\max_{\theta \in \Theta} \log p(\theta \mid I^D).$$

This requires computation of the conditional probabilities $p(\theta \mid I^D) = \dfrac{p(I^D, \theta)}{p(I^D)}$. The multiple atlas orbit model randomizes over the denumerable set of atlases $\{I_a, a \in \mathcal{A}\}$. The model on images in the orbit take the form of a multi-modal mixture distribution:

$$p(I^D, \theta) = \sum_{a \in \mathcal{A}} p(I^D, \theta \mid I_a) \pi_{\mathcal{A}}(a).$$

The conditional Gaussian model has been examined heavily for inexact matching in dense images and for landmark matching.

Dense Emage Matching

Model $I^D(x), x \in X$ as a conditionally Gaussian random field conditioned, mean field, $\varphi_1 \cdot I \doteq I(\varphi_1^{-1}), \varphi_1 \in Diff_V$. For uniform variance the endpoint error terms plays the role of the log-conditional (only a function of the mean field) giving the endpoint term:

$$-\log p(I^D \mid I(g)) \simeq E(\varphi_1) \doteq \frac{1}{2\sigma^2} \| I^D - I \circ \varphi_1^{-1} \|^2 . \text{ (Conditional-Gaussian)}$$

Landmark Matching

Model $Y = \{y_1, y_2, \ldots\}$ as conditionally Gaussian with mean field $\varphi_1(x_i), i = 1, 2, \ldots, \varphi_1 \in Diff_V$, constant noise variance independent of landmarks. The log-conditional (only a function of the mean field) can be viewed as the endpoint term:

$$-\log p(I^D \mid I(g)) \simeq E(\varphi_1) \doteq \frac{1}{2\sigma^2} \sum_i \| y_i - \varphi_1(x_i) \|^2 .$$

MAP Segmentation based on Multiple Atlases

The random orbit model for multiple atlases models the orbit of shapes as the union over multiple anatomical orbits generated from the group action of diffeomorphisms, $\mathcal{I} = \bigcup_{a \in \mathcal{A}} Diff_V \cdot I_a$, with each atlas having a template and predefined segmentation field $(I_a, W_a), a = a_1, a_2, \ldots$ incorporating the parcellation into anatomical structures of the coordinate of the MRI. The pairs are indexed over the voxel lattice $I_a(x_i), W_a(x_i), x_i \in X \subset \mathbb{R}^3$ with an MRI image and a dense labelling of every voxel coordinate. The anatomical labelling of parcellated structures are manual delineations by neuroanatomists.

The Bayes segmentation problem is given measurement I^D with mean field and parcellation (I, W), the anatomical labelling $\theta \doteq W$ must be estimated for the measured MRI image. The mean field of the observable I^D image is modelled as a random deformation from one of the templates I^D, which is also randomly selected, $I \doteq \varphi \cdot I_a$. The optimal diffeomorphism $A = a$ is hidden and acts on the background space of coordinates of the randomly selected template image $\varphi \in \mathcal{G}$. Given a single atlas I_a, the likelihood model for inference is determined by the joint probability $p(I^D, W \mid A = a)$ with multiple atlases, the fusion of the likelihood functions yields the multi-modal mixture model with the prior averaging over models.

The MAP estimator of segmentation W_a is the maximizer $\max_w \log p(W \mid I^D)$ given I^D, which involves the mixture over all atlases.

$$\hat{W} \doteq \arg\max_W \log p(I^D, W) \text{ with } p(I^D, W) = \sum_{a \in \mathcal{A}} p(I^D, W \mid A = a)\pi_A(a).$$

The quantity $p(I^D, W)$ is computed via a fusion of likelihoods from multiple deformable atlases, with $\pi_A(a)$ being the prior probability that the observed image evolves from the specific template image I_a.

The MAP segmentation can be iteratively solved via the expectation-maximization(EM) algorithm

$$W^{new} \doteq \arg\max_W \int \log p(W, I^D, A, \varphi)dp(A, \varphi \mid W^{old}, I^D).$$

MAP Estimation of Volume Templates from Populations and the EM Algorithm

Generating templates empirically from populations is a fundamental operation ubiquitous to the discipline. Several methods based on Bayesian statistics have emerged for submanifolds and dense image volumes. For the dense image volume case, given the observable $I^{D_1}, I^{D_2}, \ldots$ the problem is to estimate the template in the orbit of dense images $I \in \mathcal{I}$. Ma's procedure takes an initial hypertemplate $I_0 \in \mathcal{I}$ as the starting point, and models the template in the orbit under the unknown to be estimated diffeomorphism $I \doteq \phi_0 \cdot I_0$, with the parameters to be estimated the log-coordinates $\theta \doteq v_0$ determining the geodesic mapping of the hyper-template $\mathrm{Exp}_{id}(v_0) \cdot I_0 = I \in \mathcal{I}$.

In the Bayesian random orbit model of computational anatomy the observed MRI images I^{D_i} are modelled as a conditionally Gaussian random field with mean field $\phi_i \cdot I$, with ϕ_i a random unknown transformation of the template. The MAP estimation problem is to estimate the unknown template $I \in \mathcal{I}$ given the observed MRI images.

Ma's procedure for dense imagery takes an initial hypertemplate $I_0 \in \mathcal{I}$ as the starting point, and models the template in the orbit under the unknown to be estimated diffeomorphism. The observables are modelled as conditional random fields, $I \doteq \phi_0 \cdot I_0$. a conditional-Gaussian random field with mean field I^{D_i}. The unknown variable to be estimated explicitly by MAP is the mapping of the hyper-template $\phi_i \cdot I \doteq \phi_i \cdot \phi_0 \cdot I_0 \cdot$, with the other mappings considered as nuisance or hidden variables which are integrated out via the Bayes procedure. This is accomplished using the expectation-maximization (EM) algorithm.

The orbit-model is exploited by associating the unknown to be estimated flows to their log-coordinates $v_i, i = 1, \ldots$ via the Riemannian geodesic log and exponential for computational anatomy the initial vector field in the tangent space at the identity so that

$\mathrm{Exp}_{\mathrm{id}}(v_i) \doteq \phi_i$, with $\mathrm{Exp}_{\mathrm{id}}(v_0)$ the mapping of the hyper-template. The MAP estimation problem becomes:

$$\max_{v_0} p(I^D, \theta = v_0) = \int p(I^D, \theta = v_0 \mid v_1, v_2, \ldots) \pi(v_1, v_2, \ldots) dv$$

The EM algorithm takes as complete data the vector-field coordinates parameterizing the mapping, $v_i, i = 1, \ldots$ and compute iteratively the conditional-expectation:

$$Q(\theta = v_0; \theta^{old} = v_0^{old}) \quad = -E(\log p(I^D, \theta = v_0 \mid v_1, v_2, \ldots) \mid I^D, \theta^{old})$$
$$= - \| (\overline{I}^{old} - I_0 \circ \mathrm{Exp}_{\mathrm{id}}(v_0)^{-1}) \sqrt{\beta^{old}} \|^2 - \| v_0 \|_V^2$$

- Compute new template maximizing Q-function setting:

$$\theta^{new} \doteq v_0^{new} = \arg\max_{\theta = v_0} Q(\theta; \theta^{old} = v_0^{old}) = - \| (\overline{I}^{old} - I_0 \circ \mathrm{Exp}_{\mathrm{id}}(v_0)^{-1}) \sqrt{\beta^{old}} \|^2 - \| v_0 \|_V^2$$

- Compute the mode-approximation for the expectation updating the expected-values for the mode values:

$$v_i^{new} = \arg\max_{v:\phi=v \circ \phi} - \int_0^1 \| v_t \|_V^2 \, dt - \| I^{D_i} - I_0 \circ \mathrm{Exp}_{\mathrm{id}}(v_0^{old})^{-1} \circ \mathrm{Exp}_{\mathrm{id}}(v)^{-1} \|^2 \ . i = 1, 2, \ldots$$

$$\beta^{new}(x) = \sum_{i=1}^n | D\mathrm{Exp}_{\mathrm{id}}(v_i^{new})(x) |, with \, \overline{I}^{new}(x) = \frac{\sum_{i=1}^n I^{D_i} \circ \mathrm{Exp}_{\mathrm{id}}(v_i^{new}) | D\mathrm{Exp}_{\mathrm{id}}(v_i^{new})(x) |}{\beta^{old}(x)}$$

Bayesian Estimation of Templates in Computational Anatomy

Statistical shape analysis and statistical shape theory in computational anatomy (CA) is performed relative to templates, therefore it is a local theory of statistics on shape. Template estimation in computational anatomy from populations of observations is a fundamental operation ubiquitous to the discipline. Several methods for template estimation based on Bayesian probability and statistics in the random orbit model of CA have emerged for submanifolds and dense image volumes.

The Deformable Template Model of Shapes and Forms via Diffeomorphic Group Actions

Linear algebra is one of the central tools of modern engineering. Central to linear algebra is the notion of an orbit of vectors, with the matrices forming groups (matrices with inverses and identity) which act on the vectors. In linear algebra the equations describing the orbit elements the vectors are linear in the vectors being acted upon by the matrices. In computational anatomy the space of all shapes and forms is modeled as an orbit similar to the vectors in linear-algebra, however the groups do not act linear as the matrices do, and the shapes and forms are not additive. In computational anatomy addition is essentially replaced by the law of composition.

The central group acting CA defined on volumes in $\mathbb{R}^3$ are the diffeomorphisms $\mathcal{G} \doteq Diff$ which are mappings with 3-components $\phi(\cdot) = (\phi_1(\cdot), \phi_2(\cdot), \phi_3(\cdot))$, law of composition of functions $\phi \circ \phi'(\cdot) \doteq \phi(\phi'(\cdot))$, with inverse $\phi \circ \phi^{-1}(\cdot) = \phi(\phi^{-1}(\cdot)) = id$.

Groups and group are familiar to the Engineering community with the universal popularization and standardization of linear algebra as a basic model.

A popular group action is on scalar images, $I(x), x \in \mathbb{R}^3$, with action on the right via the inverse:

$$\phi \cdot I(x) = I \circ \phi^{-1}(x), x \in \mathbb{R}^3.$$

For sub-manifolds $X \subset \mathbb{R}^3 \in \mathcal{M}$, , parametrized by a chart or immersion $m(u), u \in U$, , the diffeomorphic action the flow of the position:

$$\phi \cdot m(u) \doteq \phi \circ m(u), u \in U.$$

Several group actions in computational anatomy have been defined.

Geodesic Positioning via the Riemannian Exponential

For the study of deformable shape in CA, a more general diffeomorphism group has been the group of choice, which is the infinite dimensional analogue. The high-dimensional diffeomorphism groups used in computational anatomy are generated via smooth flows $\phi_t, t \in [0,1]$ which satisfy the Lagrangian and Eulerian specification of the flow fields satisfying the ordinary differential equation:

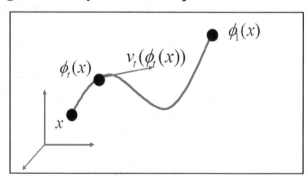

$$\frac{d}{dt}\phi_t = v_t \circ \phi_t, \phi_0 = id \; ; \text{ (Lagrangian Flow)}$$

with $v \doteq (v_1, v_2, v_3)$ the vector fields on $\mathbb{R}^3$ termed the Eulerian velocity of the particles at position ϕ of the flow. The vector fields are functions in a function space, modelled as a smooth Hilbert space with the vector fields having 1-continuous derivative. For $v_t = \dot{\phi}_t \circ \phi_t^{-1}, t \in [0,1]$, with the inverse for the flow given by:

$$\frac{d}{dt}\phi_t^{-1} = -(D\phi_t^{-1})v_t, \phi_0^{-1} = id \; , \quad \text{(Eulerianflow)}$$

and the 3×3 Jacobian matrix for flows in $\mathbb{R}^3$ given as $D\phi \doteq \left(\dfrac{\partial \phi_i}{\partial x_j} \right)$.

Flows were first introduced for large deformations in image matching; $\dot{\phi}_t(x)$ is the instantaneous velocity of particle x at time t. with the vector fields termed the Eulerian velocity of the particles at position of the flow. The modelling approach used in CA enforces a continuous differentiability condition on the vector fields by modelling the space of vector fields $(V, \|\cdot\|_V)$ as a reproducing kernel Hilbert space (RKHS), with the norm defined by a 1-1, differential operator $A : V \to V^*,,$ Green's inverse $K = A^{-1}$. The norm according to $\| v \|_V^2 \doteq \int_X Av \cdot v dx, v \in V,$ where for $\sigma(v) \doteq Av \in V^*$ a generalized function or distribution, then $(\sigma \mid w) \doteq \int_{\mathbb{R}^3} \sum_i w_i(x)\sigma_i(dx)$. Since A is a differential operator, finiteness of the norm-square $\int_X Av \cdot v dx < \infty$ includes derivatives from the differential operator implying smoothness of the vector fields.

To ensure smooth flows of diffeomorphisms with inverse, the vector fields $(V, \|\cdot\|_V)$ must be at least 1-time continuously differentiable in space which are modelled as elements of the Hilbert space $v_i \in H_0^3, i = 1, 2, 3,$ using the Sobolev embedding theorems so that each element has 3-square-integrable derivatives. Thus $(V, \|\cdot\|_V)$ embed smoothly in 1-time continuously differentiable functions. The diffeomorphism group are flows with vector fields absolutely integrable in Sobolev norm:

$$Diff_V \doteq \{\varphi = \phi_1 : \dot{\phi}_t = v_t \circ \phi_t, \phi_0 = id, \int_0^1 \| v_t \|_V \, dt < \infty\}. \text{ (Diffeomorphism Group)}$$

The Bayes Model of Computational Anatomy

The central statistical model of computational anatomy in the context of medical imaging is the source-channel model of Shannon theory; the source is the deformable template of images $I \in \mathcal{I}$, the channel outputs are the imaging sensors with observables $I^D \in \mathcal{I}^D$. The variation in the anatomical configurations are modelled separately from the Medical imaging modalities Computed Axial Tomography machine, MRI machine, PET machine, and others. The Bayes theory models the prior on the source of images $\pi_{\mathcal{I}}(\cdot)$ on $I \in \mathcal{I},,$ and the conditional density on the observable imagery $p(\cdot \mid I)$ on $I^D \in \mathcal{I}^D$, conditioned on $I \in \mathcal{I}..$ For images with diffeomorphism group action $I \doteq \phi \cdot I_{\text{temp}}, \phi \in Diff_V$, then the prior on the group $\pi_{Diff_V}(\cdot)$ induces the prior on images $\pi_{\mathcal{I}}(\cdot),,$ written as densities the log-posterior takes the form:

$$\log p(\phi \cdot I \mid I^D) \simeq \log p(I^D \mid \phi \cdot I) + \log \pi_{\text{Diff}_V}(\phi).$$

Maximum a posteriori estimation (MAP) estimation is central to modern statistical theory. Parameters of interest $\theta \in \Theta$ take many forms including (i) disease type such as neurodegenerative or neurodevelopmental diseases, (ii) structure type such as cortical or subcorical structures in problems associated with segmentation of images, and (iii) template reconstruction from populations. Given the observed image I^D, MAP estimation maximizes the posterior:

$$\hat{\theta} \doteq \arg\max_{\theta \in \Theta} \log p(\theta \mid I^D).$$

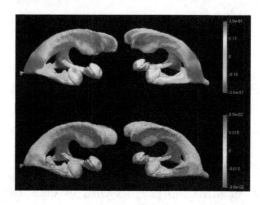

Shown are shape templates of amygdala, hippocampus, and ventricle generated from 754 ADNI samples Topcd surface area group differences between normal ageing and Alzheimer disease (positive represents atrophy in Alzheimer whereas negative suggests expansion). Bottom panel denotes the group differences in the annualized rates of change in the localized surface areas (positive represents faster atrophy rates (or slower expansion rates) in Alzheimer whereas negative suggests faster expansion rates (or slower atrophy rates) in Alzheimer).

This requires computation of the conditional probabilities $p(\theta \mid I^D) = \dfrac{p(I^D, \theta)}{p(I^D)}$. The multiple atlas orbit model randomizes over the denumerable set of atlases $\{I_a, a \in \mathcal{A}\}$. The model on images in the orbit take the form of a multi-modal mixture distribution

$$p(I^D, \theta) = \sum_{a \in \mathcal{A}} p(I^D, \theta \mid I_a) \pi_{\mathcal{A}}(a).$$

Surface Templates for Computational Neuroanatomy and Subcortical Structures

The study of sub-cortical neroanatomy has been the focus of many studies. Since the original publications by Csernansky and colleagues of hippocampal change in Schizophrenia, Alzheimer's disease, and Depression, many neuroanatomical shape statistical studies have now been completed using templates built from all of the subcortical structures for depression, Alzheimer's, Bipolar disorder, ADHD, autism, and Huntington's Disease. Templates were generated using Bayesian template estimation data back to Ma, Younes and Miller.

Shown in the accompanying figure is an example of subcortical structure templates generated from T1-weighted magnetic resonance imagery by Tang et al. for the study of Alzheimer's disease in the ADNI population of subjects.

Surface Estimation in Cardiac Computational Anatomy

Showing population atlases identifying regional differences in radial thickness at end-systolic cardiac phase between patients with hypertrophic cardiomyopathy (left) and hypertensive heart disease (right). Grey mesh shows the common surface template to the population, with the color map representing basilar septal and anterior epicardial wall with larger radial thickness in patients with hypertrophic cardiomyopathy vs. hypertensive heart disease.

Numerous studies have now been done on cardiac hypertrophy and the role of the structural integrates in the functional mechanics of the heart. Siamak Ardekani has been working on populations of Cardiac anatomies reconstructing atlas coordinate systems from populations. The figure on the right shows the computational cardiac anatomy method being used to identify regional differences in radial thickness at end-systolic cardiac phase between patients with hypertrophic cardiomyopathy (left) and hypertensive heart disease (right). Color map that is placed on a common surface template (grey mesh) represents region (basilar septal and the anterior epicardial wall) that has on average significantly larger radial thickness in patients with hypertrophic cardiomyopathy vs. hypertensive heart disease.

MAP Estimation of Volume Templates from Populations and the EM Algorithm

Generating templates empirically from populations is a fundamental operation ubiquitous to the discipline. Several methods based on Bayesian statistics have emerged for submanifolds and dense image volumes. For the dense image volume case, given the observable $I^{D_1}, I^{D_2}, \ldots$ the problem is to estimate the template in the orbit of dense images $I \in \mathcal{I}$. Ma's procedure takes an initial hypertemplate $I_0 \in \mathcal{I}$ as the starting point, and models the template in the orbit under the unknown to be estimated diffeomorphism $I \doteq \phi_0 \cdot I_0$,, with the parameters to be estimated the log-coordinates $\theta \doteq v_0$ determining the geodesic mapping of the hyper-template $\text{Exp}_{\text{id}}(v_0) \cdot I_0 = I \in \mathcal{I}$.

In the Bayesian random orbit model of computational anatomy the observed MRI images I^{D_i} are modelled as a conditionally Gaussian random field with mean field $\phi_i \cdot I$, with ϕ_i a random unknown transformation of the template. The MAP estimation problem is to estimate the unknown template $I \in \mathcal{I}$ given the observed MRI images.

Ma's procedure for dense imagery takes an initial hypertemplate $I_0 \in \mathcal{I}$ as the starting point, and models the template in the orbit under the unknown to be estimated diffeomorphism. The observables are modelled as conditional random fields, $I \doteq \phi_0 \cdot I_0$. a conditional-Gaussian random field with mean field I^{D_i}. The unknown variable to be estimated explicitly by MAP is the mapping of the hyper-template $\phi_i \cdot I \doteq \phi_i \cdot \phi_0 \cdot I_0$., with the other mappings considered as nuisance or hidden variables which are integrated out via the Bayes procedure. This is accomplished using the expectation-maximization (EM) algorithm.

The orbit-model is exploited by associating the unknown to be estimated flows to their log-coordinates $v_i, i = 1, \ldots$ via the Riemannian geodesic log and exponential for computational anatomy the initial vector field in the tangent space at the identity so that $\text{Exp}_{\text{id}}(v_i) \doteq \phi_i$, with $\text{Exp}_{\text{id}}(v_0)$ the mapping of the hyper-template. The MAP estimation problem becomes:

$$\max_{v_0} p(I^D, \theta = v_0) = \int p(I^D, \theta = v_0 \mid v_1, v_2, \ldots) \pi(v_1, v_2, \ldots) dv$$

The EM algorithm takes as complete data the vector-field coordinates parameterizing the mapping, $v_i, i = 1, \ldots$ and compute iteratively the conditional-expectation:

$$Q(\theta = v_0; \theta^{\text{old}} = v_0^{\text{old}}) \quad = -E(\log p(I^D, \theta = v_0 \mid v_1, v_2, \ldots) \mid I^D, \theta^{\text{old}})$$

$$= -\| (\bar{I}^{\text{old}} - I_0 \circ \text{Exp}_{\text{id}}(v_0)^{-1}) \sqrt{\beta^{\text{old}}} \|^2 - \| v_0 \|_V^2$$

- Compute new template maximizing Q-function setting:

$$\theta^{\text{new}} \doteq v_0^{\text{new}} = \arg\max_{\theta = v_0} Q(\theta; \theta^{\text{old}} = v_0^{\text{old}}) = -\| (\bar{I}^{\text{old}} - I_0 \circ \text{Exp}_{\text{id}}(v_0)^{-1}) \sqrt{\beta^{\text{old}}} \|^2 - \| v_0 \|_V^2$$

- Compute the mode-approximation for the expectation updating the expected-values for the mode values:

$$v_i^{\text{new}} = \arg\max_{v: \phi = v \circ \phi} - \int_0^1 \| v_t \|_V^2 \, dt - \| I^{D_i} - I_0 \circ \text{Exp}_{\text{id}}(v_0^{\text{old}})^{-1} \circ \text{Exp}_{\text{id}}(v)^{-1} \|^2 \, .i = 1, 2, \ldots$$

$$\beta^{\text{new}}(x) = \sum_{i=1}^n |D\text{Exp}_{\text{id}}(v_i^{\text{new}})(x)|, \text{with } \bar{I}^{\text{new}}(x) = \frac{\sum_{i=1}^n I^{D_i} \circ \text{Exp}_{\text{id}}(v_i^{\text{new}}) \mid D\text{Exp}_{\text{id}}(v_i^{\text{new}})(x)|}{\beta^{\text{old}}(x)}$$

Large Deformation Diffeomorphic Metric Mapping

Large deformation diffeomorphic metric mapping (LDDMM) is a specific suite of algorithms used for diffeomorphic mapping and manipulating dense imagery based on diffeomorphic metric mapping within the academic discipline of computational anatomy, to be distinguished from its precursor based on diffeomorphic mapping. The distinction between the two is that diffeomorphic metric maps satisfy the property that the length associated with their flow away from the identity induces a metric on the group of diffeomorphisms, which in turn induces a metric on the orbit of shapes and forms within the field of Computational Anatomy. The study of shapes and forms with the metric of diffeomorphic metric mapping is called diffeomorphometry.

A diffeomorphic mapping system is a system designed to map, manipulate, and transfer information which is stored in many types of spatially distributed medical imagery.

Diffeomorphic mapping is the underlying technology for mapping and analyzing information measured in human anatomical coordinate systems which have been measured via Medical imaging. Diffeomorphic mapping is a broad term that actually refers to a number of different algorithms, processes, and methods. It is attached to many operations and has many applications for analysis and visualization. Diffeomorphic mapping can be used to relate various sources of information which are indexed as a function of spatial position as the key index variable. Diffeomorphisms are by their Latin root structure preserving transformations, which are in turn differentiable and therefore smooth, allowing for the calculation of metric based quantities such as arc length and surface areas. Spatial location and extents in human anatomical coordinate systems can be recorded via a variety of Medical imaging modalities, generally termed multi-modal medical imagery, providing either scalar and or vector quantities at each spatial location. Examples are scalar T1 or T2 magnetic resonance imagery, or as 3x3 diffusion tensor matrices diffusion MRI and diffusion-weighted imaging, to scalar densities associated with computed tomography (CT), or functional imagery such as temporal data of functional magnetic resonance imaging and scalar densities such as Positron emission tomography (PET).

Computational anatomy is a subdiscipline within the broader field of neuroinformatics within bioinformatics and medical imaging. The first algorithm for dense image mapping via diffeomorphic metric mapping was Beg's LDDMM for volumes and Joshi's landmark matching for point sets with correspondence, with LDDMM algorithms now available for computing diffeomorphic metric maps between non-corresponding landmarks and landmark matching intrinsic to spherical manifolds, curves, currents and surfaces, tensors, varifolds, and time-series. The term LDDMM was first established as part of the National Institutes of Health supported Biomedical Informatics Research Network.

In a more general sense, diffeomorphic mapping is any solution that registers or builds correspondences between dense coordinate systems in medical imaging by ensuring the solutions are diffeomorphic. There are now many codes organized around diffeomorphic registration including ANTS, DARTEL, DEMONS, StationaryLDDMM, FastLDDMM, as examples of actively used computational codes for constructing correspondences between coordinate systems based on dense images.

The distinction between diffeomorphic metric mapping forming the basis for LDDMM and the earliest methods of diffeomorphic mapping is the introduction of a Hamilton principle of least-action in which large deformations are selected of shortest length corresponding to geodesic flows. This important distinction arises from the original formulation of the Riemannian metric corresponding to the right-invariance. The lengths of these geodesics give the metric in the metric space structure of human anatomy. Non-geodesic formulations of diffeomorphic mapping in general does not correspond to any metric formulation.

Diffeomorphic mapping 3-dimensional information across coordinate systems is central to high-resolution Medical imaging and the area of Neuroinformatics within the newly emerging field of bioinformatics. Diffeomorphic mapping 3-dimensional coordinate systems as measured via high resolution dense imagery has a long history in 3-D beginning with Computed Axial Tomography (CAT scanning). In the 90's there were several solutions for image registration which were associated with linearizations of small deformation and non-linear elasticity.

The central focus of the sub-field of Computational anatomy (CA) within medical imaging is mapping information across anatomical coordinate systems at the 1 millimeter morphome scale. In CA mapping of dense information measured within Magnetic resonance image (MRI) based coordinate systems such as in the brain has been solved via inexact matching of 3D MR images one onto the other. The earliest introduction of the use of diffeomorphic mapping via large deformation flows of diffeomorphisms for transformation of coordinate systems in image analysis and medical imaging was by Christensen, Rabbitt and Miller and Trouve. The introduction of flows, which are akin to the equations of motion used in fluid dynamics, exploit the notion that dense coordinates in image analysis follow the Lagrangian and Eulerian equations of motion. This model becomes more appropriate for cross-sectional studies in which brains and or hearts are not necessarily deformations of one to the other. Methods based on linear or non-linear elasticity energetics which grows with distance from the identity mapping of the template, is not appropriate for cross-sectional study. Rather, in models based on Lagrangian and Eulerian flows of diffeomorphisms, the constraint is associated with topological properties, such as open sets being preserved, coordinates not crossing implying uniqueness and existence of the inverse mapping, and connected sets remaining connected. The use of diffeomorphic methods grew quickly to dominate the field of mapping methods post Christensen's original paper, with fast and symmetric methods becoming available.

Such methods are powerful in that they introduce notions of regularity of the solutions so that they can be differentiated and local inverses can be calculated. The disadvantages of these methods are that there was no associated global least-action property which could score the flows of minimum energy. This contrasts the geodesic motions which are central to the study of Rigid body kinematics and the many problems solved in Physics via Hamilton's principle of least action. In 1998, Dupuis, Grenander and Miller established the conditions for guaranteeing the existence of solutions for dense image matching in the space of flows of diffeomorphisms. These conditions require an action penalizing kinetic energy measured via the Sobolev norm on spatial derivatives of the flow of vector fields.

The large deformation diffeomorphic metric mapping (LDDMM) code that Faisal Beg derived and implemented for his PhD, developed the earliest algorithmic code which solved for flows with fixed points satisfying the necessary conditions for the dense image matching problem subject to least-action. Computational anatomy now has many existing codes organized around diffeomorphic registration including ANTS, DARTEL, DEMONS, LDDMM, StationaryLDDMM as examples of actively used computational codes for constructing correspondences between coordinate systems based on dense images.

These large deformation methods have been extended to landmarks without registration via measure matching, curves, surfaces, dense vector and tensor imagery, and varifolds removing orientation.

The Diffeomorphism Orbit Model in Computational Anatomy

Deformable shape in Computational Anatomy (CA) is studied via the use of diffeomorphic mapping for establishing correspondences between anatomical coordinates in Medical Imaging. In this setting, three dimensional medical images are modelled as a random deformation of some exemplar, termed the template I_{temp}, with the set of observed images element in the random orbit model of CA for images $I \in \mathcal{I} \doteq \{I = I_{temp} \circ \varphi, \varphi \in Diff_V\}$. The template is mapped onto the target by defining a variational problem in which the template is transformed via the diffeomorphism used as a change of coordinate to minimize a squared-error matching condition between the transformed template and the target.

The diffeomorphisms are generated via smooth flows $\phi_t, t \in [0,1]$, , with $\varphi \doteq \phi_1$, , satisfying the Lagrangian and Eulerian specification of the flow field associated with the ordinary differential equation:

$$\frac{d}{dt}\phi_t = v_t \circ \phi_t, \phi_0 = id,$$

with $v_t, t \in [0,1]$ the Eulerian vector fields determining the flow. The vector fields are guaranteed to be 1-time continuously differentiable $v_t \in C^1$ by modelling them to be in a smooth Hilbert $v \in V$ space supporting 1-continuous derivative. The inverse $\phi_t^{-1}, t \in [0,1]$ is defined by the Eulerian vector-field with flow given by:

$$\frac{d}{dt}\phi_t^{-1} = -(D\phi_t^{-1})v_t, \phi_0^{-1} = id . \quad \text{(Inverse Transport Flow)}$$

To ensure smooth flows of diffeomorphisms with inverse, the vector fields with components in $\mathbb{R}^3$ must be at least 1-time continuously differentiable in space which are modelled as elements of the Hilbert space $(V, \|\cdot\|_V)$ using the Sobolev embedding theorems so that each element $v_i \in H_0^3, i = 1,2,3$, has 3-times square-integrable weak-derivatives. Thus $(\ ,\|\cdot\|\ )$ embeds smoothly in 1-time continuously differentiable functions. The diffeomorphism group are flows with vector fields absolutely integrable in Sobolev norm:

$$Diff_V \doteq \{\varphi = \phi_1 : \dot{\phi}_t = v_t \circ \phi_t, \phi_0 = id, \int_0^1 \|v\|_V \ dt < \infty\} . \quad \text{(Diffeomorphism Group)}$$

The Variational Problem of Dense Image Matching and Sparse Landmark Matching

LDDMM Algorithm for Dense Image Matching

In CA the space of vector fields $(V, \|\cdot\|_V)$ are modelled as a reproducing Kernel Hilbert space (RKHS) defined by a 1-1, differential operator $A : V \rightarrow V^*$ determining the norm $\|v\|_V^2 \doteq \int_{R^3} Av \cdot v dx, v \in V$, where the integral is calculated by integration by parts when is a generalized function in the dual space V^*. The differential operator is selected so that the Green's kernel, the inverse of the operator, is continuously differentiable in each variable implying that the vector fields support 1-continuous derivative; for the necessary conditions on the norm for existence of solutions.

The original large deformation diffeomorphic metric mapping (LDDMM) algorithms of Beg, Miller, Trouve, Younes was derived taking variations with respect to the vector field parameterization of the group, since $v = \dot{\phi} \circ \phi^{-1}$ are in a vector spaces. Beg solved the dense image matching minimizing the action integral of kinetic energy of diffeomorphic flow while minimizing endpoint matching term according to:

$$\min_{v:\dot{\phi}=v\circ\phi,\phi_0=id} C(v) \doteq \frac{1}{2}\int_0^1 \int_{R^3} Av_t \cdot v_t dxdt + \frac{1}{2}\int_{R^3} |I \circ \phi_1^{-1} - J|^2 \ dx \quad \text{(Variational Problem Images)}$$

- Beg's Iterative Algorithm for Dense Image Matching.

Update until convergence, $\phi_t^{old} \leftarrow \phi_t^{new}$ each iteration, with $\phi_{t1} \doteq \phi_1 {}^{\circ} \phi_t^{-1}$:

$$\begin{cases} v_t^{new}(\cdot) = v_t^{old}(\cdot) - \epsilon(v_t^{old} - \int_{R^3} K(\cdot, y)(I^{\circ}\phi_t^{-1old}(y) - J^{\circ}\phi_{t1}^{old}(y))\nabla(I^{\circ}\phi_t^{-1old}(y)) \mid D\phi_{t1}^{old}(y) \mid dy), t \in [0,1] \\ \dot{\phi}_t^{new} = v_t^{new}{}^{\circ}\phi_t^{new}, t \in [0,1] \end{cases}$$

(Beg-LDDMM-iteration)

This implies that the fixed point at $t = 0$ satisfies:

$$\mu_0^* = Av_0^* = (I - J^{\circ}\phi_1^*)\nabla I \mid D\phi_1^* \mid,$$

which in turn implies it satisfies the Conservation equation given by the Endpoint Matching Condition according to:

$$Av_t^* = (D\phi_t^{*-1})^T Av_0^*{}^{\circ}\phi_t^{*-1} \mid D\phi_t^{*-1} \mid$$

LDDMM Registered Landmark Matching

The landmark matching problem has a pointwise correspondence defining the endpoint condition with geodesics given by the following minimum:

$$\min_{v\dot{\phi}_t = v_t {}^{\circ}\phi_t} C(v) \doteq \frac{1}{2}\int_0^1 \int_{R^3} Av_t \cdot v_t dxdt + \frac{1}{2}\sum_i (\phi_1(x_i) - y_i)\cdot(\phi_1(x_i) - y_i);$$

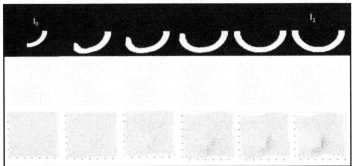

LDMM dense image matching. Top row shows transport of the image under the flow $v_{,}$; middle row shows sequence of vector fields $I^{\circ}\phi_t^{-1}$; t=0,1/5,2/5,3/5,4/5,1; bottom row shows the sequence of grids under ϕ_t.

- Iterative Algorithm for Landmark Matching Joshi originally defined the registered landmark matching probleme,. Update until convergence, $\phi_t^{old} \leftarrow \phi_t^{new}$ each iteration, with : $\phi_{t1} \doteq \phi_1{}^{\circ}\phi_t^{-1}$:

$$\begin{cases} v_t^{new}(\cdot) = v_t^{old}(\cdot) - \grave{o}(v_t^{old} + \sum_i K(\cdot, \phi_t^{old}(x_i))(D\phi_{t1})^{oldT}\mid_{\phi_t^{old}(x_i)} (y_i - \phi_1^{old}(x_i)), t \in [0,1] \\ \dot{\phi}_t^{new} = v_t^{new} {}^{\circ} \phi_t^{new}, t \in [0,1] \end{cases}$$

(Landmark-LDDMM-iteration)

This implies that the fixed point satisfy:

$$Av_0 = -\sum_i (D\phi_1)(x_i)^T (y_i - \phi_1(x_i))\delta_{x_i}$$

with,

$$Av_t = -\sum_i (D\phi_{t1})^T |_{\phi_t(x_i)} (y_i - \phi_1(x_i))\delta_{\phi_t(x_i)}.$$

Variations for LDDMM Dense Image and Landmark Matching

The Calculus of variations was used in beg to derive the iterative algorithm as a solution which when it converges satisfies the necessary maximizer conditions given by the necessary conditions for a first order variation requiring the variation of the endpoint with respect to a first order variation of the vector field. The directional derivative calculates the Gateaux derivative as calculated in Beg's original paper and show.

First Order Variation of the Flow and Vector Field for Dense Image and Landmark Matching.

LDDMM Diffusion Tensor Image Matching

LDDMM matching based on the principal eigen vector of the diffusion tensor matrix takes the image $I(x), x \in \mathbb{R}^3$ as a unit vector field defined by the first eigen vector. The group action becomes:

$$\varphi \cdot I = \begin{cases} \dfrac{D_{\varphi^{-1}}\varphi I \circ \varphi^{-1} \, \| I \circ \varphi^{-1} \|}{\| D_{\varphi^{-1}}\varphi I \circ \varphi^{-1} \|} & I \circ \varphi \neq 0, \\ 0 & \text{otherwise.} \end{cases}$$

where $\|\cdot\|$ that denotes image squared-error norm.

LDDMM matching based on the entire tensor matrix has group action $\varphi \cdot M = (\lambda_1 \hat{e}_1 \hat{e}_1^T + \lambda_2 \hat{e}_2 \hat{e}_2^T + \lambda_3 \hat{e}_3 \hat{e}_3^T) \circ \varphi^{-1}$, transformed eigenvectors:

$$\hat{e}_1 = \frac{D\varphi e_1}{\| D\varphi e_1 \|}, \quad \hat{e}_2 = \frac{D\varphi e_2 - \langle \hat{e}_1, D\varphi e_2 \rangle \hat{e}_1}{\sqrt{\| D\varphi e_2 \|^2 - \langle \hat{e}_1, D\varphi e_2 \rangle^2}}, \quad \hat{e}_3 = \hat{e}_1 \times \hat{e}_2.$$

Dense Matching Problem onto Principle Eigenvector of DTI

The variational problem matching onto vector image $I'(x), x \in \mathbb{R}^3$ with endpoint

$$E(\phi_1) \doteq \alpha \int_{\mathbb{R}^3} \| \phi_1 \cdot I - I' \|^2 dx + \beta \int_{\mathbb{R}^3} (\| .\phi_1 \cdot I \| - \| I' \|)^2 dx)$$

becomes:

$$\min_{v:\dot{\phi}\circ\phi^{-1}} \frac{1}{2}\int_0^1\int_{R^3} Av_t\cdot v_t dxdt + \alpha\int_{\mathbb{R}^3}\|\phi_1\cdot I - I'\|^2 dx + \beta\int_{\mathbb{R}^3}(\|\phi_1\cdot I\| - \|I'\|)^2 dx.$$

Dense Matching Problem Onto DTI MATRIX

The variational problem matching onto: $M'(x), x \in \mathbb{R}^3$ with endpoint:

$$E(\phi_1) \doteq \int_{R^3}\|\phi_1\cdot M(x) - M'(x)\|_F^2\ dx$$

with $\|\cdot\|_F$ Frobenius norm, giving variational problem:

$$\min_{v:v=\dot{\phi}\circ\phi^{-1}} \frac{1}{2}\int_0^1\int_{\mathbb{R}^3} Av_t\cdot v_t dxdt + \alpha\int_{\mathbb{R}^3}\|\phi_1\cdot M(x) - M'(x)\|_F^2\ dx$$

(Dense TensorDTI-Matching).

LDDMM ODF

High angular resolution diffusion imaging (HARDI) addresses the well-known limitation of DTI, that is, DTI can only reveal one dominant fiber orientation at each location. HARDI measures diffusion along n uniformly distributed directions on the sphere and can characterize more complex fiber geometries by reconstructing an orientation distribution function (ODF) that characterizes the angular profile of the diffusion probability density function of water molecules. The ODF is a function defined on a unit sphere, $\mathbb{S}^2$. Denote the square-root ODF ($\sqrt{\text{ODF}}$) as $\psi(\mathbf{s})$, where $\psi(\mathbf{s})$ is non-negative to ensure uniqueness and $\int_{\mathbf{s}\in\mathbb{S}^2}\psi^2(\mathbf{s})d\mathbf{s}=1$. The metric defines the distance between two $\sqrt{\text{ODF}}$ functions $\psi_1,\psi_2 \in \Psi$ as:

$$\rho(\psi_1,\psi_2) = \|\log_{\psi_1}(\psi_2)\|_{\psi_1} = \cos^{-1}\langle\psi_1,\psi_2\rangle = \cos^{-1}(\int_{\mathbf{s}\in\mathbb{S}^2}\psi_1(\mathbf{s})\psi_2(\mathbf{s})d\mathbf{s}),$$

where $\langle\cdot,\cdot\rangle$ is the normal dot product between points in the sphere under the L^2 metric. The template and target are denoted $\psi_{\text{temp}}(\mathbf{s},x), \psi_{\text{targ}}(\mathbf{s},x), \mathbf{s} \in \mathbb{S}^2\ x \in X$ indexed across the unit sphere and the image domain, with the target indexed similarly.

Define the variational problem assuming that two ODF volumes can be generated from one to another via flows of diffeomorphisms $\phi_t,$, which are solutions of ordinary differential equations $\dot{\phi}_t = v_t(\phi_t), t \in [0,1], \phi_0 = id,$. The group action of the diffeomorphism on the template is given according to $\phi_1 \psi(x) \doteq (D\phi_1)\psi \circ \phi_1^{-1}(x), x \in X$, where $(D\phi_1)$ is the Jacobian of the affined transformed ODF and is defined as:

$$(D\phi_1)\psi \circ \phi_1^{-1}(x) = \sqrt{\frac{\det\left(D_{\phi_1^{-1}\phi_1}\right)^{-1}}{\left\|\left(D_{\phi_1^{-1}\phi_1}\right)^{-1}\mathbf{s}\right\|^3}} \quad \psi\left(\frac{\left(D_{\phi_1^{-1}\phi_1}\right)^{-1}\mathbf{s}}{\left\|\left(D_{\phi_1^{-1}\phi_1}\right)^{-1}\mathbf{s}\right\|}, \phi_1^{-1}(x)\right).$$

The LDDMM variational problem is defined as:

$$\min_{v:\dot\phi_t = v_t \circ \phi_t, \phi_0 = id} \int_0^1 \int_{R^3} Av_t \cdot v_t dx\, dt + \lambda \int_{R^3} \left\| \log_{(D\phi_1)\psi_{temp} \circ \phi_1^{-1}(x)} \left(\psi_{targ}(x)\right) \right\|^2_{(D\phi_1)\psi_{temp}\circ\phi_1^{-1}(x)} dx$$

Hamiltonian LDDMM for Dense Image Matching

Beg solved the early LDDMM algorithms by solving the variational matching taking variations with respect to the vector fields. Another solution by Vialard, reparameterizes the optimization problem in terms of the state $q_t \doteq I \circ \phi_t^{-1}, q_0 = I$, for image $I(x), x \in X = R^3$, with the dynamics equation controlling the state by the control given in terms of the advection equation according to $\dot q_t = -\nabla q_t \cdot v_t$. The endpoint matching term $E(q_1) \doteq \frac{1}{2}\| q_1 - J \|^2$ gives the variational problem:

$$\min_{v.\dot q = v \circ q} C(v) \doteq \frac{1}{2}\int_0^1 \int_{\mathbb{R}^3} Av_t \cdot v_t dx dt + \frac{1}{2}\int_{\mathbb{R}^3} | q_1(x) - J(x) |^2 \, dx$$

(Advective-State-Image-Matching)

$$\begin{cases} \text{Hamiltonian Dynamics} & \begin{aligned} \dot q_t &= -\nabla q_t \cdot v_t \\ \dot p_t &= -\text{div}(p_t v_t), \quad t \in [0,1] \\ Av_t &= \mu_t = -p_t \nabla q_t \end{aligned} \\[2em] \text{Endpoint Condition} & p_1 = -\frac{\partial E}{\partial q_1}(q_1) = -(q_1 - J) = -(I \circ \phi_1^{-1} - J) \\[1em] & Av_1 = \mu_1 = (I \circ \phi_1^{-1} - J)\nabla(I \circ \phi_1^{-1}) \; t = 1. \\[1em] \text{Conserved Dynamics} & p_t = -(I \circ \phi_t^{-1} - J \circ \phi_{t1}) | D\phi_{t1} |, \; t \in [0,1]. \end{cases}$$

(Hamiltonian Matching Condition)

Computational Genomics

Computational genomics (often referred to as Computational Genetics) refers to the use of computational and statistical analysis to decipher biology from genome sequences and related data, including both DNA and RNA sequence as well as other "post-genomic" data (i.e., experimental data obtained with technologies that require the genome sequence, such as genomic DNA microarrays). These, in combination with computational and statistical approaches to understanding the function of the genes and statistical association analysis, this field is also often referred to as Computational and Statistical Genetics/genomics. As such, computational genomics may be regarded as a subset of bioinformatics and computational biology, but with a focus on using whole genomes (rather than individual genes) to understand the principles of how the DNA of a species controls its biology at the molecular level and beyond. With the current abundance of massive biological datasets, computational studies have become one of the most important means to biological discovery.

The roots of computational genomics are shared with those of bioinformatics. During the 1960s, Margaret Dayhoff and others at the National Biomedical Research Foundation assembled databases of homologous protein sequences for evolutionary study. Their research developed a phylogenetic tree that determined the evolutionary changes that were required for a particular protein to change into another protein based on the underlying amino acid sequences. This led them to create a scoring matrix that assessed the likelihood of one protein being related to another.

Beginning in the 1980s, databases of genome sequences began to be recorded, but this presented new challenges in the form of searching and comparing the databases of gene information. Unlike text-searching algorithms that are used on websites such as Google or Wikipedia, searching for sections of genetic similarity requires one to find strings that are not simply identical, but similar. This led to the development of the Needleman-Wunsch algorithm, which is a dynamic programming algorithm for comparing sets of amino acid sequences with each other by using scoring matrices derived from the earlier research by Dayhoff. Later, the BLAST algorithm was developed for performing fast, optimized searches of gene sequence databases. BLAST and its derivatives are probably the most widely used algorithms for this purpose.

The emergence of the phrase "computational genomics" coincides with the availability of complete sequenced genomes in the mid-to-late 1990s. The first meeting of the Annual Conference on Computational Genomics was organized by scientists from The Institute for Genomic Research (TIGR) in 1998, providing a forum for this speciality and effectively distinguishing this area of science from the more general fields of Genomics or Computational Biology. The first use of this term in scientific literature, according to MEDLINE abstracts, was just one year earlier in Nucleic Acids Research. The final Computational Genomics conference was held in 2006, featuring a keynote talk by Nobel Laureate Barry Marshall, co-discoverer of the link between Helicobacter pylori and stomach ulcers. As of 2014, the leading conferences in the field include Intelligent Systems for Molecular Biology (ISMB) and Research in Computational Molecular Biology (RECOMB).

The development of computer-assisted mathematics (using products such as Mathematica or Matlab) has helped engineers, mathematicians and computer scientists to start operating in this domain, and a public collection of case studies and demonstrations is growing, ranging from whole genome comparisons to gene expression analysis. This has increased the introduction of different ideas, including concepts from systems and control, information theory, strings analysis and data mining. It is anticipated that computational approaches will become and remain a standard topic for research and teaching, while students fluent in both topics start being formed in the multiple courses created in the past few years.

Contributions of Computational Genomics Research to Biology

Contributions of computational genomics research to biology include:

- Proposing cellular signalling networks.

- Proposing mechanisms of genome evolution.

- Predict precise locations of all human genes using comparative genomics techniques with several mammalian and vertebrate species.

- Predict conserved genomic regions that are related to early embryonic development.

- Discover potential links between repeated sequence motifs and tissue-specific gene expression.

- Measure regions of genomes that have undergone unusually rapid evolution.

Computational Neuroscience

Computational neuroscience is a branch of neuroscience which uses computational approaches, to study the nervous system. Computational approaches include mathematics, statistics, computer simulations, and abstractions which are used across many subareas of neuroscience including development, structure, physiology and cognitive abilities of the nervous system.

The computational neuroscience discipline roughly divides into two subfields. A first, which may be called theoretical neuroscience focuses on principled approaches towards arriving at meaningful models of the nervous system. This field contains many aspects of mathematical neuroscience which employs mathematical techniques to arrive at models. Models in theoretical neuroscience are often aimed at capturing the essential features of the biological system at multiple spatial-temporal scales, from membrane currents, and chemical coupling via network oscillations, columnar and topographic architecture, all the way up to behavior. These computational models frame hypotheses that can often be directly tested by biological or psychological experiments. A second subfield, which is often called neural data science focuses on approaches towards making sense of the progressively larger datasets in neuroscience. This may include the processing of electrophysiological or imaging data, the fitting of models to data, and the comparison of models. These two subfields are highly synergistic and many papers draw from both traditions.

Research in computational neuroscience can be roughly categorized into several lines of inquiry. Most computational neuroscientists collaborate closely with experimentalists in analyzing novel data and synthesizing new models of biological phenomena.

Single-neuron Modelling

Even single neurons have complex biophysical characteristics and can perform computations (e.g.). Hodgkin and Huxley's original model only employed two voltage-sensitive currents (Voltage sensitive ion channels are glycoprotein molecules which extend through the lipid bilayer, allowing ions to traverse under certain conditions through the axolemma), the fast-acting sodium and the inward-rectifying potassium. Though successful in predicting the timing and qualitative features of the action potential, it nevertheless failed to predict a number of important features such as adaptation and shunting. Scientists now believe that there are a wide variety of voltage-sensitive currents, and the implications of the differing dynamics, modulations, and sensitivity of these currents is an important topic of computational neuroscience.

The computational functions of complex dendrites are also under intense investigation. There is a large body of literature regarding how different currents interact with geometric properties of neurons. Some models are also tracking biochemical pathways at very small scales such as spines or synaptic clefts.

There are many software packages, such as GENESIS and NEURON, that allow rapid and systematic *in silico* modelling of realistic neurons. Blue Brain, a project founded by Henry Markram from the École Polytechnique Fédérale de Lausanne, aims to construct a biophysically detailed simulation of a cortical column on the Blue Gene supercomputer.

Modelling the richness of biophysical properties on the single-neuron scale can supply mechanisms that serve as the building blocks for network dynamics. However, detailed neuron descriptions are computationally expensive and this can handicap the pursuit of realistic network investigations, where many neurons need to be simulated. As a result, researchers that study large neural circuits typically represent each neuron and synapse with an artificially simple model, ignoring much of the biological detail. Hence there is a drive to produce simplified neuron models that can retain significant biological fidelity at a low computational overhead. Algorithms have been developed to produce faithful, faster running, simplified surrogate neuron models from computationally expensive, detailed neuron models.

Development, Axonal Patterning and Guidance

Computational neuroscience aims to address a wide array of questions. How do axons and dendrites form during development? How do axons know where to target and how to reach these targets? How do neurons migrate to the proper position in the central and peripheral systems? How do synapses form? We know from molecular biology that distinct parts of the nervous system release distinct chemical cues, from growth factors to hormones that modulate and influence the growth and development of functional connections between neurons.

Theoretical investigations into the formation and patterning of synaptic connection and morphology are still nascent. One hypothesis that has recently garnered some attention is the minimal wiring hypothesis, which postulates that the formation of axons and dendrites effectively minimizes resource allocation while maintaining maximal information storage.

Sensory Processing

Early models on sensory processing understood within a theoretical framework are credited to Horace Barlow. Barlow understood the processing of the early sensory systems to be a form of efficient coding, where the neurons encoded information which minimized the number of spikes. Experimental and computational work have since supported this hypothesis in one form or another.

Current research in sensory processing is divided among a biophysical modelling of different subsystems and a more theoretical modelling of perception. Current models of perception have suggested that the brain performs some form of Bayesian inference and integration of different sensory information in generating our perception of the physical world.

Motor Control

Many models of the way the brain controls movement have been developed. This includes models of processing in the brain such as the cerebellum's role for error correction, skill learning in motor cortex and the basal ganglia, or the control of the vestibulo ocular reflex. This also includes many normative models, such as those of the Bayesian or optimal control flavor which is built on the idea that the brain efficiently solves its problems.

Memory and Synaptic Plasticity

Earlier models of memory are primarily based on the postulates of Hebbian learning. Biologically relevant models such as Hopfield net have been developed to address the properties of associative (also known as "content-addressable") style of memory that occur in biological systems. These attempts are primarily focusing on the formation of medium- and long-term memory, localizing in the hippocampus. Models of working memory, relying on theories of network oscillations and persistent activity, have been built to capture some features of the prefrontal cortex in context-related memory. Additional models look at the close relationship between the basal ganglia and the prefrontal cortex and how that contributes to working memory.

One of the major problems in neurophysiological memory is how it is maintained and changed through multiple time scales. Unstable synapses are easy to train but also prone to stochastic disruption. Stable synapses forget less easily, but they are also harder to consolidate. One recent computational hypothesis involves cascades of plasticity that allow synapses to function at multiple time scales. Stereochemically detailed models of the acetylcholine receptor-based synapse with the Monte Carlo method, working at the time scale of microseconds, have been built. It is likely that computational tools will contribute greatly to our understanding of how synapses function and change in relation to external stimulus in the coming decades.

Behaviors of Networks

Biological neurons are connected to each other in a complex, recurrent fashion. These connections are, unlike most artificial neural networks, sparse and usually specific. It is not known how information is transmitted through such sparsely connected networks, although specific areas of the brain, such as the Visual cortex, are understood in some detail. It is also unknown what the computational functions of these specific connectivity patterns are, if any.

The interactions of neurons in a small network can be often reduced to simple models such as the Ising model. The statistical mechanics of such simple systems are well-characterized theoretically. There has been some recent evidence that suggests that dynamics of arbitrary neuronal networks can be reduced to pairwise interactions. It is not known, however, whether such descriptive dynamics impart any important computational function. With the emergence of two-photon microscopy and calcium imaging, we now have powerful experimental methods with which to test the new theories regarding neuronal networks.

In some cases the complex interactions between *inhibitory* and *excitatory* neurons can be simplified using mean field theory, which gives rise to the population model of neural networks. While many neurotheorists prefer such models with reduced complexity, others argue that uncovering structural-functional relations depends on including as much neuronal and network structure as possible. Models of this type are typically built in large simulation platforms like GENESIS or NEURON. There have been some attempts to provide unified methods that bridge and integrate these levels of complexity.

Visual Attention, Identification and Categorization

Visual attention can be described as a set of mechanisms that limit some processing to a subset of incoming stimuli. Attentional mechanisms shape what we see and what we can act upon. They allow for concurrent selection of some (preferably, relevant) information and inhibition of other information.In order to have a more concrete specification of the mechanism underlying visual attention and the binding of features, a number of computational models have been proposed aiming to explain psychophysical findings. In general, all models postulate the existence of a saliency or priority map for registering the potentially interesting areas of the retinal input, and a gating mechanism for reducing the amount of incoming visual information, so that the limited computational resources of the brain can handle it. Computational neuroscience provides a mathematical framework for studying the mechanisms involved in brain function and allows complete simulation and prediction of neuropsychological syndromes.

Cognition, Discrimination and Learning

Computational modelling of higher cognitive functions has only recently begun. Experimental data comes primarily from single-unit recording in primates. The frontal lobe and parietal lobe function as integrators of information from multiple sensory modalities. There are some tentative ideas regarding how simple mutually inhibitory functional circuits in these areas may carry out biologically relevant computation.

The brain seems to be able to discriminate and adapt particularly well in certain contexts. For instance, human beings seem to have an enormous capacity for memorizing and recognizing faces. One of the key goals of computational neuroscience is to dissect how biological systems carry out these complex computations efficiently and potentially replicate these processes in building intelligent machines.

The brain's large-scale organizational principles are illuminated by many fields, including biology, psychology, and clinical practice. Integrative neuroscience attempts to consolidate these observations through unified descriptive models and databases of behavioral measures and recordings. These are the bases for some quantitative modelling of large-scale brain activity.

The Computational Representational Understanding of Mind (CRUM) is another attempt at modelling human cognition through simulated processes like acquired rule-based systems in decision making and the manipulation of visual representations in decision making.

Consciousness

One of the ultimate goals of psychology/neuroscience is to be able to explain the everyday experience of conscious life. Francis Crick, Giulio Tononi and Christof Koch made some attempts to formulate consistent frameworks for future work in neural correlates of consciousness (NCC), though much of the work in this field remains speculative.

Computational Clinical Neuroscience

Computational Clinical Neuroscience is a field that brings together experts in neuroscience, neurology, psychiatry, decision sciences and computational modelling to quantitatively define and investigate problems in neurological and psychiatric diseases, and to train scientists and clinicians that wish to apply these models to diagnosis and treatment.

Controversies

Some scientists believe that computational neuroscience should focus only on the description of biologically plausible neurons (and neural systems) and their physiology and dynamics, and should therefore not be concerned about disciplines that are perceived to be biologically unrealistic such as connectionism, machine learning, artificial neural networks, artificial intelligence and computational learning theory. Other scientists believe that artificial neural networks are among the best models we currently have for neural function.

Computational Biomodelling

Simulation of biological systems has prospects for the evaluation of normal and diseased conditions, identification of the underlying mechanisms of biological function, and prediction of surgical and rehabilitative outcomes. When experimentation is limited due to feasibility and safety, computer simulations are likely to provide insight. Modelling can be utilized with constricted experimental data to extract biological properties that may not be measured directly, e.g. in vivo deformation characteristics of tissues. Simulations can link organ function to cell response. For example, it may be possible to establish the role of system level mechanical loading to cellular damage. Simulation tools and models can be used to assess health risks when experimentation is not safe. Estimation of electromagnetic radiation due to wireless devices illustrates such an application. Simulation based medicine is possible by utilizing predictive nature of computational modelling. Adequacy of intravascular stent functionality can be evaluated like the performance of other cardiovascular devices, orthopedic implants and many more. Model development procedures and numerical methods are applicable in many health related research areas including but not limited to the exploration of drug delivery systems, cellular signaling and molecular processes.

In computational modelling, one searches for the representation of the essential aspects of the biological system in a usable form. While description of the system with mathematical equations provides this form, a.k.a. model, useful information is extracted by solving these equations numerically, a.k.a. simulation. Successful realization of this process establishes virtual test beds to explore the system.

References

- Alexander, D. C.; Pierpaoli, C.; Basser, P. J.; Gee, J. C. (2001-11-01). "Spatial transformations of diffusion tensor magnetic resonance images". IEEE Transactions on Medical Imaging. 20 (11): 1131–1139. Doi:10.1109/42.963816. ISSN 0278-0062. PMID 11700739

- "Comparing algorithms for diffeomorphic registration: Stationary LDDMM and Diffeomorphic Demons (PDF Download Available)". Researchgate. Retrieved 2017-12-02

- Miller, M. I.; Younes, L. (2001-01-01). "Group Actions, Homeomorphisms, And Matching: A General Framework". International Journal of Computer Vision. 41: 61–84. Citeseerx 10.1.1.37.4816. Doi:10.1023/A:1011161132514

- M. I. Miller and S. Mori and X. Tang and D. Tward and Y. Zhang (2015-02-14). Bayesian Multiple Atlas Deformable Templates. Brain Mapping: An Encyclopedic Reference. Academic Press. ISBN 9780123973160

- Christensen, G.E.; Rabbitt, R.D.; Miller, M.I. (1996-02-01). "Deformable Templates Using Large Deformation Kinematics". IEEE Transactions on Image Processing. 5 (10): 1435–1447. Bibcode:1996ITIP....5.1435C. Doi:10.1109/83.536892. PMID 18290061

Bioinformatics

3

- **Structural Bioinformatics**
- **Sequence Analysis**
- **Sequence Alignment**
- **Alignment-free Sequence Analysis**
- **Gene Expression**
- **Protein Expression**
- **Gene Prediction**
- **BLAST (Biotechnology)**
- **Role of Bioinformatics in Biotechnology**

The interdisciplinary field which is concerned with the development of methods and software tools used for analyzing and interpreting biological data is known as bioinformatics. It branches into structural bioinformatics which focuses on the analysis and prediction of the three-dimensional structure of proteins, RNA and DNA. The topics elaborated in this chapter will help in gaining a better perspective about bioinformatics.

Bioinformatics is a hybrid science that links biological data with techniques for information storage, distribution, and analysis to support multiple areas of scientific research, including biomedicine. Bioinformatics is fed by high-throughput data-generating experiments, including genomic sequence determinations and measurements of gene expression patterns. Database projects curate and annotate the data and then distribute it via the World Wide Web. Mining these data leads to scientific discoveries and to the identification of new clinical applications. In the field of medicine in particular, a number of important applications for bioinformatics have been discovered. For example, it is used to identify correlations between gene sequences and diseases, to predict protein structures from amino acid sequences, to aid in the design of novel drugs, and to tailor treatments to individual patients based on their DNA sequences (pharmacogenomics).

The Data of Bioinformatics

The classic data of bioinformatics include DNA sequences of genes or full genomes; amino acid sequences of proteins; and three-dimensional structures of proteins, nucleic acids and protein–nucleic acid complexes. Additional "-omics" data streams include: transcriptomics, the pattern of RNA synthesis from DNA; proteomics, the distribution of proteins in cells; interactomics, the patterns of protein-protein and protein–nucleic acid interactions; and metabolomics, the nature and traffic patterns of transformations of small molecules by the biochemical pathways active in cells. In each case there is interest in obtaining comprehensive, accurate data for particular cell types and in identifying patterns of variation within the data. For example, data may fluctuate depending on cell type, timing of data collection (during the cell cycle, or diurnal, seasonal, or annual variations), developmental stage, and various external conditions. Metagenomics and metaproteomics extend these measurements to a comprehensive description of the organisms in an environmental sample, such as in a bucket of ocean water or in a soil sample.

Bioinformatics has been driven by the great acceleration in data-generation processes in biology. Genome sequencing methods show perhaps the most dramatic effects. In 1999 the nucleic acid sequence archives contained a total of 3.5 billion nucleotides, slightly more than the length of a single human genome; a decade later they contained more than 283 billion nucleotides, the length of about 95 human genomes. The U.S. National Institutes of Health has challenged researchers by setting a goal to reduce the cost of sequencing a human genome to $1,000; this would make DNA sequencing a more affordable and practical tool for U.S. hospitals and clinics, enabling it to become a standard component of diagnosis.

Storage and Retrieval of Data

In bioinformatics, data banks are used to store and organize data. Many of these entities collect DNA and RNA sequences from scientific papers and genome projects. Many databases are in the hands of international consortia. For example, an advisory committee made up of members of the European Molecular Biology Laboratory Nucleotide Sequence Database (EMBL-Bank) in the United Kingdom, the DNA Data Bank of Japan (DDBJ), and GenBank of the National Center for Biotechnology Information (NCBI) in the United States oversees the International Nucleotide Sequence Database Collaboration (INSDC). To ensure that sequence data are freely available, scientific journals require that new nucleotide sequences be deposited in a publicly accessible database as a condition for publication of an article. (Similar conditions apply to nucleic acid and protein structures.) There also exist genome browsers, databases that bring together all the available genomic and molecular information about a particular species.

The major database of biological macromolecular structure is the worldwide Protein Data Bank (wwPDB), a joint effort of the Research Collaboratory for Structural Bioinformatics (RCSB) in the United States, the Protein Data Bank Europe (PDBe) at the European Bioinformatics Institute in the United Kingdom, and the Protein Data Bank Japan. The homepages of the wwPDB partners contain links to the data files themselves, to expository and tutorial material (including news items), to facilities for deposition of new entries, and to specialized search software for retrieving structures.

Information retrieval from the data archives utilizes standard tools for identification of data items by keyword; for instance, one can type "aardvark myoglobin" into Google and retrieve the molecule's amino acid sequence. Other algorithms search data banks to detect similarities between data items. For example, a standard problem is to probe a sequence database with a gene or protein sequence of interest in order to detect entities with similar sequences.

Goals of Bioinformatics

The development of efficient algorithms for measuring sequence similarity is an important goal of bioinformatics. The Needleman-Wunsch algorithm, which is based on dynamic programming, guarantees finding the optimal alignment of pairs of sequences. This algorithm essentially divides a large problem (the full sequence) into a series of smaller problems (short sequence segments) and uses the solutions of the smaller problems to construct a solution to the large problem. Similarities in sequences are scored in a matrix, and the algorithm allows for the detection of gaps in sequence alignment.

Although the Needleman-Wunsch algorithm is effective, it is too slow for probing a large sequence database. Therefore, much attention has been given to finding fast information-retrieval algorithms that can deal with the vast amounts of data in the archives. An example is the program BLAST (Basic Local Alignment Search Tool). A development of BLAST, known as position-specific iterated- (or PSI-) BLAST, makes use of patterns of conservation in related sequences and combines the high speed of BLAST with very high sensitivity to find related sequences.

Another goal of bioinformatics is the extension of experimental data by predictions. A fundamental goal of computational biology is the prediction of protein structure from an amino acid sequence. The spontaneous folding of proteins shows that this should be possible. Progress in the development of methods to predict protein folding is measured by biennial Critical Assessment of Structure Prediction (CASP) programs, which involve blind tests of structure prediction methods.

Bioinformatics is also used to predict interactions between proteins, given individual structures of the partners. This is known as the "docking problem". Protein-protein complexes show good complementarity in surface shape and polarity and are stabilized largely by weak interactions, such as burial of hydrophobic surface, hydrogen bonds, and van der Waals forces. Computer programs simulate these interactions to predict the optimal spatial relationship between binding partners. A particular challenge, one that could have important therapeutic applications, is to design an antibody that binds with high affinity to a target protein.

Initially, much bioinformatics research has had a relatively narrow focus, concentrating on devising algorithms for analyzing particular types of data, such as gene sequences or protein structures. Now, however, the goals of bioinformatics are integrative and are aimed at figuring out how combinations of different types of data can be used to understand natural phenomena, including organisms and disease.

Structural Bioinformatics

Structural bioinformatics is the branch of bioinformatics which is related to the analysis and prediction of the three-dimensional structure of biological macromolecules such as proteins, RNA, and DNA. It deals with generalizations about macromolecular 3D structure such as comparisons of overall folds and local motifs, principles of molecular folding, evolution, and binding interactions, and structure/function relationships, working both from experimentally solved structures and from computational models. The term *structural* has the same meaning as in structural biology, and structural bioinformatics can be seen as a part of computational structural biology.

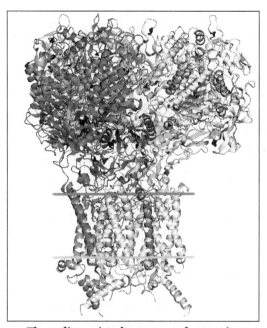

Three-dimensional structure of a protein.

Informatics approaches used in structural bioinformatics are:

- Selection of Target - Potential targets are identified by comparing them with databases of known structures and sequence. The importance of a target can be decided on the basis of published literature. Target can also be selected on the basis of its protein domain. Protein domain are building blocks that can be rearranged to form new proteins. They can be studied in isolation initially.

- Tracking X-ray crystallography trials - X-Ray crystallography can be used to reveal three-dimensional structure of a protein. But, in order to use X-ray for studying protein crystals, pure proteins crystals must be formed, which can take a lot of trials. This leads to a need for tracking the conditions and results of trials. Furthermore, supervised machine learning algorithms can be used on the stored data to identify conditions that might increase the yield of pure crystals.

- Analysis of X-Ray crystallographic data - The diffraction pattern obtained as a result of bombarding X-rays on electrons is Fourier transform of electron density distribution. There is a need for algorithms that can deconvolve Fourier transform with partial information (due to missing phase information, as the detectors can only measure amplitude of diffracted X-rays, and not the phase shifts). Extrapolation technique such as Multiwavelength anomalous dispersion can be used to generate electron density map, which uses the location of selenium atoms as a reference to determine rest of the structure. Standard Ball-and-stick model is generated from the electron density map.

- Analysis of NMR spectroscopy data - Nuclear magnetic resonance spectroscopy experiments produce two (or higher) dimensional data, with each peak corresponding to a chemical group within the sample. Optimization methods are used to convert spectra into three dimensional structures.

- Correlating Structural information with functional information - Structural studies can be used as probe for structural-functional relationship.

Sequence Analysis

In bioinformatics, sequence analysis is the process of subjecting a DNA, RNA or peptide sequence to any of a wide range of analytical methods to understand its features, function, structure, or evolution. Methodologies used include sequence alignment, searches against biological databases, and others. Since the development of methods of high-throughput production of gene and protein sequences, the rate of addition of new sequences to the databases increased exponentially. Such a collection of sequences does not, by itself, increase the scientist's understanding of the biology of organisms. However, comparing these new sequences to those with known functions is a key way of understanding the biology of an organism from which the new sequence comes. Thus, sequence analysis can be used to assign function to genes and proteins by the study of the similarities between the compared sequences. Nowadays, there are many tools and techniques that provide the sequence comparisons (sequence alignment) and analyze the alignment product to understand its biology.

Sequence analysis in molecular biology includes a very wide range of relevant topics:

1. The comparison of sequences in order to find similarity, often to infer if they are related (homologous).

2. Identification of intrinsic features of the sequence such as active sites, post translational modification sites, gene-structures, reading frames, distributions of introns and exons and regulatory elements.

3. Identification of sequence differences and variations such as point mutations and single nucleotide polymorphism (SNP) in order to get the genetic marker.

4. Revealing the evolution and genetic diversity of sequences and organisms.

5. Identification of molecular structure from sequence alone.

In chemistry, sequence analysis comprises techniques used to determine the sequence of a polymer formed of several monomers. In molecular biology and genetics, the same process is called simply "sequencing".

In marketing, sequence analysis is often used in analytical customer relationship management applications, such as NPTB models (Next Product to Buy).

In sociology, sequence methods are increasingly used to study life-course and career trajectories, patterns of organizational and national development, conversation and interaction structure, and the problem of work/family synchrony. This body of research has given rise to the emerging subfield of social sequence analysis.

Since the very first sequences of the insulin protein were characterized by Fred Sanger in 1951, biologists have been trying to use this knowledge to understand the function of molecules. He and his colleague's discoveries contributed to the successful sequencing of the first DNA-based genome. The method used.which is called the "Sanger method" or Sanger sequencing, was a milestone in sequencing long strand molecules such as DNA. This method was eventually used in the human genome project. According to Michael Levitt, sequence analysis was born in the period from 1969-1977. In 1969 the analysis of sequences of transfer RNAs was used to infer residue interactions from correlated changes in the nucleotide sequences, giving rise to a model of the tRNA secondary structure. In 1970, Saul B. Needleman and Christian D. Wunsch published the first computer algorithm for aligning two sequences. Over this time, developments in obtaining nucleotide sequence improved greatly, leading to the publication of the first complete genome of a bacteriophage in 1977. Robert Holley and his team had believed to be the first to sequence an RNA molecule.

Sequence Alignment

```
A5ASC3.1   14 SIKLWPPSQTTRLLLVERMANNLST..PSIFTRK..YGSLSKEEARENAKQIEEVACSTANQ.....HYEKEPDGDGGSAVQLYAKECSKLILEVLK 101
B4F917.1   13 SIKLWPPSESTRIMLVDRMTNNLST..ESIFSRK..YRLLGKQEAHENAKTIEELCFALADE.....HFREEPDGDGSSAVQLYAKETSKMMLEVLK 100
A9S1V2.1   23 VFKLWPPSQGTREAVRQKMALKLSS..ACFESQS..FARIELADAQEHARAIEEVAFGAAQE.....ADSGGDKTGSAVVMVYAKHASKLMLETLR 109
B9GSN7.1   13 SVKLWPPGQSTRLMLVERMTKNFIT..PSFISRK..YGLLSKEEAEEDAKKIEEVAFAAANQ.....HYEKQPDGDGSSAVQLYAKESSRLMLEVLK 100
Q8HO56.1   30 SFSIWPPTQRTRDAVVRRLVDTLGG..DTILCKR..YGAVPAADAEPAARGIEAEAFDAAAA..SGEAAATASVEEGIKALQLYSKEVSRRLLDFVK 120
Q0D4Z3.2   44 SLSIWPPSQRTRDAVVRRLVQTLVA..PSILSQR..YGAVPEAEAGRAAAAVEAEAYAAVTES.SSAAAAPASVEDGIEVLQAYSKEVSRRLLELAK 135
B9MVW8.1   56 SFSIWPPTQRTRDAIISRLIETLST..TSVLSKR..YGTIPKEEASEASRRIEEEAFSGAST.......VASSEKDGLEVLQLYSKEISKRMLETVK 141
Q0IYC5.1   29 SFAVWPPTRRTRDAVVRRLVAVLSGDTTTALRKRYRYGAVPAADAERAARAVEAQAFDAASA....SSSSSSSVEDGIETLQLYSREVSNRLLAFVR 121
A9NW46.1   13 SIKLWPPSESTRLMLVERMTDNLSS..VSFFSRK..YGLLSKEEAAENAKRIEETAFLAAND....HEAKEPNLDDSSVVQFYAREASKLMLEALK 100
Q9C5OO.1   57 SLRIWPPTQKTRDAVLNRLIETLST..ESILSKR..YGTLKSDDATTVAKLIEEEAYGVASN.......AVSSDDDGIKILELYSKEISKRMLESVK 142
Q2HRI7.1   25 NYSIWPPKQRTRDAVKNRLIETLST..PSVLTKR..YGTMSADEASAAAIQIEDEAFSVANA.......SSSTSNDNVTILEVYSKEISKRMIETVK 110
Q9M7N3.1   28 SFKIWPPTQRTREAVVRRLVETLTS..QSVLSKR..YGVIPEEDATSAARIIEEEAFSVASV.ASAASTGGRPEDEWIEVLHIYSQEIXQRVVESAK 119
Q9M7N6.1   25 SFSIWPPTQRTRDAVINRLIESLST..PSILSKR..YGTLPQDEASETARLIEEEAFAAAGS.......TASDADDGIEILQVYSKEISKRMIDTVK 110
Q9LE82.1   14 SVKMWPPSKSTRLMLVERMTKNITT..PSIFSRK..YGLLSVEEAEQDAKRIEDLAFATANK....HFQNEPDGDGTSAVHVYAKESSKLMLDVIK 101
Q9M651.2   13 SIKLWPPSLPTRKALIERITNNFSS..KTIFTEK..YGSLTKDQATENAKRIEDIAFSTANQ.....QFEREPDGDGGSAVQLYAKECSKLILEVLK 100
B9R748.1   48 SLSIWPPTQRTRDAVITRLIETLSS..PSVLSKR..YGTISHDEAESAARRIEDEAFGVANT.......ATSAEDDGLEILQLYSKEISRRMLDTVK 133
```

Example multiple sequence alignment.

There are millions of protein and nucleotide sequences known. These sequences fall into many groups of related sequences known as protein families or gene families. Relationships between these sequences are usually discovered by aligning them together and assigning this alignment a score. There are two main types of sequence alignment. Pair-wise sequence alignment only compares two sequences at a time and multiple sequence alignment compares many sequences. Two important algorithms for aligning pairs of sequences are the Needleman-Wunsch algorithm and the Smith-Waterman algorithm. Popular tools for sequence alignment include:

- Pair-wise alignment - BLAST, Dot plots.

- Multiple alignment - ClustalW, PROBCONS, MUSCLE, MAFFT, and T-Coffee.

A common use for pairwise sequence alignment is to take a sequence of interest and compare it to all known sequences in a database to identify homologous sequences. In general, the matches in the database are ordered to show the most closely related sequences first, followed by sequences with diminishing similarity. These matches are usually reported with a measure of statistical significance such as an Expectation value.

Profile Comparison

In 1987, Michael Gribskov, Andrew McLachlan, and David Eisenberg introduced the method of profile comparison for identifying distant similarities between proteins. Rather than using a single sequence, profile methods use a multiple sequence alignment to encode a profile which contains information about the conservation level of each residue. These profiles can then be used to search collections of sequences to find sequences that are related. Profiles are also known as Position Specific Scoring Matrices (PSSMs). In 1993, a probabilistic interpretation of profiles was introduced by David Haussler and colleagues using hidden Markov models. These models have become known as profile-HMMs.

In recent years, methods have been developed that allow the comparison of profiles directly to each other. These are known as profile-profile comparison methods.

Sequence Assembly

Sequence assembly refers to the reconstruction of a DNA sequence by aligning and merging small DNA fragments. It is an integral part of modern DNA sequencing. Since presently-available DNA sequencing technologies are ill-suited for reading long sequences, large pieces of DNA (such as genomes) are often sequenced by (1) cutting the DNA into small pieces, (2) reading the small fragments, and (3) reconstituting the original DNA by merging the information on various fragments.

Recently, sequencing multiple species at one time is one of the top research objectives. Metagenomics is the study of microbial communities directly obtained from the environment. Different from cultured microorganisms from the lab, the wild sample usually contains dozens, sometimes even thousands of types of microorganisms from their original habitats. Recovering the original genomes can prove to be very challenging.

Gene Prediction

Gene prediction or gene finding refers to the process of identifying the regions of genomic DNA that encode genes. This includes protein-coding genes as well as RNA genes, but may also include the prediction of other functional elements such as regulatory regions. Gene finding is one of the first and most important steps in understanding the genome of a species once it has been sequenced. In general, the prediction of bacterial genes is significantly simpler and more accurate than the prediction of genes in eukaryotic species that usually have complex intron/exon patterns. Identifying genes in long sequences remains a problem, especially when the number of genes is unknown. Hidden markov models can be part of the solution. Machine learning has played a significant role in predicting the sequence of transcription factors. Traditional sequencing analysis focused on the statistical parameters of the nucleotide sequence itself. Another method is to identify homologous sequences based on other known gene sequences. The two methods described here are focused on the sequence. However, the shape feature of these molecules such as DNA and protein have also been studied and proposed to have an equivalent, if not higher, influence on the behaviors of these molecules.

Protein Structure Prediction

The 3D structures of molecules are of great importance to their functions in nature. Since structural prediction of large molecules at an atomic level is a largely intractable problem, some biologists introduced ways to predict 3D structure at a primary sequence level. This includes the biochemical or statistical analysis of amino acid residues in local regions and structural the inference from homologs (or other potentially related proteins) with known 3D structures.

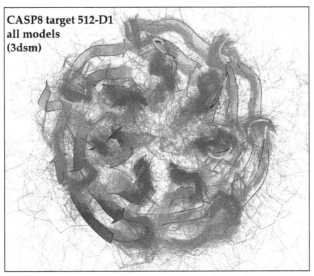

Target protein structure (3dsm, shown in ribbons), with Calpha backbones (in gray) of 354 predicted models for it submitted in the CASP8 structure-prediction experiment.

There have been a large number of diverse approaches to solve the structure prediction problem. In order to determine which methods were most effective, a structure prediction competition was founded called CASP (Critical Assessment of Structure Prediction).

Methodology

The tasks that lie in the space of sequence analysis are often non-trivial to resolve and require the use of relatively complex approaches. Of the many types of methods used in practice, the most popular include:

- DNA patterns.

- Dynamic programming.

- Artificial Neural Network.

- Hidden Markov Model.

- Support Vector Machine.

- Clustering.

- Bayesian Network.

- Regression Analysis.

- Sequence mining.

- Alignment-free sequence analysis.

Identification of Genes in a Genomic DNA Sequence

Prediction of Protein-coding Genes

Archaeal and bacterial genes typically comprise uninterrupted stretches of DNA between a start codon (usually ATG, but in a minority of genes, GTG, TTG, or CTG) and a stop codon (TAA, TGA, or TAG; alternative genetic codes of certain bacteria, such as mycoplasmas, have only two stop codons). Rare exceptions to this rule involve important but rare mechanisms, such as programmed frameshifts. There seem to be no strict limits on the length of the genes. Indeed, the Mgene *rpmJ* encoding the ribosomal protein L36 is only 111 bp long in most bacteria, whereas the gene for *B. subtilis* polyketide synthase PksK is 13,343 bp long. In practice, mRNAs shorter than 30 codons are poorly translated, so protein-coding genes in prokaryotes are usually at least 100 bases in length. In prokaryotic genome-sequencing projects, open reading frames (ORFs) shorter than 100 bases are rarely taken into consideration, which does not seem to result in substantial underprediction. In contrast, in multicellular eukaryotes, most genes are interrupted by introns. The mean length of an exon is ~50 codons, but some exons are much shorter; many of the introns are extremely long, resulting in genes occupying up to several megabases of genomic DNA. This makes prediction of eukaryotic genes a far more complex (and still unsolved) problem than prediction of prokaryotic genes.

Prokaryotes

For most common purposes, a prokaryotic gene can be defined simply as the longest ORF for a given region of DNA. Translation of a DNA sequence in all six reading frames is a straightforward task, Of course, this approach is oversimplified and may result in a certain number of incorrect gene predictions, although the error rate is rather low. Firstly, DNA sequencing errors may result in incorrectly assigned or missed start and stop codons, because of which a gene might be truncated, overextended, or missed altogether. Secondly, on rare occasions, among two overlapping ORFs (on the same or the opposite DNA strand), the shorter one might be the real gene.

The existence of a long "shadow" ORF opposite a protein-coding sequence is more likely than in a random sequence because of the statistical properties of the coding regions. Indeed, consider the simple case where the first base in a codon is a purine and the third base is a pyrimidine (the RNY codon pattern). Obviously, the mirror frame in the complementary strand would follow the same pattern, resulting in a deficit of stop codons. Figure shows the ORFs of at least 100 bp located in a 10-kb fragment of the *E. coli* genome (from 3435250 to 3445250) that encodes potassium transport protein TrkA, mechanosensitive channel MscL, transcriptional regulator YhdM, RNA polymerase alpha subunit RpoA, preprotein translocase subunit SecY, and ribosomal proteins RplQ (L17), RpsD (S4), RpsK (S11), RpsM (S13), RpmJ (L36), RplO (L15), RpmD (L30), RpsE (S5), RplR (L18), RplF (L6), RpsH (S8), RpsN (S14), RplE (L5), and RplX (L24). Although the two ORFs in frame +1 (top line, on the right) are longer (207 aa and 185 aa) than the ORFs in frame −3 (bottom line, 117 aa, 177 aa, 130 aa, and 101 aa), it is the latter that encode real proteins, namely the ribosomal proteins RplR, RplF, RpsH, and RpsN.

Open reading frames of ≥100 bp encoded on a 10-kb fragment of the Escherichia coli K12 genome from 3435250 to 3445250The figure was generated using the program ORF finder at the NCBI web site. The six horizontal lines represent frames 1, 2, 3, −1, −2, and −3, respectively. ORFs in each frame are shown as green boxes.

Because of these complications, it is always desirable to have some additional evidence that a particular ORF actually encodes a protein. Such evidence comes along many different lines and can be obtained using various methods, e.g. the following ones:

- The ORF in question encodes a protein that is similar to previously described ones (search the protein database for homologs of the given sequence).

- The ORF has a typical GC content, codon frequency, or oligonucleotide composition (calculate the codon bias and other statistical features of the sequence, compare to those for known protein-coding genes from the same organism).

- The ORF is preceded by a typical ribosome-binding site (search for a Shine-Dalgarno sequence in front of the predicted coding sequence).

- The ORF is preceded by a typical promoter (if consensus promoter sequences for the given organism are known, check for the presence of a similar upstream region).

The most reliable of these approaches is a database search for homologs. In several useful tools, DNA translation is seamlessly bound to the database searches. In the ORF finder, for example, the user can submit the translated sequence for a BLASTP or TBLASTN search against the NCBI sequence databases. In addition, there is an opportunity to compare the translated sequence to the COG database.

Other methods take advantage of the statistical properties of the coding sequences.

For organisms with highly biased GC content, for example, the third position in each codon has a highly biased (very high or very low) frequency of G and C. The most useful and popular gene prediction programs, such as GeneMark and Glimmer, build Markov models of the known coding regions for the given organism and then employ them to estimate the coding potential of uncharacterized ORFs.

Inferring genes based on the coding potential and on the similarity of the encoded protein sequences to those of other proteins represent the intrinsic and extrinsic approaches to gene prediction, which ideally should be combined. Two programs that implement such a combination, developed specifically for analysis of prokaryotic genomes, are ORPH and CRITICA Several other algorithms that incorporate both these approaches are aimed primarily at eukaryotic genomes.

Unicellular Eukaryotes

Genomes of unicellular eukaryotes are extremely diverse in size, the proportion of the genome that is occupied by protein-encoding genes and the frequency of introns. Clearly, the smaller the intergenic regions and the fewer introns are there, the easier it is to identify genes. Fortunately, genomes of at least some simple eukaryotes are quite compact and contain very few introns. Thus, in yeast S. cerevisiae, at least 67% of the genome is protein-coding, and only 233 genes (less than 4% of the total) appear to have introns. Although these include some biologically important and extensively studied genes, e.g. those for aminopeptidase APE2, ubiquitin-protein ligase UBC8, subunit 1 of the mitochondrial cytochrome oxidase COX1, and many ribosomal proteins, introns comprise less than 1% of the yeast genome. The tiny genome of the intracellular eukaryotic parasite Encephalitozoon cuniculi appears to contain introns in only 12 genes and is practically prokaryote-like in terms of the "wall-to-wall" gene arrangement. Malaria parasite Plasmodium falciparum is a more complex case, with ~43% of the genes located on chromosome 2 containing one or more introns. Protists with larger genomes often have fairly high intron density. In the slime mold Physarum polycephalum, for example, the average gene has 3.7 introns. Given that the average exon size in this organism (165 ± 85 bp) is comparable to the length of an average intron (138 ± 103 bp), homology-based prediction of genes becomes increasingly complicated.

Because of this genome diversity, there is no single way to efficiently predict protein-coding genes in different unicellular eukaryotes. For some of them, such as yeast, gene prediction can be done by using more or less the same approaches that are routinely employed in prokaryotic genome analysis. For those with intron-rich genomes, the gene model has to include information on the intron splice sites, which can be gained from a comparison of the genomic sequence against a set of ESTs from the same organism. This necessitates creating a comprehensive library of ESTs that have to be sequenced in a separate project. Such dual EST/genomic sequencing projects are currently under way for several unicellular eukaryotes.

Multicellular Eukaryotes

In most multicellular eukaryotes, gene organization is so complex that gene identification poses a major problem. Indeed, eukaryotic genes are often separated by large intergenic regions, and the genes themselves contain numerous introns, many of them long. Figure shows a typical distribution of exons and introns in a human gene, the X chromosome-located gene encoding iduronate 2-sulfatase (IDS_HUMAN), a lysosomal enzyme responsible for removing sulfate groups from heparan sulfate and dermatan sulfate. Mutations causing iduronate sulfatase deficiency result in the lysosomal accumulation of these glycosaminoglycans, clinically known as Hunter's syndrome or type II mucopolysaccharidosis (OMIM entry 309900). A number of clinical cases have been shown to result from aberrant alternative splicing of this gene's mRNA, which emphasizes the importance of reliable prediction of gene structure.

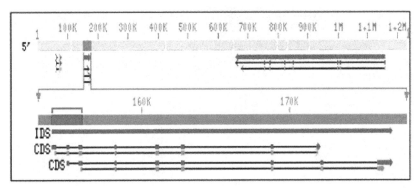

Organization of the human iduronate 2-sulfatase gene.

This gene is located in positions 152960–177995 of human X chromosome and encodes a 550-aa precursor protein that contains a 25-aa N-terminal signal sequence, followed by eight amino acids that are removed in the course of protein maturation. Mutations in this gene cause mucopolysaccharidosis type II, also known as Hunter's disease, which results in tissue deposits of chondroitin sulfate and heparin sulfate. The symptoms of Hunter's disease include dysostosis with dwarfism, coarse facial features, hepatosplenomegaly, cardiovascular disorders, deafness, and, in some cases, progressive mental retardation. The top line indicates the X chromosome and shows the location of the iduronate sulfatase gene (thick line in the middle). Thin lines on the bottom indicate two alternative transcripts. Exons are shown with small rectangles. The square bracket above the iduronate sulfatase gene marks the region of the gene.

Obviously, the coding regions compose only a minor portion of the gene. In this case, positions of the exons could be unequivocally determined by mapping the cDNA sequence (i.e. iduronate sulfatase mRNA) back to the chromosomal DNA. Because of the clinical phenotype of the mutations in the iduronate sulfatase gene, we already know the "correct" mRNA sequence and can identify various alternatively spliced variants as mutations. However, for many, perhaps the majority of the human genes, multiple alternative forms are part of the regular expression pattern, and correct gene prediction ideally should identify all of these forms, which immensely complicates the task.

Ideally, gene prediction should identify all exons and introns, including those in the 5′-untranslated region (5′-UTR) and the 3′-UTR of the mRNA, in order to precisely reconstruct the predominant mRNA species. For practical purposes, however, it is useful to assemble at least the coding exons correctly because this allows one to deduce the protein sequence.

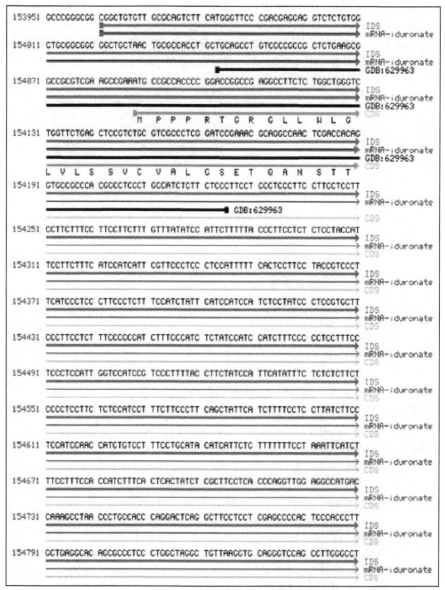

Sequence of the first two exons of human iduronate sulfatase gene.

The figure shows the DNA sequence of the positions 15391–15571 of human X chromosome. The iduronate sulfatase mRNA and its coding sequence are shown as thick lines;

the corresponding amino acid residues are shown underneath. "Variation" indicates the positions of mapped mutations causing type II mucopolysaccharidosis.

Correct identification of the exon boundaries relies on the recognition of the splice sites, which is facilitated by the fact that the great majority of splice sites conform to consensus sequences that include two nearly invariant dinucleotides at the ends of each intron, a GT at the 5' end and an AG at the 3' end. Non-canonical splice signals are rare and come in several variants. In the 5' splice sites, the GC dinucleotide is sometimes found instead of GT. The second class of exceptions to the splice site consensus includes so-called "AT-AC" introns that have the highly conserved /(A,G)TATCCT(C,T) sequence at their 5' sites. There are additional variants of non-canonical splice signals, which further complicate prediction of the gene structure.

The available assessments of the quality of eukaryotic gene prediction achieved by different programs show a rather gloomy picture of numerous errors in exon/intron recognition. Even the best tools correctly predict only ~40% of the genes. The most serious errors come from genes with long introns, which may be predicted as intragenic sequences, resulting in erroneous gene fission, and pairs of genes with short intergenic regions, which may be predicted as introns, resulting in false gene fusion. Nevertheless, most of the popular gene prediction programs reasonable performance in predicting the coding regions in the sense that, even if a small exon is missed or overpredicted, the majority of exons are identified correctly.

Another important parameter that can affect ORF prediction is the fraction of sequencing errors in the analyzed sequence. Indeed, including frameshift corrections was found to substantially improve the overall quality of gene prediction. Several algorithms were described that could detect frameshift errors based on the statistical properties of coding sequences. On the other hand, error correction techniques should be used with caution because eukaryotic genomes contain numerous pseudogenes, and non-critical frameshift correction runs the risk of wrongly "rescuing" pseudogenes. The problem of discriminating between pseudogenes and frameshift errors is actually quite complex and will likely be solved only through whole-genome alignments of different species or, in certain cases, by direct experimentation, e.g., expression of the gene(s) in question.

Algorithms and Software Tools for Gene Identification

recognizing genes in the DNA sequences remains one of the most pressing problems in genome analysis. Several different approaches to gene prediction have been developed, and there are several popular programs that are most commonly used for this task. Some of these tools perform gene prediction *ab initio*, relying only on the statistical parameters in the DNA sequence for gene identification. In contrast, homology-based methods rely primarily on identifying homologous sequences in other genomes and in public databases using BLAST or Smith-Waterman algorithms. Many of the commonly used methods combine these two approaches.

Software Tools for Ab initio Gene Prediction

The absence of introns and relatively high gene density in most genomes of prokaryotes and some unicellular eukaryotes provides for effective use of sequence similarity searches as the first step in genome annotation. Genes identified by homology can be used as the training set for one of the statistical methods for gene recognition, and the resulting statistical model can then be used for analyzing the remaining parts of the genome. In most eukaryotes, the abundance of introns and long intergenic regions makes it difficult to use homology-based methods as the first step unless, of course, one can rely on synteny between several closely related genomes (e.g. human, mouse, and rat). As a result, gene prediction for genome sequences of multicellular eukaryotes usually starts with *ab initio* methods, followed by similarity searches with the initial exon assemblies.

A detailed comparison of the algorithms and tools for gene prediction. each of these methods has its own advantages and limitations, and none of them is perfect. Therefore, it is advisable to use at least two different programs for gene prediction in a new DNA sequence, especially if it comes from a eukaryote or a poorly characterized prokaryote. A comparison of predictions generated by different programs reveals the cases where a given program performs the best and helps in achieving consistent quality of gene prediction. Such a comparison can be performed, which employs a voting scheme to combine predictions of different gene-finding programs, such as GeneMark, GlimmerM, GRAIL, GenScan, and Fgenes.

GeneMark

GeneMark mirrored at the EBI web site was developed by Mark Borodovsky and James McIninch in 1993. GeneMark was the first tool for finding prokaryotic genes that employed a non-homogeneous Markov model to classify DNA regions into protein-coding, non-coding, and non-coding but complementary to coding. It has been shown previously that, by multivariate codon usage analysis, the *E. coli* genes could be classified into so-called typical, highly typical, and atypical gene sets, with the latter two groups apparently corresponding to highly expressed genes and horizontally transferred genes. Accordingly, more than one Markov model was required to adequately describe different groups of genes in the same genome.

Like other gene prediction programs, GeneMark relies on organism-specific recognition parameters to partition the DNA sequence into coding and non-coding regions and thus requires a sufficiently large training set of known genes from a given organism for best performance. The program has been repeatedly updated and modified and now exists in separate variants for gene prediction in prokaryotic, eukaryotic, and viral DNA sequences.

Glimmer

Gene Locator and Interpolated Markov Modeler, is a system for finding genes in prokaryotic genomes. To identify coding regions and distinguish them from noncoding DNA, Glimmer uses interpolated Markov models, i.e. series of Markov models with the order of the model increasing at each step and the predictive power of each model separately evaluated. Like GeneMark, Glimmer requires a training set, which is usually selected among known genes, genes coding for proteins with strong database hits, and simply long ORFs. Glimmer is used as the primary gene finder tool at TIGR, where it has been applied to the annotation of numerous microbial genomes.

Recently, Salzberg and coworkers developed GlimmerM, a modified version of Glimmer specifically designed for gene recognition in small eukaryotic genomes, such as the malaria parasite Plasmodium falciparum.

Grail

Gene Recognition and Assembly Internet Link, is a tool that identifies exons, polyA sites, promoters, CpG islands, repetitive elements, and frameshift errors in DNA sequences by comparing them to a database of known human and mouse sequence elements. Exon and repetitive element prediction is also available for *Arabidopsis* and *Drosophila* sequences.

Grail has been recently incorporated into the Oak Ridge genome analysis pipeline, which provides a unified web interface to a number of convenient analysis tools. For prokaryotes, it offers gene prediction using Glimmer and Generation programs, followed by BLASTP searches of predicted ORFs against SWISS-PROT and NR databases and a HMMer search against Pfam. There is also an option of BLASTN search of the submitted DNA sequence against a variety of nucleotide sequence databases.

For human and mouse sequences, the Oak Ridge pipeline offers gene prediction using GrailEXP and GenScan, also followed by BLASTP searches of predicted ORFs against SWISS-PROT and NR databases and a HMMer search against Pfam. Again, the user can perform BLASTN search of the submitted DNA sequence against a variety of nucleotide sequence databases, as well as search for CpG islands, repeat fragments, tRNAs, and BAC-end pairs, the possibility to directly compare gene predictions made by two different programs is a valuable feature, which is available at the Oak Ridge web site.

GenScan

GenScan was developed by Chris Burge and Samuel Karlin and is currently hosted in the Burge laboratory at the MIT Department of Biology. This program uses a complex probabilistic model of the gene structure that is based on actual biological information about the properties of transcriptional, translational, and splicing signals. In addition, it utilizes various statistical properties of coding and noncoding regions. To account for the heterogeneity of the human genome that affects gene structure and gene density, GenScan derives different sets of gene models for genome regions with different GC content. Its high speed and accuracy make GenScan the method of choice for the initial analysis of large (in the megabase range) stretches of eukaryotic genomic DNA. GenScan has being used as the principal tool for gene prediction in the International Human Genome Project.

GeneBuilder

GeneBuilder performs *ab initio* gene prediction using numerous parameters, such as GC content, dicodon frequencies, splicing site data, CpG islands, repetitive elements, and others. It also utilizes a unique approach that is based on evaluating relative frequencies of synonymous and nonsynonymous substitutions to identify likely coding sequences. In addition, it performs BLAST searches of predicted genes against protein and EST databases, which helps to refine the boundaries of predicted exons using the BLAST hits as guides. The program allows the user to change certain parameters, which permits interactive gene structure prediction. As a result, GeneBuilder is sometimes able to predict the gene structure with a good accuracy, even when the similarity of the predicted ORF to a homologous protein sequence is low.

Splice Site Prediction

Programs for predicting intron splice sites, which are commonly used as subroutines in the gene prediction tools, can also be used as stand-alone programs to verify positions of splice sites or predict alternative splicing sites. Such programs can be particularly useful for predicting non-coding exons, which are commonly missed in gene prediction studies.

Combining Various Gene Prediction Tools

While the first step of gene identification in long genomic sequences utilizes *ab initio* programs that can rapidly and with reasonable accuracy predict multiple genes, the next step validates these predictions through similarity searches. Predicted genes are compared to nucleotide sequence databases, including EST databases, and protein sequences encoded by these predicted genes are compared to protein sequence databases. These data are then combined with the information about repetitive elements, CpG islands, and transcription factor binding sites and used for further refinement of gene structure. Thus, homology information is ultimately incorporated into every gene prediction pipeline. There are, however, several programs that primarily rely on similarity search for gene prediction. Although differing in details, they all search for the best alignment of the given piece of DNA to the homologous nucleotide or protein sequences in the database.

Principles of Sequence Similarity Searches

initial characterization of any new DNA or protein sequence starts with a database search aimed at finding out whether homologs of this gene (protein) are already available, and if they are, what is known about them. Clearly, looking for exactly the same sequence is quite straightforward. One can just take the first letter of the query sequence, search for its first occurrence in the database, and then check if the second letter of the query is the same in the subject. If it is indeed the same, the program could check the third letter, then the fourth, and continue this comparison to the end of the query. If the second letter in the subject is different from the second letter in the query, the program should search for another occurrence of the first letter, and so on. This will identify all the sequences in the database that are identical to the query sequence (or include it). Of course, this approach is primitive computation-wise, and there are sophisticated algorithms for text matching that do it much more efficiently.

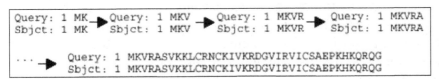

```
Query: 1 MK    Query: 1 MKV    Query: 1 MKVR    Query: 1 MKVRA
Sbjct: 1 MK    Sbjct: 1 MKV    Sbjct: 1 MKVR    Sbjct: 1 MKVRA


   ...    Query: 1 MKVRASVKKLCRNCKIVKRDGVIRVICSAEPKHKQRQG
          Sbjct: 1 MKVRASVKKLCRNCKIVKRDGVIRVICSAEPKHKQRQG
```

Note that, in the example above, we looked only for sequences that exactly match the query. The algorithm would not even find a sequence that is identical to the query with the exception of the first letter. To find such sequences, the same analysis should be conducted with the fragments starting from the second letter of the original query, then from the third one, and so on.

```
Query1: 1   KVRASVKKLCRNCKIVKRDGVIRVICSAEPKHKQRQG
Query2: 1   VRASVKKLCRNCKIVKRDGVIRVICSAEPKHKQRQG
Query3: 1   RASVKKLCRNCKIVKRDGVIRVICSAEPKHKQRQG
Query4: 1   ASVKKLCRNCKIVKRDGVIRVICSAEPKHKQRQG
```

Such search quickly becomes time-consuming, and we are still dealing only with identical sequences. Finding close relatives would introduce additional conceptual and technical problems. Let us assume that sequences that are 99% identical are definitely homologous. What should one select as the threshold to consider sequences not to be homologous: 50% identity, 33%, or perhaps 25%? These are legitimate questions that need to be answered before one goes any further. The example of two lysozymes shows that sequences with as low as 8% identity may belong to orthologous proteins and perform the same function.

As a matter of fact, when comparing nucleic acid sequences, there is very little one could do. All the four nucleotides, A, T, C, and G, are found in the database with approximately the same frequencies and have roughly the same probability of mutating one into another. As a result, DNA-DNA comparisons are largely based on straightforward text matching, which makes them fairly slow and not particularly sensitive, although a variety of heuristics have been developed to overcome this.

Amino acid sequence comparisons have several distinct advantages over nucleotide sequence comparisons, which, at least potentially, lead to a much greater sensitivity.

Firstly, because there are 20 amino acids but only four bases, an amino acid match carries with it >4 bits of information as opposed to only two bits for a nucleotide match. Thus, statistical significance can be ascertained for much shorter sequences in protein comparisons than in nucleotide comparisons. Secondly, because of the redundancy of the genetic code, nearly one-third of the bases in coding regions are under a weak (if any) selective pressure and represent noise, which adversely affects the sensitivity of the searches. Thirdly, nucleotide sequence databases are much larger than protein databases because of the vast amounts of non-coding sequences coming out of eukaryotic genome projects, and this further lowers the search sensitivity. Finally, and probably most importantly, unlike in nucleotide sequence, the likelihoods of different amino acid substitutions occurring during evolution are substantially different, and taking this into account greatly improves the performance of database search methods as described below. Given all these advantages, comparisons of any coding sequences are typically carried out at the level of protein sequences; even when the goal is to produce a DNA-DNA alignment (e.g. for analysis of substitutions in silent codon positions), it is usually first done with protein sequences, which are then replaced by the corresponding coding sequences. Direct nucleotide sequence comparison is indispensable only when non-coding regions are analyzed.

Substitution Scores and Substitution Matrices

The fact that each of the 20 standard protein amino acids has its own unique properties means that the likelihood of the substitution of each particular residue for another residue during evolution should be different. Generally, the more similar the physico-chemical properties of two residues, the greater the chance that the substitution will not have an adverse effect on the protein's function and, accordingly, on the organism's fitness. Hence, in sequence comparisons, such a substitution should be penalized less than a replacement of amino acid residue with one that has dramatically different properties. This is, of course, an oversimplification, because the effect of a substitution depends on the structural and functional environment where it occurs. For example, a cysteine-to-valine substitution in the catalytic site of an enzyme will certainly abolish the activity and, on many occasions, will have a drastic effect on the organism's fitness. In contrast, the same substitution within a β-strand may have little or no effect. Unfortunately, in general, we do not have *a priori* knowledge of the location of a particular residue in the protein structure, and even with such knowledge, incorporating it in a database search algorithm is an extremely complex task. Thus, a generalized measure of the likelihood of amino acid substitutions is required so that each substitution is given an appropriate score (weight) to be used in sequence comparisons. The score for a substitution between amino acids i and j always can be expressed by the following intuitively plausible formula, which shows how likely a particular substitution is given the frequencies of each the two residues in the analyzed database:

$$S_{ij} = kln\left(q_i \,/\, p_i p_i\right)$$

where k is a coefficient, q_{ij} is the observed frequency of the given substitution, and p_i, p_j are the background frequencies of the respective residues. Obviously, here the product $p_i p_j$ is the expected frequency of the substitution and, if $q_{ij} = p_i p_j$ ($S_{ij} = 0$), the substitution occurs just as often as expected. The scores used in practice are scaled such that the expected score for aligning a random pair of amino acid sequences is negative.

There are two fundamentally different ways to come up with a substitution score matrix, i.e. a triangular table containing 210 numerical score values for each pair of amino acids, including identities (diagonal elements of the matrix. As in many other situations in computational biology, the first approach works *ab initio*, whereas the second one is empirical. One *ab initio* approach calculates the score as the number of nucleotide substitutions that are required to transform a codon for one amino acid in a pair into a codon for the other. In this case, the matrix is obviously unique (as long as alternative genetic codes are not considered) and contains only four values, 0, 1, 2, or 3. Accordingly, this is a very coarse grain matrix that is unlikely to work well. The other *ab initio* approach assigns scores on the basis of similarities and differences in the physico-chemical properties of amino acids. Under this approach, the number of possible matrices is infinite, and they may have as fine a granularity as desirable, but a degree of arbitrariness is inevitable because our understanding of protein physics is insufficient to make informed decisions on what set of properties "correctly" reflects the relationships between amino acids.

```
A    6
R   -7   8
N   -4  -6   8
D   -3 -10   2   8
C   -6  -8 -11 -14  10
Q   -4  -2  -3  -2 -14   8
E   -2  -9  -2   2 -14   1   8
G   -2  -9  -3  -3  -9  -7  -4   6
H   -7  -2   0  -4  -7   1  -5  -9   9
I   -5  -5  -5  -7  -6  -8  -5 -11  -9   8
L   -6  -8  -7 -12 -15  -5  -9 -10  -6  -1   7
K   -7   0  -1  -4 -14  -3  -4  -7  -6  -6  -8   7
M   -5  -4  -9 -11 -13  -4  -7  -8 -10  -1   1  -2  11
F   -8  -9  -9 -15 -13 -13 -14  -9  -6  -2  -3 -14  -4   9
P   -2  -4  -6  -8  -8  -3  -5  -6  -4  -8  -7  -6  -8 -10   8
S    0  -3   0  -4  -3  -5  -4  -2  -6  -7  -8  -4  -5  -6  -2   6
T   -1  -6  -2  -5  -8  -5  -6  -6  -7  -2  -7  -3  -4  -9  -4   0   7
W  -13  -2  -8 -15 -15 -13 -17 -15  -7 -14  -6 -12 -13  -4 -14  -5 -13  13
Y   -8 -10  -4 -11  -4 -12  -8 -14  -3  -6  -7  -9 -11   2 -13  -7  -6  -5  10
V   -2  -8  -8  -8  -6  -7  -6  -5  -6   2  -2  -9  -1  -8  -6  -6  -3 -15  -7   7
B   -3  -7   6   6 -12  -3   1  -1  -1  -6  -9  -2 -10 -10  -7  -1  -3 -10  -6  -8   6
Z   -3  -4  -3   1 -14   6   6  -5  -1  -6  -7  -4  -5 -13  -4  -5  -6 -14  -9  -6   0   6
X   -3  -6  -3  -5  -9  -5  -5  -5  -5  -5  -6  -5  -5  -8  -5  -3  -4 -11  -7  -5  -5  -5  -5
     A   R   N   D   C   Q   E   G   H   I   L   K   M   F   P   S   T   W   Y   V   B   Z   X
```

The PAM30 substitution matrix.

The numbers indicate the substitution scores for each replacement. The greater the number, the lesser the penalty for the given substitution. Note the high penalty for replacing Cys and aromatic amino acids (Phe, Tyr, and Trp) with any other residues and, accordingly, the high reward for conservation of these residues (see the diagonal elements).

The meaning of the numbers is the same as for PAM30. Note the relatively lower reward for conservation of Cys, Phe, Tyr, and Trp and lower penalties for replacing these amino acids than in the PAM30 matrix. This trend is even stronger in lower series members (e.g. BLOSUM45) because drastic amino acid changes are more likely at larger evolutionary distances.

Empirical approaches, which historically came first, attempt to derive the characteristic frequencies of different amino acid substitutions from actual alignments of homologous protein families. In other words, these approaches strive to determine the actual likelihood of each substitution occurring during evolution. Obviously, the outcome of such efforts critically depends on the quantity and quality of the available alignments, and even now, any alignment database is far from being complete or perfectly correct. Furthermore, simple counting of different types of substitutions will not suffice if alignments of distantly related proteins are included because, in many cases, multiple substitutions might have occurred in the same position. Ideally, one should construct the phylogenetic tree for each family, infer the ancestral sequence for each internal node, and then count the substitutions exactly. This is not practicable in most cases, and various shortcuts need to be taken.

	A	R	N	D	C	Q	E	G	H	I	L	K	M	F	P	S	T	W	Y	V	X
R	-1	5																			
N	-2	0	6																		
D	-2	-2	1	6																	
C	0	-3	-3	-3	9																
Q	-1	1	0	0	-3	5															
E	-1	0	0	2	-4	2	5														
G	0	-2	0	-1	-3	-2	-2	6													
H	-2	0	1	-1	-3	0	0	-2	8												
I	-1	-3	-3	-3	-1	-3	-3	-4	-3	4											
L	-1	-2	-3	-4	-1	-2	-3	-4	-3	2	4										
K	-1	2	0	-1	-3	1	1	-2	-1	-3	-2	5									
M	-1	-1	-2	-3	-1	0	-2	-3	-2	1	2	-1	5								
F	-2	-3	-3	-3	-2	-3	-3	-3	-1	0	0	-3	0	6							
P	-1	-2	-2	-1	-3	-1	-1	-2	-2	-3	-3	-1	-2	-4	7						
S	1	-1	1	0	-1	0	0	0	-1	-2	-2	0	-1	-2	-1	4					
T	0	-1	0	-1	-1	-1	-1	-2	-2	-1	-1	-1	-1	-2	-1	1	5				
W	-3	-3	-4	-4	-2	-2	-3	-2	-2	-3	-2	-3	-1	1	-4	-3	-2	11			
Y	-2	-2	-2	-3	-2	-1	-2	-3	2	-1	-1	-2	-1	3	-3	-2	-2	2	7		
V	0	-3	-3	-3	-1	-2	-2	-3	-3	3	1	-2	1	-1	-2	-2	0	-3	-1	4	
X	0	-1	-1	-1	-2	-1	-1	-1	-1	-1	-1	-1	-1	-1	-2	0	0	-2	-1	-1	-1

The BLOSUM 62 substitution matrix.

Several solutions to these problems have been proposed, each resulting in a different set of substitution scores. The first substitution matrix, constructed by Dayhoff and Eck in 1968, was based on an alignment of closely related proteins, so that the ancestral sequence could be deduced and all the amino acid replacements could be considered occurring just once. This model was then extrapolated to account for more distant relationships. PAM (Accepted Point Mutation) is a unit of evolutionary divergence of protein sequences, corresponding to one amino acid change per 100 residues. Thus, for example, the PAM30 matrix is supposed to apply to proteins that differ, on average, by 0.3 change per aligned residue, whereas PAM250 should reflect evolution of sequences with an average of 2.5 substitutions per position. Accordingly, the former matrix should be employed for constructing alignments of closely related sequences, whereas the latter is useful in database searches aimed at detection of distant relationships. Using an approach similar to that of Dayhoff, combined with rapid algorithms for protein sequence clustering and alignment, Jones, Taylor, and Thornton produced the series of the so-called JTT matrices, which are essentially an update of the PAMs.

The PAM and JTT matrices, however, have obvious limitations because of the fact that they have been derived from alignments of closely related sequences and extrapolated to distantly related ones. This extrapolation may not be fully valid because the underlying evolutionary model might not be adequate, and the trends that determine sequence divergence of closely related sequences might not apply to the evolution at larger distances.

In 1992, Steven and Jorja Henikoff developed a different series of substitution matrices using conserved ungapped alignments of related proteins from the BLOCKS database. The use of these alignments offered three important advantages over the alignments used for constructing the PAM matrices. First, the BLOCKS collection obviously included a much larger number and, more importantly, a much greater diversity of protein families than the collection that was available to Dayhoff and coworkers in the 1970's. Second, coming from rather distantly related proteins, BLOCKS alignments better reflected the amino acid changes that occur over large phylogenetic distances and thus produced substitution scores that represented sequence divergence in distant homologs directly, rather than through extrapolation. Third, in these distantly related proteins, BLOCKS included only the most confidently aligned regions, which are likely to best represent the prevailing evolutionary trends. These substitution matrices, named the BLOSUM (= BLOcks SUbstitution Matrix) series, were tailored to particular evolutionary distances by ignoring the sequences that had more than a certain percent identity. In the BLOSUM62 matrix, for example, the substitution scores were derived from the alignments of sequences that had no more than 62% identity; the substitution scores of the BLOSUM45 matrix were calculated from the alignments that contained sequences with no more than 45% identity. Accordingly, BLOSUM matrices with high numbers, such as BLOSUM80, are best suited for comparisons of closely related sequences (it is also advisable to use BLOSUM80 for database searches with short sequences, see), whereas low-number BLOSUM matrices, such as BLOSUM45, are better for distant relationships. In addition to the general-purpose PAM, JTT, and BLOSUM series, some specialized substitution matrices were developed, for example, for integral membrane proteins], but they never achieved comparable recognition.

Several early studies found the PAM matrices based on empirical data consistently resulted in greater search sensitivity than any of the *ab initio* matrices (see). An extensive empirical comparison showed that: (i) BLOSUM matrices consistently outperformed PAMs in BLAST searches, and (ii) on average, BLOSUM62 performed best in the series; this matrix is currently used as the default in most sequence database searches. It is remarkable that so far, throughout the 30-plus-year history of amino acid substitution matrices, empirical matrices have consistently outperformed those based on theory, either physico-chemical or evolutionary. This is not to say, of course, that theory is powerless in this field, but to point out that we currently do not have a truly adequate theory to describe protein evolution. Clearly, the last word has not been said on amino acid substitution matrices, and one can expect that eventually the BLOSUM series will be replaced by new matrices based on greater amounts of higher quality alignment data and more realistic evolutionary models. A recently reported maximum-likelihood model for substitution frequency estimation has already been claimed to describe individual protein families better than the Dayhoff and JTT models. It remains to be seen how this and other new matrices perform in large-scale computational experiments on real databases. AAindex lists 66 different substitution matrices, both *ab initio* and empirical, and there is no doubt that this list will continue to grow.

Statistics of Protein Sequence Comparison

It is impossible to explain even the basic principles of statistical analysis of sequence similarities without invoking some mathematics. To introduce these concepts in the least painful way, let us consider the same protein sequence (*E. coli* RpsJ) as above

```
Query: 1 MKVRASVKKLCRNCKIVKRDGVIRVICSAEPKHKQRQG 38
```

and check how many times segments of this sequence of different lengths are found in the database (we chose fragments starting from the second position in the sequence because nearly every protein in the database starts with a methionine). Not unexpectedly, we find that the larger the fragment, the smaller the number of exact matches in the database.

Table: Dependence of the number of exact database matches on the length of the query word.

Sequence	Occurrences in the database
KV	488,559
KVR	28,592
KVRA	2,077
KVRAS	124
KVRASV	23
KVRASVK	8
KVRASVKK	4
KVRASVKKL	1
KVRASVKKLC	1

Dependence of the number of exact database matches on the length of the query word. Perhaps somewhat counterintuitively, a 9-mer is already unique. With the decrease in the number of database hits, the likelihood that these hits are biologically relevant, i.e. belong to homologs of the query protein, increases. Thus, 13 of the 23 occurrences of the string KVRASV and all 8 occurrences of the string KVRASVK are from RpsJ orthologs.

The number of occurrences of a given string in the database can be roughly estimated as follows. The probability of matching one amino acid residue is 1/20 (assuming equal frequencies of all 20 amino acids in the database; this not being the case, the probability is slightly greater). The probability of matching two residues in a row is then $(1/20)^2$, and the probability of matching n residues is $(1/20)^n$. Given that the protein database currently contains $N \sim 2 \times 10^8$ letters, one should expect a string of n letters to match approximately $N \times (1/20)^n$ times, which is fairly close to the numbers in table.

Searching for perfect matches is the simplest and, in itself, obviously insufficient form of sequence database search, although, it is important as one of the basic steps in currently used search algorithms. the goal of a search is finding homologs, which can have drastically different sequences such that, in distant homologs, only a small fraction of the amino acid residues are identical or even similar. Even in close homologs, a region of high similarity is usually flanked by dissimilar regions like in the following alignment of *E. coli* RpmJ with its ortholog from *Vibrio cholerae*:

```
E. coli RpmJ:    1 MKVRASVKKLCR---NCKIVKRDGVIRVICSAEPKHKQRQG
                   MKV +S+K       +C+IVKR G + VIC + P+ K   Q
Vibrio VC0879: 1 MKVLSSLKSAKNRHPDCQIVKRRGRLYVICKSNPRFKAVQR
```

In this example, the region of highest similarity is in the middle of the alignment, but including the less conserved regions on both sides improves the overall score (taking into account the special treatment of gaps, which is introduced below). Further along the alignment, the similarity almost disappears so that inclusion of additional letters into the alignment would not increase the overall score or would even decrease it. Such fragments of the alignment of two sequences whose similarity score cannot be improved by adding or trimming any letters, are referred to as high-scoring segment pairs (HSPs). For this approach to work, the expectation of the score for random sequences must be negative, and the scoring matrices used in database searches are scaled accordingly.

So, instead of looking for perfect matches, sequence comparisons programs actually search for HSPs. Once a set of HSPs is found, different methods, such as Smith-Waterman, FASTA, or BLAST, deal with them in different fashions. However, the principal issue that any database search method needs to address is identifying those HSPs that are unlikely to occur by chance and, by inference, are likely to belong to homologs and to be biologically relevant. This problem has been solved by Samuel Karlin and Stephen Altschul, who showed that maximal HSP scores follow the extreme value distribution. Accordingly, if the lengths of the query sequence (m) and the database (n) are sufficiently high, the expected number of HSPs with a score of at least S is given by the formula:

$$E = mn2^{S'}$$

Here, S is the so-called raw score calculated under a given scoring system, and K and λ are natural scaling parameters for the search space size and the scoring system, respectively. Normalizing the score according to the formula:

$$S' = (\lambda S - Ink)/In2$$

gives the bit score, which has a standard unit accepted in information theory and computer science. Then,

$$E = Kmn2^{-\lambda S}$$

and, since it can be shown that the number of random HSPs with score $\geq S'$ is described by Poisson distribution, the probability of finding at least one HSP with bit score $\geq S'$ is:

$$P = 1 - E^{-E}$$

Equation $P = 1 - E^{-E}$ links two commonly used measures of sequence similarity, the probability (P-value) and expectation (E-value). For example, if the score S is such that three HSPs with this score (or greater) are expected to be found by chance, the probability of finding at least one such HSP is ($1 - e^{-3}$), ~0.95. By definition, P-values vary from 0 to 1, whereas E-values can be much greater than 1. The BLAST programs report E-values, rather than P-values, because E-values of, for example, 5 and 10 are much easier to comprehend than P-values of 0.993 and 0.99995. However, for E < 0.01, P-value and E-value are nearly identical.

The product mn defines the search space, a critically important parameter of any database search. Equations $S' = (\lambda S - Ink)/In2$ and $E = Kmn2^{-\lambda S}$ codify the intuitively obvious notion that the larger the search space, the higher the expectation of finding an HSP with a score greater than any given value. There are two corollaries of this that might take some getting used to: (i) the same HSP may come out statistically significant in a small database and not significant in a large database; with the natural growth of the database, any given alignment becomes less and less significant (but by no means less important because of that) and (ii) the same HSP may be statistically significant in a small protein (used as a query) and not significant in a large protein.

Clearly, one can easily decrease the E-value and the P-value associated with the alignment of the given two sequences by lowering n in equation $E = mn2^{S'}$, i.e. by searching a smaller database. However, the resulting increase in significance is false, although such a trick can be useful for detecting initial hints of subtle relationships that should be subsequently verified using other approaches. It is the experience of the authors that the simple notion of E(P)-value is often misunderstood and interpreted as if these values applied just to a single pairwise comparison (i.e., if an E-value of 0.001 for an HSP with score S is reported, then, in a database of just a few thousand sequences, one expects to find a score $>S$ by chance). It is critical to realize that the size of the search space is already factored in these E-values, and the reported value corresponds to the database size at the time of search (thus, it is certainly necessary to indicate, in all reports of sequence analysis, which database was searched, and desirably, also on what exact date).

Speaking more philosophically (or futuristically), one could imagine that, should the genomes of all species that inhabit this planet be sequenced, it would become almost impossible to demonstrate statistical significance for any but very close homologs in standard database searches. Thus, other approaches to homology detection are required that counter the problems created by database growth by taking advantage of the simultaneously increasing sequence diversity.

The Karlin-Altschul statistics has been rigorously proved to apply only to sequence alignments that do not contain gaps, whereas statistical theory for the more realistic gapped alignments remains an open problem. However, extensive computer simulations have shown that these alignments also follow the extreme value distribution to a high precision; therefore, at least for all practical purposes, the same statistical formalism is applicable.

Protein Sequence Complexity: Compositional Bias

The existence of a robust statistical theory of sequence comparison, in principle, should allow one to easily sort search results by statistical significance and accordingly assign a level of confidence to any homology identification. However, a major aspect of protein molecule organization substantially complicates database search interpretation and may lead to gross errors in sequence analysis. Many proteins, especially in eukaryotes, contain low (compositional) complexity regions, in which the distribution of amino acid residues is non-random, i.e. deviates from the standard statistical model. In other words, these regions typically have biased amino acid composition, e.g. are rich in glycine or proline, or in acidic or basic amino acid residues. The ultimate form of low complexity is, of course, a homopolymer, such as a Q-linker. Other low-complexity sequences have a certain amino acid periodicity, sometimes subtle, such as, for example, in coiled-coil and other non-globular proteins (e.g. collagen or keratin).

The notion of compositional complexity was encapsulated in the SEG algorithm and the corresponding program, which partitions protein sequences into segments of low and high (normal) complexity. An important finding made by John Wootton is that low-complexity sequences correspond to non-globular portions of proteins. In other words, a certain minimal level of complexity is required for a sequence to fold into a globular structure. Low-complexity regions in proteins, although devoid of enzymatic activity, have important biological functions, most often promoting protein-protein interactions or cellular adhesion to various surfaces and to each other.

In a detailed empirical study, a set of parameters of the SEG program was identified that allowed reasonably accurate partitioning of a protein sequence into predicted globular and non-globular parts. The mastermind protein of *Drosophila* is a component of the Notch-dependent signaling pathway and plays an important role in the development of the nervous system of the fruit fly. In spite of this critical biological function, this protein consists mostly of stretches of only three amino acid residues, Gln, Asn, and Gly, and is predicted to have a predominantly non-globular structure. Recently discovered human homologs of mastermind are also involved in Notch-dependent transcriptional regulation and similarly appear to be almost entirely non-globular.

Sequence of the Drosophila mastermind protein: partitioning into predicted non-globular (left column) and globular (right column) regions.

The SEG program was run with the parameters optimized for detection of non-globular regions: window length 45, trigger complexity 3.4, extension complexity 3.7. Asn, Gln, and Gly residues are shown in bold. Note that, because the existence of globular domains consisting of <50 amino acids is unlikely, mastermind probably contains only one globular domain, between amino acid residues 122 and 195. Prediction of short segments as 'globular' appears to be a SEG artifact.

Low-complexity regions represent a major problem for database searches. Since the λ parameter of equation 4.2 is calculated for the entire database, Karlin-Altschul statistics breaks down when the composition of the query or a database sequence or both significantly deviates from the average composition of the database. The result is that low-complexity regions with similar composition (e.g. acidic or basic) often produce "statistically significant" alignments that have nothing to with homology and are completely irrelevant. The SEG program can be used to overcome this problem in a somewhat crude manner: the query sequence, the database, or both can be partitioned into normal complexity and low-complexity regions, and the latter are masked (i.e. amino acid symbols are replaced with the corresponding number of X's). For the purpose of a database search, such filtering is usually done using short windows so that only the segments with a strongly compositional bias are masked. Low-complexity filtering has been indispensable for making database search methods, in particular BLAST, into reliable tools. Without masking low-complexity regions, false results would have been produced for a substantial fraction of proteins, especially eukaryotic ones (an early estimate held that low-complexity regions comprise ~15% of the protein sequences in the SWISS-PROT database). These false results would have badly polluted any large-scale database search, and the respective proteins would have been refractory to any meaningful sequence analysis. For these reasons, for several years, SEG filtering had been used as the default for BLAST searches to mask low-complexity segments in the query sequence. However, this procedure is not without its drawbacks. Not all low-complexity sequences are captured, and false-positives still occur in database searches. The opposite problem also hampers database searches for some proteins: when short low-complexity sequences are parts of conserved regions, statistical significance of an alignment may be underestimated, sometimes grossly.

In a recent work of Alejandro Schäffer and colleagues, a different, less arbitrary approach for dealing with compositionally biased sequences was introduced. This method, called composition-based statistics, recalculates the λ parameter and, accordingly, the E values for each query and each database sequence, thus correcting the inordinately low ("significant") E-values for sequences with similarly biased amino acid composition. This improves the accuracy of the reported E-values and eliminates most false-positives. Composition-based statistics is currently used as the default for the NCBI BLAST. In,

Algorithms for Sequence Alignment and Similarity Search

The Basic Alignment Concepts and Principal Algorithms

similarity searches aim at identifying the homologs of the given query protein (or nucleotide) sequence among all the protein (or nucleotide) sequences in the database. An alignment of homologous protein sequences reveals their common features that are ostensibly important for the structure and function of each of these proteins; it also reveals poorly conserved regions that are less important for the common function but might define the specificity of each of the homologs. In principle, the only way to identify homologs is by aligning the query sequence against all the sequences in the database (below we will discuss some important heuristics that allow an algorithm to skip sequences that are obviously unrelated to the query), sorting these hits based on the degree of similarity, and assessing their statistical significance that is likely to be indicative of homology. Thus, before considering algorithms and programs used to search sequence databases.

It is important to make a distinction between a global (i.e. full-length) alignment and a local alignment, which includes only parts of the analyzed sequences (subsequences). Although, in theory, a global alignment is best for describing relationships between sequences, in practice, local alignments are of more general use for two reasons. Firstly, it is common that only parts of compared proteins are homologous (e.g. they share one conserved domain, whereas other domains are unique). Secondly, on many occasions, only a portion of the sequence is conserved enough to carry a detectable signal, whereas the rest have diverged beyond recognition. Optimal global alignment of two sequences was first realized in the Needleman-Wunsch algorithm, which employs dynamic programming. The notion of optimal local alignment (the best possible alignment of two subsequences from the compared sequences) and the corresponding dynamic programming algorithm were introduced by Smith and Waterman. Both of these are $O(n^2)$ algorithms.

the time and memory required to generate an optimal alignment are proportional to the product of the lengths of the compared sequences (for convenience, the sequences are assumed to be of equal length n in this notation). Optimal alignment algorithms for multiple sequences have the $O(n^k)$ complexity (where k is the number of compared sequences). Such algorithms for $k > 3$ are not feasible on any existing computers, therefore all available methods for multiple sequence alignments produce only approximations and do not guarantee the optimal alignment.

It might be useful, at this point, to clarify the notion of optimal alignment. Algorithms like Needleman-Wunsch and Smith-Waterman guarantee the optimal alignment (global and local, respectively) for any two compared sequences. It is important to keep in mind, however, that this optimality is a purely formal notion, which means that, given a scoring function, the algorithm outputs the alignment with the highest possible score. This has nothing to with statistical significance of the alignment, which has to be estimated separately (e.g. using the Karlin-Altschul statistics as outlined above), let alone the biological relevance of the alignment.

For better or worse, alignment algorithms treat protein or DNA as simple strings of letters without recourse to any specific properties of biological macromolecules. Therefore, it might be useful to illustrate the principles of local alignments using a text free of biological context as an example. Below is the text of stanzas I and IV of one of the most famous poems of all times; we shall compare them line by line, observing along the way various problems involved in sequence alignment (the alignable regions are shown in bold):

> I
> "Once upon a midnight dreary, while I pondered, weak and weary,
> Over many a quaint and curious volume of forgotten lore,
> While I nodded, nearly napping, suddenly there came a tapping,
> As of some one gently rapping, rapping at my chamber door.
> "'Tis some visitor," I muttered, "tapping at my chamber door-
> Only this, and nothing more."
>
> IV
> "Presently my soul grew stronger; hesitating then no longer,
> "Sir," said I, "or Madam, truly your forgiveness I implore;
> But the fact is I was napping, and so gently you came rapping,
> And so faintly you came tapping, tapping at my chamber door,
> That I scarce was sure I heard you"- here I opened wide the door;-
> Darkness there, and nothing more. "

It is easy to see that, in the first two lines of the two stanzas, the longest common string consists of only five letters, with one mismatch:

```
...I pondered ...                                    (I)
...stronger...
```

The second lines align better, with two similar blocks separated by spacers of variable lengths, which requires gaps to be introduced, in order to combine them in one alignment:

```
...of forgotten--- - ---lore           (II)
your forgiv-eness I implore
```

In the third lines, there are common words of seven, four, and six letters, again separated by gaps:

```
...napping sud -  den-ly there came a tapping,  (III)
...napping and so gently you-- came - rapping
```

The fourth lines align very well, with a long string of near identity at the end:

```
As of some one gently --- ---- rapping rapping at my chamber door (IV)
An d- so-- --f aintly you came tapping tapping at my chamber door
```

In contrast, there is no reasonable alignment between the fifth lines, except for the identical word 'door'. Obviously, however, the fourth line of the second stanza may be aligned not only with the fourth (IV), but also with the fifth line of the first stanza:

```
...   I muttered tapping at my chamber door    (IV')
... came tapping tapping at my chamber door
```

Alignments (IV) and (IV') can thus be combined to produce a multiple alignment:

```
...rapping rapping at my chamber door       (IV'')
...tapping tapping at my chamber door
...-------- tapping at my chamber door
```

Finally, sixth lines of the two stanzas could be aligned at their ends:

```
Only  this- and nothing more              (V)
Darkness  there and nothing more
```

This simple example seems to capture several important issues that emerge in sequence alignment analysis. Firstly, remembering that an optimal alignment can be obtained for any two sequences, we should ask: Which alignments actually reflect homology of the respective lines? The alignments III, IV, IV' (and the derivative IV''), and V seem to be relevant beyond reasonable doubt. However, are they really correct? In particular, aligning en-ly/ently in III and ntly/ntly in IV require introducing gaps into both sequences. Is this justified? We cannot answer this simple question without a statistical theory for assessing the significance of an alignment, including a way to introduce some reasonable gap penalties.

The treatment of gaps is one of the hardest and still unsolved problems of alignment analysis. There is no theoretical basis for assigning gap penalties relative to substitution penalties (scores). Deriving these penalties empirically is a much more complicated task than deriving substitution penalties as in PAM and BLOSUM series because, unlike the alignment of residues in highly conserved blocks, the number and positions of gaps in alignments tend to be highly uncertain (see, for example alignment IV: Is it correct to place gaps both before and after 'so' in the second line?). Thus, gap penalties typically are assigned on the basis of two notions that stem both from the existing understanding of protein structure and from empirical examinations of protein family alignments: (i) deletion or insertion resulting in a gap is much less likely to occur than even the most radical amino acid substitution and should be heavily penalized, and (ii) once a deletion (insertion) has occurred in a given position, deletion or insertion of additional residues (gap extension) becomes much more likely. Therefore a linear function:

$$G = a + bx, a \gg b$$

where a is the gap opening penalty, b is the gap extension penalty, and x is the length of the gap is used to deal with gaps in most alignment methods. Typically, $a = 10$ and $b = 1$ is a reasonable choice of gap penalties to be used in conjunction with the BLOSUM62 matrix. Using these values, the reader should be able to find out whether gaps should have been introduced in alignments III and IV above. In principle, objective gap penalties could be produced through analysis of distributions of gaps in structural alignments, and such a study suggested using convex functions for gap penalties. However, this makes alignment algorithms much costlier computationally, and the practical advantages remain uncertain, so linear gap penalties are still universally employed.

The feasibility of alignments (IV) and (IV') creates the problem of choice: Which of these is the correct alignment? Alignment (IV) wins because it clearly has a longer conserved region. What is, then, the origin of line 5 in the first stanza and, accordingly, of alignment (IV')? It is not too difficult to figure out that this is a repeat, a result of duplication of line 4 (this is what we have to conclude given that line 4 is more similar to the homologous line in the second stanza). Such duplications are common in protein sequences, too, and often create major problems for alignment methods.

We concluded that lines 3, 4, and 6 in each stanza of "Raven" are homologous, i.e. evolved from common ancestors with some subsequent divergence. In this case, the conclusion is also corroborated by the fact that we recognize the English words in these lines and see that they are indeed nearly the same and convey similar meanings, albeit differing in nuances. What about alignments (I) and (II)? The content here tells us that no homology is involved, even though alignment (II) looks "believable". However, it would not have been recognized as statistically significant in a search of any sizable database, such as, for example, the "Complete poems of Edgar Allan Poe" at the American Verse Project.

Most of the existing alignment methods utilize modifications of the Smith-Waterman algorithm. the latest developments in sequence alignment, the reader has to keep in mind that this remains an active research field, with a variety of algorithms and tools being developed, which at least claim improvements over the traditional ones appearing at a high rate. Just one recent example is BALSA, a Bayesian local alignment algorithm that explores series of substitution matrices and gap penalty values and assesses their posterior probabilities, thus overcoming some of the shortcomings of the Smith-Waterman algorithm.

Pairwise alignment methods are important largely in the context of a database search. For analysis of individual protein families, multiple alignment methods are critical. We believe that anyone routinely involved in protein family analysis would agree that, so far, no one has figured out the best way to do it. As indicated above, optimal alignment of more than three sequences is not feasible in the foreseeable future; so all the available methods are approximations. The main principle underlying popular algorithms is hierarchical clustering that roughly approximates the phylogenetic tree and guides the alignment (to our knowledge, this natural idea was first introduced by Feng and Doolittle). The sequences are first compared using a fast method and clustered by similarity scores to produce a guide tree. Sequences are then aligned step-by-step in a bottom-up succession, starting from terminal clusters in the tree and proceeding to the internal nodes until the root is reached. Once two sequences are aligned, their alignment is fixed and treated essentially as a single sequence with a modification of dynamic programming. Thus, the hierarchical algorithms essentially reduce the $O(n^k)$ multiple alignment problem to a series of $O(n^2)$ problems, which makes the algorithm feasible but potentially at the price of alignment quality. The hierarchical algorithms attempt to minimize this problem by starting with most similar sequences where the likelihood of incorrect alignment is minimal, in the hope that the increased weight of correctly aligned positions precludes errors even on the subsequent steps. The most commonly used method for hierarchical multiple alignment is Clustal, which is currently used in the ClustalW or ClustalX variants.

Clustal is fast and tends to produce reasonable alignments, even for protein families with limited sequence conservation, provided the compared proteins do not differ in length too much. A combination of length differences and low sequence conservation tends to result in gross distortions of the alignment. The T-Coffee program is a recent modification of Clustal that incorporates heuristics partially solving these problems.

Sequence Database Search Algorithms

Smith-waterman

Any pairwise sequence alignment method in principle can be used for database search in a straightforward manner. All that needs to be done is to construct alignments of the query with each sequence in the database, one by one, rank the results by sequence similarity, and estimate statistical significance.

The classic Smith-Waterman algorithm is a natural choice for such an application, and it has been implemented in several database search programs, the most popular one being SSEARCH written by William Pearson and distributed as part of the FASTA package. It is currently available on numerous servers around the world. The major problem preventing SSEARCH and other implementations of the Smith-Waterman algorithm from becoming the standard choice for routine database searches is the computational cost, which is orders of magnitude greater than it is for the heuristic FASTA and BLAST methods (see below). Since extensive comparisons of the performance of these methods in detecting structurally relevant relationships between proteins failed to show a decisive advantage of SSEARCH, the fast heuristic methods dominate the field. Nevertheless, on a case-by-case basis, it is certainly advisable to revert to full Smith-Waterman search when other methods do not reveal a satisfactory picture of homologous relationship for a protein of interest. On a purely empirical and even personal note, the authors have not had much success with this, but undoubtedly, even rare findings may be important. A modified, much faster version of the Smith-Waterman algorithm has been implemented in the MPSRCH program.

FASTA

FASTA, introduced in 1988 by William Pearson and David Lipman, was the first database search program that achieved search sensitivity comparable to that of Smith-Waterman but was much faster. FASTA looks for biologically relevant global alignments by first scanning the sequence for short exact matches called "words"; a word search is extremely fast. The idea is that almost any pair of homologous sequences is expected to have at least one short word in common. Under this assumption, the great majority of the sequences in the database that do not have common words with the query can be skipped without further examination with a minimal waste of computer time. The sensitivity and speed of the database search with FASTA are inversely related and depend on the "k-tuple" variable, which specifies the word size; typically, searches are run with $k = 3$, but, if high sensitivity at the expense of speed is desired, one may switch to $k = 2$.

Subsequently, Pearson introduced several improvements to the FASTA algorithm, which are implemented in the FASTA3 program available on the EBI server at. A useful FASTA-based tool for comparing two sequences, LALIGN.

Motifs, Domains and Profiles

Protein Sequence Motifs and Methods for Motif Detection

Let us ask a very general question: What distinguishes biologically important sequence similarities from spurious ones? By looking at just one alignment of the query and its database hit showing more or less scattered identical and similar residues as in this, already familiar alignment:

```
E. coli RpmJ:     1 MKVRASVKKLCR---NCKIVKRDGVIRVICSAEPKHKQRQG
                    MKV +S+K        +C+IVKR G + VIC + P+ K   Q
Vibrio VC0879:    1 MKVLSSLKSAKNRHPDCQIVKRRGRLYVICKSNPRFKAVQR
```

it might be hard to tell one from the other. However, as soon as we align more homologous sequence, particularly from distantly related organisms, as it is done for L36 in figure, we will have a clue as to the nature of the distinction. Note two pairs of residues that are conserved in the great majority of L36 sequences: Cx(2)Cx(12)Cx(4–5)H [here x(n) indicates n residues whose identity does not concern us]. Those familiar with protein domains might have already noticed that this conserved pattern resembles the pattern of metal-coordinating residues in the so-called Zn-fingers and Zn-ribbons, extremely widespread metal-binding domains, which mediate protein-nucleic acid and protein-protein interactions. Indeed, L36 has been shown to bind Zn^{2+}, and those very cysteines and histidines are involved. Such constellation of conserved amino acid residues associated with a particular function is called a sequence motif. Typically, motifs are confined to short stretches of protein sequences, usually spanning 10 to 30 amino acid residues. The notion of a motif, arguably one of the most important concepts in computational biology, was first explicitly introduced by Russell Doolittle in 1981. Fittingly and, to our knowledge, quite independently, the following year, John Walker and colleagues described what is probably the most prominent sequence motif in the entire protein universe, the phosphate-binding site of a vast class of ATP/GTP-utilizing enzymes, which subsequently has been named P-loop. Discovery of sequence motifs characteristic of a vast variety of enzymatic and binding activities of proteins proceeded first at an increasing and then, apparently, at a steady rate, and the motifs, in the form of amino acid patterns, were swiftly incorporated by Amos Bairoch in the PROSITE database.

The P-loop, which we already encountered in is usually presented as the following pattern of amino acid residues:

$$[GA]x(4)GK[ST]$$

Note that there are two strictly conserved residues in this pattern and two positions where one of two residues is allowed. By running this pattern against the entire protein sequence database using, for example, the FPAT program available through the ExPASy server program or any other pattern-matching program (even the UNIX 'grep' command will do), one immediately realizes just how general and how useful this pattern is. Indeed, such a search retrieves sequences of thousands of experimentally characterized ATPases and GTPases and their close homologs. However, only about one-half of the retrieved sequences are known or predicted NTPases of the P-loop class, whereas the rest are false-positives (E.V.K., unpublished). This is not surprising given the small number of residues in this pattern, which results in the probability of chance occurrence of about:

$$(1/10)(1/20)(1/20)(1/10)=2.5\times10^{-5}$$

(this is an approximate estimate because the actual amino acid frequencies are not taken into account, but it is close enough). With the current database size of about 3.2 × 10^8 residues, the expected number of matches is about 8,000.

This simple calculation shows that this and many other similar patterns, although they include the most conserved amino acid residues of important motifs, are insufficiently selective to be good diagnostic tools. The specificity of a pattern can be increased by taking into account adjacent residues that tend to have conserved properties. In particular, for the P-loop pattern, it can be required that there are at least three bulky, hydrophobic residues among the five residues upstream of the first glycine (structurally, this is a hydrophobic β-strand in ATPases and GTPases). This would greatly reduce the number of false-positives in a database search but would require a more sophisticated search method (as implemented, for example, in the GREF program of the SEALS package. Still, this does not solve the problem of motif identification. Figure shows the alignment of a small set of selected P-loops that were chosen for their sequence diversity. Obviously, not even a single amino is conserved in all these sequences, although they all represent the same motif that has a conserved function and, in all likelihood, is monophyletic, i.e. evolved only once. Given this lack of strict conservation of amino acid residues in an enzymatic motif, this trend is even more pronounced in motifs associated with macromolecular interactions, in which invariant residues are the exception rather than the norm. Pattern search remains a useful first-approximation method for motif identification, especially because a rich pattern collection, PROSITE, can be searched using a rapid and straightforward program like SCANPROSITE. However, by the very nature of the approach, patterns are either insufficiently selective or too specific and, accordingly, are not adequate descriptions of motifs.

```
RecB_Ecoli      ERLIEASAGTGKTFTIAALYLRLL
SbcC_Ecoli      LFAITGPTGAGKTTLLDAICLALY
MutS_Ecoli      MLIITGPNMGGKSTYMRQTALIAL
Adk_Ecoli       RIILLGAPGAGKGTQAQFIMEKYG
MCM2_HUMAN      NVLLCGDPGTAKSQFLKYIEKVSS
UvsX_T4         LLILAGPSKSFKSNFGLTMVSSYM
CmpK_Mjan       VITVSGLAGSGTTTLCRNLAKHYG
Pta_Ecoli       IMLIPTGTSVGLTSVSLGVIRAME
```

Alignment of P-loops from diverse ATPases and GTPases
The most conserved residues are shown in bold.

The way to properly capture the information contained in sequence motifs is to represent them as amino acid frequency profiles, which incorporate the frequencies of each of the 20 amino acid residues in each position of the motif. Even in the absence of invariant residues, non-randomness of a motif may be quite obvious in a profile representation. Utilization of frequency profiles for database searches had a profound effect on the quality and depth of sequence and structure analysis.

```
Csp1_Hs    KTSDSTFLVFMSIGIRE------GICGKKHSEQVPDILQ-LNAIFNMLNT--3-PSLKDKPKVIIIQACRGD-SPGVVWF
Csp2_Hs    RVTDSCIVALLSIGVE-------GAIYGVDG----KLLQ-LQEVFQLFDN--3-PSLQNKPKMFFIQACRGDETDRGVDQ
Csp3_Hs    SKRSSFVCVLLSIGEE-------GIIFGTN-----GPVD-LKKITNFFRG--3-RSLTGKPKLFIIQACRGTELDCGIET
Csp9_Hs    GALDCCVVVILSIGCQASHLQFPGAVYGTDG----CPVS-VEKIVNIFNG--3-PSLGGKPKLFFIQACGGEQKDHGFEV
Csp10_Hs   ADGDCFVFCILTIGRF-------GAVYSSDE----ALIP-IREIMSHFTA--3-PRLAEKPKLFFIQACQGEEIQPSVSI
CED3_Ce    G--DSAILVILSIGEE-------NVIIGVDD----IPIS-THEIYDLLNA--3-PRLANKPKIVFVQACRGERRDNGFPV

PC_Hs      DKGVYGLLYYAGIGYEN-----FGNSFMVPVD---APNPYRSENCLCVQN--5-QEKETGLNVFLLDMCRKRNDYDDTIP
PC_Ce      GNGVYAVFYFVGIGFEV-----NGQCYLLGVD---APADAHQPQHSMSMD--6-RHKTPDLNLLLLDVCRKFVPYDAISA
PC_Dd      QSYIEVVVYYAGIGRSD-----NGNLKLIMT----DGNPVQLSIIASTLT--2-IKNSDSLCLFIVDCCRDGENVLPFHY
Mlr2366_Ml YNADLAVIFYAGIGMQV-----DGKNYL-------IPVDADLTSPAYLKT-11-LPADPAVGVIILDACRDNPLGRTLAA
Mlr1804_Ml IGADMAVFYYAGIALQY-----NGQNLL-------LPVDTRISSAKEVAA-12-KNDPVGVKVFILDACRNNPVAKEKGL
Mll2372_Ml RGADVALFFYAGIGLQV-----SGKNYL-------LPVDAALEDETSLDF-11-MSRETSIRLVFLDACRDNPLADVLAK
Mlr3463_Ml EGAGVGLFYYAGIGLQV-----DGRNYI-------VPVDAKLDMPVKLQL-11-MEQQTKVSLVFLDACRNNPFARSLSR
Mll5190_Ml KGADVALVFSGIGVEI------SGDNRL-------LPVDADASSVDQLDK-12-VAATAKVGLIVLDACRSDPFSASSGD
Mlr1170_Ml EGADVAFIYYSGIGIEA------GGEN------YLVPVDADVSSLKDAGQ-11-LKKTVPVTIMLLDACRTNPFPADAVV
YOR197w_Sc QPNDSLFLHYSGIGGQTED--LDGDEEDGM-DDVIYPVDFETQGPIIDDE--8-PLQQGVRLTALFDSCHSGTVLDLPYT

MC1_At     TAGDSLVFHYSGIGSRQRN--YNGDEVDGY-DETLCPLDFETQGMIVDDE--7-PLPHGVKLHSIIDACHSGTVLDLPFL
MC2_At     KPGDSLVFHFSGIGNNQMD--DNGDEVDGF-DETLLPVDHRTSGVIVDDE--7-PLPYGVKLHAIVDACHSGTVMDLPYL
MC3_At     KPGDVLVVHYSGIGTRLPA--ETGEDDDTGYDECIVPCD-MNLITDDEFR--4-KVPKEAHITIISDSCHSGGLIDEAKE
Mlr3300_Ml QRDDFVYLHLSGIGAQQPER-AKGDETDGLDE-IFLPVDIEKWINRDAGV-15-IRNKGAFVWAVFDCCHSGTATRAVEV
MCH_Rsph   EPGGIFLMSYAGIGAQIGDFDEGDGPDRDRLDETLCLHD-AMLV-DDELY--4-AFREGVRVVAVFDSCHSGSILRASAN
MCH_Gsul   GKGDIFMLSYSGIGGQVP---DTSNDEPDGVDETWCLFD-GELI-DDELY--4-KFAAGVRVLVFSDSCHSGTVVKMAYY
```

AConserved catalytic motifs in the caspase-like superfamily of proteases

A. Multiple alignment of the catalytic motifs around the two active residues (His and Cys) of caspases (Csp, top group), paracaspases (PC, middle group), and metacaspases; see more about these proteases in. Note the conservation in the stretches preceding each of the catalytic residues and corresponding to the two main β-strands of the caspase domain. Conserved hydrophobic residues are highlighted in yellow; conserved small residues (Gly, Ser, Ala, Cys) are shown on a green background. The species abbreviations are: Hs, human; Ce, C. elegans; Dd, Dictyostelium; Ml, M. loti; Sc, yeast; At, Arabidopsis; Rsph, Rhodobacter sphaeroides; Gsul, Geobacter sulfurreducens.

Protein Domains, PSSMs and Advanced Methods for Database Search

Sequence motifs are extremely convenient descriptors of conserved, functionally important short portions of proteins. However, motifs are not the natural units of protein structure and evolution. Such distinct units are protein domains. In structural biology, domains are defined as structurally compact, independently folding parts of protein molecules. In comparative genomics and sequence analysis in general, the central, "atomic" objects are parts of proteins that have distinct evolutionary trajectories, i.e. occur either as stand-alone proteins or as parts of variable domain architectures (we refer to the linear order of domains in protein sequences as domain or multidomain architecture), but are never split into parts. Very often, probably in the majority of cases, such units of protein evolution exactly correspond to structural domains. However, in some groups of proteins, an evolutionary unit may consist of two or more domains. For example, from a purely structural viewpoint, trypsin-like proteases have two domains. However, at least so far, separation of these domains has not been observed, and therefore, they should be treated as a single evolutionary unit. It might be desirable to propose a special name for these units of protein evolution, but to our knowledge, this has not been done, and in comparative-genomic literature, including this book, they are commonly referred to as domains. On rare occasions, a domain consists of a single motif, as in the case of AT-hooks shown in figure However, much more often, domains are relatively large, comprising 100 to 300 amino acid residues and including two or more distinct motifs. Motifs are highly conserved patches in multiple alignments of domains that tend to be separated by regions of less pronounced sequence conservation and often of variable length; in other words, motifs may be conceptualized (and visualized) as peaks on sequence conservation profiles. In the 3D structure of most domains, the distinct motifs are juxtaposed and function together, which explains their correlated conservation. Figure illustrates the juxtaposition of motifs that center around the two catalytic residues in the alignment of the catalytic domain of caspase-related proteases from figure.

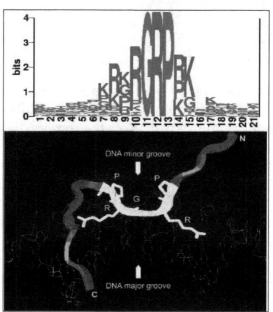

Profile representation of a conserved sequence motif and
the corresponding 3D structure of the DNA-binding AT-hook domain. The
pictorial form of the profile was produced using the Sequence Logo method.

The notion of protein motifs has been employed directly in algorithms that construct multiple sequence alignments as a chain of motifs separated by unaligned regions. The first of such methods, Multiple Alignment Construction and Analysis Workbench (MACAW), originally used a BLAST-like method for approximately delineating conserved sequence blocks (motifs) and then allowed the user to determine whether inclusion of additional alignment columns increased the significance of the block alignment.

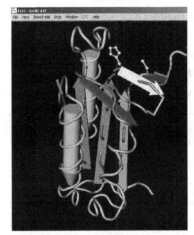

Conserved catalytic motifs in the caspase-like superfamily of proteases.

B. Structure of the human caspase-7 (PDB entry 1I51). The figure is generated using Cn3D representation of the MMDB entry. The conserved histidine and cysteine residues are shown in ball-and-stick representation in the upper part of the structure.

MACAW is a very convenient, accurate, and flexible alignment tool; however, the algorithm is $O(n^k)$ and, accordingly, becomes prohibitively computationally expensive for a large number of sequences. MACAW is an interactive tool that embodies the important notion that completely automatic methods are unlikely to capture all important motifs in cases of subtle sequence conservation, particularly in proteins that substantially differ in length. For many occasions, it remains the method of choice when careful alignment analysis is required, although, in the current situation of explosive growth of sequence data, the computational cost severely limits MACAW's utility. Subsequently, Charles Lawrence, Andrew Neuwald, and coworkers adapted the Gibbs sampling strategy for motif detection and developed the powerful (if not necessarily user-friendly) PROBE method that allows delineation of multiple, subtle motifs in large sets of sequences Importantly, Gibbs sampler is an $O(n)$ algorithm, which allows analysis of large numbers of sequences. Gibbs sampling has been incorporated into MACAW as one of the methods for conserved block detection. In principle, this should enable MACAW to efficiently align numerous sequences.

Arguably, the most important methodological advance based on the concepts of domains and motifs was the development of position-specific weight matrices (PSSMs) and their use in database searches as an incomparably more powerful substitute for regular matrices, such as BLOSUMs and PAMs. A PSSM is a rectangular table, which consists of n columns (n is the number of positions in the multiple alignment for which the PSSM is made) and 20 rows and contains, in each cell, the score (weight) for the given amino acid in the given position of the multiple alignment. In the simplest case, this score can be the frequency of the amino acid in the given position. It is easy to realize, however, that, on most occasions, residue frequencies taken from any given alignment are unlikely to adequately describe the respective domain family. Firstly, we certainly never know the full range of family members, and moreover, there is no evidence that we have a representative set. Therefore, if a residue is missing in a particular alignment column, this does not justify a 0 score in a PSSM. In reality, a PSSM never includes a score of exactly 0, although scores for some residues might be extremely low, and rounding sometimes may result in 0 values. Instead, a finite score is assigned to the missing residue using so-called regularizers, i.e. various mathematical techniques that strive to derive the correct distribution of amino acids for a given position on the basis of a limited sample. It is easy to realize that the score given to a missing residue depends on two factors: the distribution actually found in the sample of available superfamily members and the size of the sample. Clearly, if a set of 1,000 diverse sequences invariably contains, for example, a serine residue in a particular position, the probability of finding any other residue in this position is extremely low. Nevertheless, threonine, as a residue that is structurally close to serine and, according to substitution matrices like BLOSUMs and PAMs, is often exchangeable with serine in proteins, certainly should receive a higher score than, say, lysine.

One of course, could argue that an invariant serine is most likely to be part of a catalytic center of an enzyme and as such is more likely to be replaced by cysteine than by threonine (such replacements in enzymes, e.g. proteases and acyltransferases, are well documented, e.g. This level of sophistication seems to be beyond the capabilities of current automatic methods for PSSM generation, although, in principle, a PSSM for a particular domain could be tailored manually. Another aspect of PSSM construction that requires formal treatment beyond calculating and regularizing amino acid residue scores stems from the fact that many protein families available to us are enriched with closely related sequences (this might be the result of a genuine proliferation of a particular subset of a family or could be caused by sequencing bias). Obviously, an overrepresented subfamily will sway the entire PSSMs toward detection of additional closely related sequences and hamper the performance. To overcome this problem, different weighting schemes are applied to PSSMs to downweigh closely related sequences and increase the contribution of diverse ones. Optimal PSSM construction remains an important problem in sequence analysis, and even small improvements have the potential of significantly enhancing the power of database search methods. Some of the recent developments that we do not have the opportunity to seem to hold considerable promise. Once a PSSM is constructed, using it in a database search is straightforward and not particularly different from using a single query sequence combined with a regular substitution matrix, e.g. BLOSUM62. The common database search methods, such as BLAST, can work equally well with a PSSM, and the same statistics apply.

To our knowledge, the notion of a PSSM and its use for detecting weak sequence similarities was first introduced by Michael Gribskov, Andrew McLachlan, and David Eisenberg in 1987. However, their method was initially of limited utility because it depended on a pre-constructed multiple sequence alignment and consequently could not be used with the speed and ease comparable to those of using FASTA or BLAST. An important additional step was combining the use of PSSMs with iterative search strategy. To our knowledge, this was first done by Gribskov. Under this approach, after the first run of a PSSM-based similarity search against a sequence database, newly detected sequences (with the similarity to PSSM above a certain cut-off) are added to the alignment, the PSSM is rebuilt, and the cycle is repeated until no new members of the family are detected. This approach was implemented in a completely automated fashion in the Motif Search Tool (MoST) program, which also included a rigorous statistical method for evaluating resulting similarities but only worked with ungapped alignment blocks.

A decisive breakthrough in the evolution of PSSM-based methods for database searching was the development of the Position-Specific Iterating (PSI)-BLAST program. This program first performs a regular BLAST search of a protein query against a protein database. It then uses all the hits with scores greater than a certain cut-off to generate a multiple alignment and create a PSSM, which is used for the second search iteration. The search goes on until convergence or for a desired number of iterations. Obviously, the first PSI-BLAST iteration must employ a regular substitution matrix, such as BLOSUM62, to calculate HSP scores. For the subsequent iterations, the PSSM regularization procedure was designed in such a way that the contribution of the initial matrix to the position-specific scores decreases, whereas the contribution of the actual amino acid frequencies in the alignment increases with the growth of the number of retrieved sequences. PSI-BLAST also employs a simple sequence-weighting scheme, which is applied for PSSM construction at each iteration. Since its appearance in 1997, PSI-BLAST has become the most common method for in-depth protein sequence analysis. The method owes its success to its high speed (each iteration takes only slightly longer than a regular BLAST run), the ease of use (no additional steps are required, the search starts with a single sequence, and alignments and PSSMs are constructed automatically on the fly), and high reliability, especially when composition-based statistics are invoked. The practical aspects of using PSI-BLAST are considered at some length in 4.3.5.

Hidden Markov Models (HMMs) of multiple sequence alignments are a popular alternative to PSSMs. HMMs can be trained on unaligned sequences or pre-constructed multiple alignments and, similarly to PSI-BLAST, can be iteratively run against a database in an automatic regime. A variety of HMM-based search programs are included in the HMMer2 package; Sean Eddy's web site displays a recommendation to pronounce the name of this package "hammer" as in "a more precise mining tool than a BLAST"). HMM search is slower than PSI-BLAST, but there have been reports of greater sensitivity of HMMs (e.g). In the extensive albeit anecdotal experience of the authors, the results of protein superfamily analysis using PSI-BLAST and HMMer2 are remarkably similar.

The availability of techniques for constructing models of protein families and using them in database searches naturally leads to a vision of the future of protein sequence analysis. The methods such as PSI-BLAST and HMMer, start with a protein sequence and gradually build a model that allows detection of homologs with low sequence similarity to the query. Clearly, this approach can be reversed such that a sequence query is run against a pre-made collection of protein family models. In principle, if models were developed for all protein families, the problem of classifying a new protein sequence would have been essentially solved. In addition to family classification, regular database searches like BLAST also provide information on the most closely related homologs of the query, thus giving an indication of its evolutionary affinity. In itself, a search of a library of family models does not yield such information, but an extension of this approach is easily imaginable whereby a protein sequence, after being assigned to a family through PSSM and HMM search, is then fit into a phylogenetic tree. Searching the COG database may be viewed as a rough prototype of this approach. Such a system seems to have the potential of largely replacing current methods with an approach that is both much faster and more informative. Given the explosive growth of sequence databases, transition to searching databases of protein family models as the primary sequence analysis approach seems inevitable in a relatively near future. Only for discovering new domains will it be necessary to revert to searching the entire database, and since the protein universe is finite, these occasions are expected to become increasingly rare.

Presently, sequence analysis has not reached such an advanced stage, but searches against large, albeit far from complete, databases of domain-specific PSSMs and HMMs have already become extremely useful approaches in sequence analysis. Pfam, SMART, and CDD, which were introduced in 3.2, are the principal tools of this type. Pfam and SMART perform searches against HMMs generated from curated alignments of a variety of proteins domains. The CDD server compares a query sequence to the PSSM collection in the CDD using the Reversed Position-Specific (RPS)-BLAST program. Algorithmically, RPS-BLAST is similar to BLAST, with minor modifications; Karlin-Altschul statistics applies to E-value calculation for this method. RPS-BLAST searches the library of PSSMs derived from CDD, finding single- or double-word hits and then performing ungapped extension on these candidate matches. If a sufficiently high-scoring ungapped alignment is produced, a gapped extension is done, and the alignments with E-values below the cut-off are reported. Since the search space is equal to nm where n is the length of the query and m is the total length of the PSSMs in the database (which, at the time of writing, contains ~5,000 PSSMs), RPS-BLAST is ~100 times faster than regular BLAST.

Pattern-Hit-Initiated BLAST (PHI-BLAST) is a variant of BLAST that searches for homologs of the query that contain a particular sequence pattern. Pattern search often is insufficiently selective. PHI-BLAST partially rectifies this by first selecting the subset of database sequences that contain the given pattern and then searching this limited database using the regular BLAST algorithm. Although the importance of this method is not comparable to that of PSI-BLAST, it can be useful for detecting homologs with a very low overall similarity to the query that nevertheless retain a specific pattern.

Stand-alone (non-web) BLAST. However, the web-based approach is not suitable for large-scale searches requiring extensive post-processing, which are common in genome analysis. For these tasks, one has to use the stand-alone version of BLAST, which can be obtained from NCBI via ftp and installed locally under the Unix or Windows operation systems. Although the stand-alone BLAST programs do not offer all the conveniences available on the web, they do provide some additional and useful opportunities. In particular, stand-alone PSI-BLAST can be automatically run for the specified number of iterations or until convergence.

With the help of simple additional scripts, the results of stand-alone BLAST can be put to much use beyond the straightforward database search. Searches with thousands of queries can be run automatically, followed with various post-processing steps; The BLASTCLUST program (written by Ilya Dondoshansky in collaboration with Yuri Wolf and E.V.K.), which is also available from NCBI via ftp and works only with stand-alone BLAST, allows clustering sequences by similarity using the results of an all-against-all BLAST search within an analyzed set of sequences as the input. It identifies clusters using two criteria: (i) level of sequence similarity, which may be expressed either as percent identity or as score density (number of bits per aligned position), and (ii) the length of HSP relative to the length of the query and subject (e.g. one may require that, for the given two sequences to be clustered, the HSP(s) should cover at least 70% of each sequence). BLASTCLUST can be used, for example, to eliminate protein fragments from a database or to identify families of paralogs.

Sequence Alignment

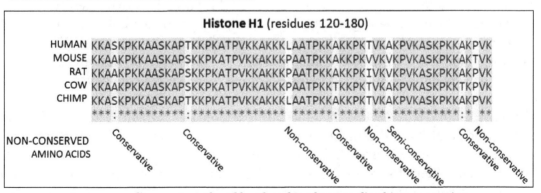

A sequence alignment, produced by ClustalO, of mammalian histone proteins.

Sequences are the amino acids for residues 120-180 of the proteins. Residues that are conserved across all sequences are highlighted in grey. Below the protein sequences is a key denoting conserved sequence (*), conservative mutations (:), semi-conservative mutations (.), and non-conservative mutations ( ).

In bioinformatics, a sequence alignment is a way of arranging the sequences of DNA, RNA, or protein to identify regions of similarity that may be a consequence of functional, structural, or evolutionary relationships between the sequences. Aligned sequences of nucleotide or amino acid residues are typically represented as rows within a matrix. Gaps are inserted between the residues so that identical or similar characters are aligned in successive columns. Sequence alignments are also used for non-biological sequences, such as calculating the distance cost between strings in a natural language or in financial data.

Interpretation

If two sequences in an alignment share a common ancestor, mismatches can be interpreted as point mutations and gaps as indels (that is, insertion or deletion mutations) introduced in one or both lineages in the time since they diverged from one another. In sequence alignments of proteins, the degree of similarity between amino acids occupying a particular position in the sequence can be interpreted as a rough measure of how conserved a particular region or sequence motif is among lineages. The absence of substitutions, or the presence of only very conservative substitutions (that is, the substitution of amino acids whose side chains have similar biochemical properties) in a particular region of the sequence, suggest that this region has structural or functional importance. Although DNA and RNA nucleotide bases are more similar to each other than are amino acids, the conservation of base pairs can indicate a similar functional or structural role.

Alignment Methods

Very short or very similar sequences can be aligned by hand. However, most interesting problems require the alignment of lengthy, highly variable or extremely numerous sequences that cannot be aligned solely by human effort. Instead, human knowledge is applied in constructing algorithms to produce high-quality sequence alignments, and occasionally in adjusting the final results to reflect patterns that are difficult to represent algorithmically (especially in the case of nucleotide sequences). Computational approaches to sequence alignment generally fall into two categories: *global alignments* and *local alignments*. Calculating a global alignment is a form of global optimization that "forces" the alignment to span the entire length of all query sequences. By contrast, local alignments identify regions of similarity within long sequences that are often widely divergent overall. Local alignments are often preferable, but can be more difficult to calculate because of the additional challenge of identifying the regions of similarity. A variety of computational algorithms have been applied to the sequence alignment problem. These include slow but formally correct methods like dynamic programming. These also include efficient, heuristic algorithms or probabilistic methods designed for large-scale database search, that do not guarantee to find best matches.

Representations

Alignments are commonly represented both graphically and in text format. In almost all sequence alignment representations, sequences are written in rows arranged so that aligned residues appear in successive columns. In text formats, aligned columns containing identical or similar characters are indicated with a system of conservation symbols. As in the image above, an asterisk or pipe symbol is used to show identity between two columns; other less common symbols include a colon for conservative substitutions and a period for semiconservative substitutions. Many sequence visualization programs also use color to display information about the properties of the individual sequence elements; in DNA and RNA sequences, this equates to assigning each nucleotide its own color. In protein alignments, such as the one in the image above, color is often used to indicate amino acid properties to aid in judging the conservation of a given amino acid substitution. For multiple sequences the last row in each column is often the consensus sequence determined by the alignment; the consensus sequence is also often represented in graphical format with a sequence logo in which the size of each nucleotide or amino acid letter corresponds to its degree of conservation.

Sequence alignments can be stored in a wide variety of text-based file formats, many of which were originally developed in conjunction with a specific alignment program or implementation. Most web-based tools allow a limited number of input and output formats, such as FASTA format and GenBank format and the output is not easily editable. Several conversion programs that provide graphical and command line interfaces are available, such as READSEQ and EMBOSS. There are also several programming packages which provide this conversion functionality, such as BioPython, BioRuby and BioPerl. The SAM/BAM files use the CIGAR (Compact Idiosyncratic Gapped Alignment Report) string format to represent an alignment of a sequence to a reference by encoding a sequence of events (e.g. match/mismatch, insertions, deletions).

Global and Local Alignments

Global alignments, which attempt to align every residue in every sequence, are most useful when the sequences in the query set are similar and of roughly equal size. (This does not mean global alignments cannot start and end in gaps.) A general global alignment technique is the Needleman–Wunsch algorithm, which is based on dynamic programming. Local alignments are more useful for dissimilar sequences that are suspected to contain regions of similarity or similar sequence motifs within their larger sequence context. The Smith–Waterman algorithm is a general local alignment method based on the same dynamic programming scheme but with additional choices to start and end at any place.

Hybrid methods, known as semi-global or "glocal" (short for global-local) methods, search for the best possible partial alignment of the two sequences (in other words, a combination of one or both starts and one or both ends is stated to be aligned). This can be especially useful when the downstream part of one sequence overlaps with the upstream part of the other sequence. In this case, neither global nor local alignment is entirely appropriate: a global alignment would attempt to force the alignment to extend beyond the region of overlap, while a local alignment might not fully cover the region of overlap. Another case where semi-global alignment is useful is when one sequence is short (for example a gene sequence) and the other is very long (for example a chromosome sequence). In that case, the short sequence should be globally (fully) aligned but only a local (partial) alignment is desired for the long sequence.

Fast expansion of genetic data challenges speed of current DNA sequence alignment algorithms. Essential needs for an efficient and accurate method for DNA variant discovery demand innovative approaches for parallel processing in real time. Optical computing approaches have been suggested as promising alternatives to the current electrical implementations, yet their applicability remains to be tested.

Pairwise Alignment

Pairwise sequence alignment methods are used to find the best-matching piecewise (local or global) alignments of two query sequences. Pairwise alignments can only be used between two sequences at a time, but they are efficient to calculate and are often used for methods that do not require extreme precision (such as searching a database for sequences with high similarity to a query). The three primary methods of producing pairwise alignments are dot-matrix methods, dynamic programming, and word methods; however, multiple sequence alignment techniques can also align pairs of sequences. Although each method has its individual strengths and weaknesses, all three pairwise methods have difficulty with highly repetitive sequences of low information content - especially where the number of repetitions differ in the two sequences to be aligned. One way of quantifying the utility of a given pairwise alignment is the 'maximum unique match' (MUM), or the longest subsequence that occurs in both query sequences. Longer MUM sequences typically reflect closer relatedness.

Dot-matrix Methods

The dot-matrix approach, which implicitly produces a family of alignments for individual sequence regions, is qualitative and conceptually simple, though time-consuming to analyze on a large scale. In the absence of noise, it can be easy to visually identify certain sequence features—such as insertions, deletions, repeats, or inverted repeats—from a dot-matrix plot. To construct a dot-matrix plot, the two sequences are written along the top row and leftmost column of a two-dimensional matrix and a dot is placed at any point where the characters in the appropriate columns match—this is a typical recurrence plot. Some implementations vary the size or intensity of the dot depending on the degree of similarity of the two characters, to accommodate conservative substitutions. The dot plots of very closely related sequences will appear as a single line along the matrix's main diagonal.

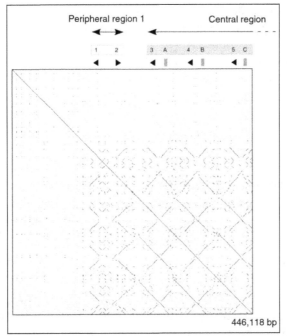

Self comparison of a part of a mouse strain genome. The dot-plot shows
a patchwork of lines, demonstrating duplicated segments of DNA.

Problems with dot plots as an information display technique include: noise, lack of
clarity, non-intuitiveness, difficulty extracting match summary statistics and match positions on the two sequences. There is also much wasted space where the match data
is inherently duplicated across the diagonal and most of the actual area of the plot is
taken up by either empty space or noise, and, finally, dot-plots are limited to two sequences. None of these limitations apply to Miropeats alignment diagrams but they
have their own particular flaws.

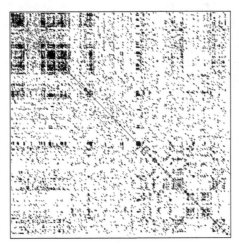

A DNA dot plot of a human zinc finger transcription factor (GenBank ID NM_002383),
showing regional self-similarity. The main diagonal represents the sequence's alignment

with itself; lines off the main diagonal represent similar or repetitive patterns within the sequence. This is a typical example of a recurrence plot.

Dot plots can also be used to assess repetitiveness in a single sequence. A sequence can be plotted against itself and regions that share significant similarities will appear as lines off the main diagonal. This effect can occur when a protein consists of multiple similar structural domains.

Dynamic Programming

The technique of dynamic programming can be applied to produce global alignments via the Needleman-Wunsch algorithm, and local alignments via the Smith-Waterman algorithm. In typical usage, protein alignments use a substitution matrix to assign scores to amino-acid matches or mismatches, and a gap penalty for matching an amino acid in one sequence to a gap in the other. DNA and RNA alignments may use a scoring matrix, but in practice often simply assign a positive match score, a negative mismatch score, and a negative gap penalty. (In standard dynamic programming, the score of each amino acid position is independent of the identity of its neighbors, and therefore base stacking effects are not taken into account. However, it is possible to account for such effects by modifying the algorithm.) A common extension to standard linear gap costs, is the usage of two different gap penalties for opening a gap and for extending a gap. Typically the former is much larger than the latter, e.g. -10 for gap open and -2 for gap extension. Thus, the number of gaps in an alignment is usually reduced and residues and gaps are kept together, which typically makes more biological sense. The Gotoh algorithm implements affine gap costs by using three matrices.

Dynamic programming can be useful in aligning nucleotide to protein sequences, a task complicated by the need to take into account frameshift mutations (usually insertions or deletions). The framesearch method produces a series of global or local pairwise alignments between a query nucleotide sequence and a search set of protein sequences, or vice versa. Its ability to evaluate frameshifts offset by an arbitrary number of nucleotides makes the method useful for sequences containing large numbers of indels, which can be very difficult to align with more efficient heuristic methods. In practice, the method requires large amounts of computing power or a system whose architecture is specialized for dynamic programming. The BLAST and EMBOSS suites provide basic tools for creating translated alignments (though some of these approaches take advantage of side-effects of sequence searching capabilities of the tools). More general methods are available from open-source software such as Genewise.

The dynamic programming method is guaranteed to find an optimal alignment given a particular scoring function; however, identifying a good scoring function is often an empirical rather than a theoretical matter. Although dynamic programming is extensible to more than two sequences, it is prohibitively slow for large numbers of sequences or extremely long sequences.

Word Methods

Word methods, also known as k-tuple methods, are heuristic methods that are not guaranteed to find an optimal alignment solution, but are significantly more efficient than dynamic programming. These methods are especially useful in large-scale database searches where it is understood that a large proportion of the candidate sequences will have essentially no significant match with the query sequence. Word methods are best known for their implementation in the database search tools FASTA and the BLAST family. Word methods identify a series of short, nonoverlapping subsequences ("words") in the query sequence that are then matched to candidate database sequences. The relative positions of the word in the two sequences being compared are subtracted to obtain an offset; this will indicate a region of alignment if multiple distinct words produce the same offset. Only if this region is detected do these methods apply more sensitive alignment criteria; thus, many unnecessary comparisons with sequences of no appreciable similarity are eliminated.

In the FASTA method, the user defines a value k to use as the word length with which to search the database. The method is slower but more sensitive at lower values of k, which are also preferred for searches involving a very short query sequence. The BLAST family of search methods provides a number of algorithms optimized for particular types of queries, such as searching for distantly related sequence matches. BLAST was developed to provide a faster alternative to FASTA without sacrificing much accuracy; like FASTA, BLAST uses a word search of length k, but evaluates only the most significant word matches, rather than every word match as does FASTA. Most BLAST implementations use a fixed default word length that is optimized for the query and database type, and that is changed only under special circumstances, such as when searching with repetitive or very short query sequences. Implementations can be found via a number of web portals, such as EMBL FASTA and NCBI BLAST.

Multiple Sequence Alignment

Multiple sequence alignment is an extension of pairwise alignment to incorporate more than two sequences at a time. Multiple alignment methods try to align all of the sequences in a given query set. Multiple alignments are often used in identifying conserved sequence regions across a group of sequences hypothesized to be evolutionarily related. Such conserved sequence motifs can be used in conjunction with structural and mechanistic information to locate the catalytic active sites of enzymes. Alignments are also used to aid in establishing evolutionary relationships by constructing phylogenetic trees. Multiple sequence alignments are computationally difficult to produce and most formulations of the problem lead to NP-complete combinatorial optimization problems. Nevertheless, the utility of these alignments in bioinformatics has led to the development of a variety of methods suitable for aligning three or more sequences.

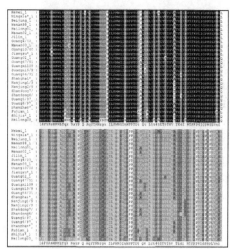

Alignment of 27 avian influenza hemagglutinin protein sequences colored
by residue conservation (top) and residue properties (bottom).

Dynamic Programming

The technique of dynamic programming is theoretically applicable to any number of sequences; however, because it is computationally expensive in both time and memory, it is rarely used for more than three or four sequences in its most basic form. This method requires constructing the n-dimensional equivalent of the sequence matrix formed from two sequences, where n is the number of sequences in the query. Standard dynamic programming is first used on all pairs of query sequences and then the "alignment space" is filled in by considering possible matches or gaps at intermediate positions, eventually constructing an alignment essentially between each two-sequence alignment. Although this technique is computationally expensive, its guarantee of a global optimum solution is useful in cases where only a few sequences need to be aligned accurately. One method for reducing the computational demands of dynamic programming, which relies on the "sum of pairs" objective function, has been implemented in the MSA software package.

Progressive Methods

Progressive, hierarchical, or tree methods generate a multiple sequence alignment by first aligning the most similar sequences and then adding successively less related sequences or groups to the alignment until the entire query set has been incorporated into the solution. The initial tree describing the sequence relatedness is based on pairwise comparisons that may include heuristic pairwise alignment methods similar to FASTA. Progressive alignment results are dependent on the choice of "most related" sequences and thus can be sensitive to inaccuracies in the initial pairwise alignments. Most progressive multiple sequence alignment methods additionally weight the sequences in the query set according to their relatedness, which reduces the likelihood of making a poor choice of initial sequences and thus improves alignment accuracy.

Many variations of the Clustal progressive implementation are used for multiple sequence alignment, phylogenetic tree construction, and as input for protein structure prediction. A slower but more accurate variant of the progressive method is known as T-Coffee.

Iterative Methods

Iterative methods attempt to improve on the heavy dependence on the accuracy of the initial pairwise alignments, which is the weak point of the progressive methods. Iterative methods optimize an objective function based on a selected alignment scoring method by assigning an initial global alignment and then realigning sequence subsets. The realigned subsets are then themselves aligned to produce the next iteration's multiple sequence alignment. Various ways of selecting the sequence subgroups and objective function are reviewed in.

Motif Finding

Motif finding, also known as profile analysis, constructs global multiple sequence alignments that attempt to align short conserved sequence motifs among the sequences in the query set. This is usually done by first constructing a general global multiple sequence alignment, after which the highly conserved regions are isolated and used to construct a set of profile matrices. The profile matrix for each conserved region is arranged like a scoring matrix but its frequency counts for each amino acid or nucleotide at each position are derived from the conserved region's characte r distribution rather than from a more general empirical distribution. The profile matrices are then used to search other sequences for occurrences of the motif they characterize. In cases where the original data set contained a small number of sequences, or only highly related sequences, pseudocounts are added to normalize the character distributions represented in the motif.

Techniques Inspired by Computer Science

A variety of general optimization algorithms commonly used in computer science have also been applied to the multiple sequence alignment problem. Hidden Markov models have been used to produce probability scores for a family of possible multiple sequence alignments for a given query set; although early HMM-based methods produced underwhelming performance, later applications have found them especially effective in detecting remotely related sequences because they are less susceptible to noise created by conservative or semiconservative substitutions. Genetic algorithms and simulated annealing have also been used in optimizing multiple sequence alignment scores as judged by a scoring function like the sum-of-pairs method.

The Burrows–Wheeler transform has been successfully applied to fast short read alignment in popular tools such as Bowtie and BWA.

Structural Alignment

Structural alignments, which are usually specific to protein and sometimes RNA sequences, use information about the secondary and tertiary structure of the protein or RNA molecule to aid in aligning the sequences. These methods can be used for two or more sequences and typically produce local alignments; however, because they depend on the availability of structural information, they can only be used for sequences whose corresponding structures are known (usually through X-ray crystallography or NMR spectroscopy). Because both protein and RNA structure is more evolutionarily conserved than sequence, structural alignments can be more reliable between sequences that are very distantly related and that have diverged so extensively that sequence comparison cannot reliably detect their similarity.

Structural alignments are used as the "gold standard" in evaluating alignments for homology-based protein structure prediction because they explicitly align regions of the protein sequence that are structurally similar rather than relying exclusively on sequence information. However, clearly structural alignments cannot be used in structure prediction because at least one sequence in the query set is the target to be modeled, for which the structure is not known. It has been shown that, given the structural alignment between a target and a template sequence, highly accurate models of the target protein sequence can be produced; a major stumbling block in homology-based structure prediction is the production of structurally accurate alignments given only sequence information.

DALI

The DALI method, or distance matrix alignment, is a fragment-based method for constructing structural alignments based on contact similarity patterns between successive hexapeptides in the query sequences. It can generate pairwise or multiple alignments and identify a query sequence's structural neighbors in the Protein Data Bank (PDB). It has been used to construct the FSSP structural alignment database (Fold classification based on Structure-Structure alignment of Proteins, or Families of Structurally Similar Proteins). A DALI webserver can be accessed at DALI and the FSSP is located at The Dali Database.

SSAP

SSAP (sequential structure alignment program) is a dynamic programming-based method of structural alignment that uses atom-to-atom vectors in structure space as comparison points. It has been extended since its original description to include multiple as well as pairwise alignments, and has been used in the construction of the CATH (Class, Architecture, Topology, Homology) hierarchical database classification of protein folds. The CATH database can be accessed at CATH Protein Structure Classification.

Combinatorial Extension

The combinatorial extension method of structural alignment generates a pairwise structural alignment by using local geometry to align short fragments of the two proteins being analyzed and then assembles these fragments into a larger alignment. Based on measures such as rigid-body root mean square distance, residue distances, local secondary structure, and surrounding environmental features such as residue neighbor hydrophobicity, local alignments called "aligned fragment pairs" are generated and used to build a similarity matrix representing all possible structural alignments within predefined cutoff criteria. A path from one protein structure state to the other is then traced through the matrix by extending the growing alignment one fragment at a time. The optimal such path defines the combinatorial-extension alignment. A web-based server implementing the method and providing a database of pairwise alignments of structures in the Protein Data Bank is located at the Combinatorial Extension website.

Phylogenetic Analysis

Phylogenetics and sequence alignment are closely related fields due to the shared necessity of evaluating sequence relatedness. The field of phylogenetics makes extensive use of sequence alignments in the construction and interpretation of phylogenetic trees, which are used to classify the evolutionary relationships between homologous genes represented in the genomes of divergent species. The degree to which sequences in a query set differ is qualitatively related to the sequences' evolutionary distance from one another. Roughly speaking, high sequence identity suggests that the sequences in question have a comparatively young most recent common ancestor, while low identity suggests that the divergence is more ancient. This approximation, which reflects the "molecular clock" hypothesis that a roughly constant rate of evolutionary change can be used to extrapolate the elapsed time since two genes first diverged (that is, the coalescence time), assumes that the effects of mutation and selection are constant across sequence lineages. Therefore, it does not account for possible difference among organisms or species in the rates of DNA repair or the possible functional conservation of specific regions in a sequence. (In the case of nucleotide sequences, the molecular clock hypothesis in its most basic form also discounts the difference in acceptance rates between silent mutations that do not alter the meaning of a given codon and other mutations that result in a different amino acid being incorporated into the protein). More statistically accurate methods allow the evolutionary rate on each branch of the phylogenetic tree to vary, thus producing better estimates of coalescence times for genes.

Progressive multiple alignment techniques produce a phylogenetic tree by necessity because they incorporate sequences into the growing alignment in order of relatedness. Other techniques that assemble multiple sequence alignments and phylogenetic trees score and sort trees first and calculate a multiple sequence alignment from the highest-scoring tree. Commonly used methods of phylogenetic tree construction are mainly heuristic because the problem of selecting the optimal tree, like the problem of selecting the optimal multiple sequence alignment, is NP-hard.

Assessment of Significance

Sequence alignments are useful in bioinformatics for identifying sequence similarity, producing phylogenetic trees, and developing homology models of protein structures. However, the biological relevance of sequence alignments is not always clear. Alignments are often assumed to reflect a degree of evolutionary change between sequences descended from a common ancestor; however, it is formally possible that convergent evolution can occur to produce apparent similarity between proteins that are evolutionarily unrelated but perform similar functions and have similar structures.

In database searches such as BLAST, statistical methods can determine the likelihood of a particular alignment between sequences or sequence regions arising by chance given the size and composition of the database being searched. These values can vary significantly depending on the search space. In particular, the likelihood of finding a given alignment by chance increases if the database consists only of sequences from the same organism as the query sequence. Repetitive sequences in the database or query can also distort both the search results and the assessment of statistical significance; BLAST automatically filters such repetitive sequences in the query to avoid apparent hits that are statistical artifacts.

Methods of statistical significance estimation for gapped sequence alignments are available in the literature.

Assessment of Credibility

Statistical significance indicates the probability that an alignment of a given quality could arise by chance, but does not indicate how much superior a given alignment is to alternative alignments of the same sequences. Measures of alignment credibility indicate the extent to which the best scoring alignments for a given pair of sequences are substantially similar. Methods of alignment credibility estimation for gapped sequence alignments are available in the literature.

Scoring Functions

The choice of a scoring function that reflects biological or statistical observations about known sequences is important to producing good alignments. Protein sequences are frequently aligned using substitution matrices that reflect the probabilities of given character-to-character substitutions. A series of matrices called PAM matrices (Point Accepted Mutation matrices, originally defined by Margaret Dayhoff and sometimes referred to as "Dayhoff matrices") explicitly encode evolutionary approximations regarding the rates and probabilities of particular amino acid mutations. Another common series of scoring matrices, known as BLOSUM (Blocks Substitution Matrix), encodes empirically derived substitution probabilities. Variants of both types of matrices are used to detect sequences with differing levels of divergence, thus allowing users of BLAST or FASTA to restrict searches to more closely related matches or expand to detect more divergent sequences. Gap penalties account for the introduction of a gap - on the evolutionary model, an insertion or deletion mutation - in both nucleotide and protein sequences, and therefore the penalty values should be proportional to the expected rate of such mutations. The quality of the alignments produced therefore depends on the quality of the scoring function.

It can be very useful and instructive to try the same alignment several times with different choices for scoring matrix and gap penalty values and compare the results. Regions where the solution is weak or non-unique can often be identified by observing which regions of the alignment are robust to variations in alignment parameters.

Other Biological Uses

Sequenced RNA, such as expressed sequence tags and full-length mRNAs, can be aligned to a sequenced genome to find where there are genes and get information about alternative splicing and RNA editing. Sequence alignment is also a part of genome assembly, where sequences are aligned to find overlap so that *contigs* (long stretches of sequence) can be formed. Another use is SNP analysis, where sequences from different individuals are aligned to find single basepairs that are often different in a population.

Non-biological Uses

The methods used for biological sequence alignment have also found applications in other fields, most notably in natural language processing and in social sciences, where the Needleman-Wunsch algorithm is usually referred to as Optimal matching. Techniques that generate the set of elements from which words will be selected in natural-language generation algorithms have borrowed multiple sequence alignment techniques from bioinformatics to produce linguistic versions of computer-generated mathematical proofs. In the field of historical and comparative linguistics, sequence alignment has been used to partially automate the comparative method by which linguists traditionally reconstruct languages. Business and marketing research has also applied multiple sequence alignment techniques in analyzing series of purchases over time.

Alignment-free Sequence Analysis

In bioinformatics, alignment-free sequence analysis approaches to molecular sequence and structure data provide alternatives over alignment-based approaches.

The emergence and need for the analysis of different types of data generated through biological research has given rise to the field of bioinformatics. Molecular sequence and structure data of DNA, RNA, and proteins, gene expression profiles or microarray data, metabolic pathway data are some of the major types of data being analysed in bioinformatics. Among them sequence data is increasing at the exponential rate due to advent of next-generation sequencing technologies. Since the origin of bioinformatics, sequence analysis has remained the major area of research with wide range of applications in database searching, genome annotation, comparative genomics, molecular phylogeny and gene prediction. The pioneering approaches for sequence analysis were based on sequence alignment either global or local, pairwise or multiple sequence alignment. Alignment-based approaches generally give excellent results when the sequences under study are closely related and can be reliably aligned, but when the sequences are divergent, a reliable alignment cannot be obtained and hence the applications of sequence alignment are limited. Another limitation of alignment-based approaches is their computational complexity and are time-consuming and thus, are limited when dealing with large-scale sequence data. The advent of next-generation sequencing technologies has resulted in generation of voluminous sequencing data. The size of this sequence data poses challenges on alignment-based algorithms in their assembly, annotation and comparative studies.

Alignment-free Methods

Alignment-free methods can broadly be classified into five categories: a) methods based on k-mer/word frequency, b) methods based on the length of common substrings, c) methods based on the number of (spaced) word matches, d) methods based on micro-alignments, e) methods based on information theory and f) methods based on graphical representation. Alignment-free approaches have been used in sequence similarity searches, clustering and classification of sequences, and more recently in phylogenetics. Such molecular phylogeny analyses employing alignment-free approaches are said to be part of next-generation phylogenomics. The AFproject is an international collaboration to benchmark and compare software tools for alignment-free sequence comparison.

Methods based on k-mer/word Frequency

The popular methods based on k-mer/word frequencies include feature frequency profile (FFP), Composition vector (CV), Return time distribution (RTD), frequency chaos game representation (FCGR) and Spaced Words.

Feature Frequency Profile

The methodology involved in FFP based method starts by calculating the count of each possible k-mer (possible number of k-mers for nucleotide sequence: 4^k, while that for protein sequence: 20^k) in sequences. Each k-mer count in each sequence is then normalized by dividing it by total of all k-mers' count in that sequence. This leads to conversion of each sequence into its feature frequency profile. The pair wise distance between two sequences is then calculated Jensen–Shannon (JS) divergence between their respective FFPs. The distance matrix thus obtained can be used to construct phylogenetic tree using clustering algorithms like neighbor-joining, UPGMA etc.

Composition Vector

In this method frequency of appearance of each possible k-mer in a given sequence is calculated. The next characteristic step of this method is the subtraction of random background of these frequencies using Markov model to reduce the influence of random neutral mutations to highlight the role of selective evolution. The normalized frequencies are put a fixed order to form the composition vector (CV) of a given sequence. Cosine distance function is then used to compute pairwise distance between CVs of sequences. The distance matrix thus obtained can be used to construct phylogenetic tree using clustering algorithms like neighbor-joining, UPGMA etc. This method can be extended through resort to efficient pattern matching algorithms to include in the computation of the composition vectors: (i) all k-mers for any value of k, (ii) all substrings of any length up to an arbitrarily set maximum k value, (iii) all maximal substrings, where a substring is maximal if extending it by any character would cause a decrease in its occurrence count.

Return Time Distribution

The RTD based method does not calculate the count of k-mers in sequences, instead it computes the time required for the reappearance of k-mers. The time refers to the number of residues in successive appearance of particular k-mer. Thus the occurrence of each k-mer in a sequence is calculated in the form of RTD, which is then summarised using two statistical parameters mean (μ) and standard deviation (σ). Thus each sequence is represented in the form of numeric vector of size $2 \cdot 4^k$ containing μ and σ of 4^k RTDs. The pair wise distance between sequences is calculated using Euclidean distance measure. The distance matrix thus obtained can be used to construct phylogenetic tree using clustering algorithms like neighbor-joining, UPGMA etc.

Frequency Chaos Game Representation

The FCGR methods have evolved from chaos game representation (CGR) technique, which provides scale independent representation for genomic sequences. The CGRs can be divided by grid lines where each grid square denotes the occurrence of oligonucleotides of a specific length in the sequence. Such representation of CGRs is termed as Frequency Chaos Game Representation (FCGR). This leads to representation of each sequence into FCGR. The pair wise distance between FCGRs of sequences can be calculated using the Pearson distance, the Hamming distance or the Euclidean distance.

Spaced-word Frequencies

While most alignment-free algorithms compare the word-composition of sequences, Spaced Words uses a pattern of care and don't care positions. The occurrence of a spaced word in a sequence is then defined by the characters at the match positions only, while the characters at the don't care positions are ignored. Instead of comparing the frequencies of contiguous words in the input sequences, this approach compares the frequencies of the spaced words according to the pre-defined pattern. Note that the pre-defined pattern can be selected by analysis of the Variance of the number of matches, the probability of the first occurrence on several models, or the Pearson correlation coefficient between the expected word frequency and the true alignment distance.

Methods based on Length of Common Substrings

The methods in this category employ the similarity and differences of substrings in a pair of sequences. These algorithms were mostly used for string processing in computer science.

Average Common Substring

In this approach, for a chosen pair of sequences (A and B of lengths n and m respectively), longest substring starting at some position is identified in one sequence (A) which exactly matches in the other sequence (B) at any position. In this way, lengths of longest substrings starting at different positions in sequence A and having exact matches at some positions in sequence B are calculated. All these lengths are averaged to derive a measure. Intuitively, larger the $L(A, B)$, the more similar the two sequences are. To account for the differences in the length of sequences, $L(A, B)$ is normalized [i.e. $L(A, B) / \log(m)$]. This gives the similarity measure between the sequences.

In order to derive a distance measure, the inverse of similarity measure is taken and a correction term is subtracted from it to assure that $d(A, A)$ will be zero.

$$d(A, B) = \left[\frac{\log m}{L(A, B)} \right] - \left[\frac{\log n}{L(A, A)} \right].$$

This measure $d(A, B)$ is not symmetric, so one has to compute $d_s(A, B) = d_s(B, A) = (d(A, B) + d(B, A)) / 2$, which gives final ACS measure between the two strings (A and B). The subsequence/substring search can be efficiently performed by using suffix trees.

k-mismatch Average Common Substring Approach

This approach is a generalization of the ACS approach. To define the distance between two DNA or protein sequences, kmacs estimates for each position i of the first sequence the longest substring starting at i and matching a substring of the second sequence with up to k mismatches. It defines the average of these values as a measure of similarity between the sequences and turns this into a symmetric distance measure. Kmacs does not compute exact k-mismatch substrings, since this would be computational too costly, but approximates such substrings.

Mutation Distances

This approach is closely related to the ACS, which calculates the number of substitutions per site between two DNA sequences using the shortest absent substring (termed as shustring).

Length Distribution of k-mismatch Common Substrings

This approach uses the program kmacs to calculate longest common substrings with up to k mismatches for a pair of DNA sequences. The phylogenetic distance between the sequences can then be estimated from a local maximum in the length distribution of the k-mismatch common substrings.

Methods based on the Number of Spaced-word Matches

D_2^S and D_2^*

These approachese are variants of the D_2 statistics that counts the number of k-mer matches between two sequences. They improve the simple D_2 statistics by taking the background distribution of the compared sequences into account.

MASH

This is an extremely fast method that uses the MinHash bottom sketch strategy for estimating the Jaccard index of the multi-sets of k-mers of two input sequences. That is, it estimates the ratio of k-mer matches to the total number of k-mers of the sequences. This can be used, in turn, to estimate the evolutionary distances between the compared sequences, measured as the number of substitutions per sequence position since the sequences evolved from their last common anchestor.

Slope-Tree

This approach calculates a distance value between two protein sequences based on the decay of the number of k-mer matches if k increases.

Slope-SpaM

This method calculates the number N_k of k-mer or spaced-word matches (*SpaM*) for different values for the word length or number of match positions k in the underlying pattern, respectively. The slope of an affine-linear function F that depends on N_k is calculated to estimate the Jukes-Cantor distance between the input sequences.

Skmer

Skmer calculates distances between species from unassembled sequencing reads. Similar to *MASH*, it uses the Jaccard index on the sets of k-mers from the input sequences. In contrast to *MASH*, the program is still accurate for low sequencing coverage, so it can be used for *genome skimming*.

Methods based on Micro-alignments

Strictly spoken, these methods are not *alignment-free*. They are using simple gap-free *micro-alignments* where sequences are required to match at certain pre-defined positions. The positions aligned at the remaining positions of the *micro-alignments* where mismatches are allowed, are then used for phylogeny inference.

Co-phylog

This method searches for so-called *structures* that are defined as pairs of k-mer matches between two DNA sequences that are one position apart in both sequences. The two k-mer matches are called the *context*, the position between them is called the *object*. Co-phylog then defines the distance between two sequences the fraction of such *structures* for which the two nucleotides in the *object* are different. The approach can be applied to unassembled sequencing reads.

ANDi

ANDi estimates phylogenetic distances between genomic sequences based on ungapped local alignments that are flanked by maximal exact word matches. Such word matches can be efficiently found using suffix arrays. The gapfree alignments between the exact word matches are then used to estimate phylogenetic distances between genome se-quences. The resulting distance estimates are accurate for up to around 0.6 substitu-tions per position.

Filtered Spaced-word Matches

FSWM uses a pre-defined binary pattern P representing so-called match positions and don't-care positions. For a pair of input DNA sequences, it then searches for spaced-word matches w.r.t. P, i.e. for local gap-free alignments with matching nucleotides at the match positions of P and possible mismatches at the don't-care positions. Spurious low-scoring spaced-word matches are discarded, evolutionary distances between the input sequences are estimated based on the nucleotides aligned to each other at the don't-care positions of the remaining, homologous spaced-word matches. FSWM has been adapted to estimate distances based on unassembled NGS reads, this version of the program is called Read-SpaM

Prot-SpaM

Prot-SpaM (Proteome-based Spaced-word Matches) is an implementation of the FSWM algorithm for partial or whole proteome sequences.

Multi-SpaM

Multi-SpaM (MultipleSpaced-word Matches) is an approach to genome-based phy-logeny reconstruction that extends the FSWM idea to multiple sequence compari-son. Given a binary pattern P of match positions and don't-care positions, the pro-gram searches for P-blocks, i.e. local gap-free four-way alignments with matching nucleotides at the match positions of P and possible mismatches at the don't-care positions. Such four-way alignments are randomly sampled from a set of input ge-nome sequences. For each P-block, an unrooted tree topology is calculated using RAxML. The program Quartet MaxCut is then used to calculate a supertree from these trees.

Methods based on Information Theory

Information Theory has provided successful methods for alignment-free sequence analysis and comparison. The existing applications of information theory include glob-al and local characterization of DNA, RNA and proteins, estimating genome entropy to motif and region classification. It also holds promise in gene mapping, next-generation sequencing analysis and metagenomics.

Base-base Correlation

Base–base correlation (BBC) converts the genome sequence into a unique 16-dimen-sional numeric vector using the following equation:

$$T_{ij}(K) = \sum_{\ell=1}^{K} P_{ij}(\ell) \cdot \log_2 \left(\frac{P_{ij}(\ell)}{P_i P_j} \right)$$

The P_i and P_j denotes the probabilities of bases i and j in the genome. The $P_{ij}(\ell)$ in-dicates the probability of bases i and j at distance ℓ in the genome. The parameter K indicates the maximum distance between the bases i and j. The variation in the values of 16 parameters reflect variation in the genome content and length.

Information Correlation and Partial Information Correlation

IC-PIC (information correlation and partial information correlation) based method employs the base correlation property of DNA sequence. IC and PIC were calculated using following formulas,

$$IC_\ell = -2\sum_i P_i \log_2 P_i + \sum_{ij} P_{ij}(\ell) \log_2 P_{ij}(\ell)$$

$$PIC_{ij}(\ell) = (P_{ij}(\ell) - P_i P_j(\ell))^2$$

The final vector is obtained as follows:

$$V = \frac{IC_\ell}{PIC_{ij}(\ell)} \text{ where } \ell \in \{\ell_0, \ell_0 + 1, \ldots, \ell_0 + n\},$$

which defines the range of distance between bases.

The pairwise distance between sequences is calculated using Euclidean distance measure. The distance matrix thus obtained can be used to construct phylogenetic tree using clustering algorithms like neighbor-joining, UPGMA, etc.

Lempel-Ziv Compression

Lempel-Ziv complexity uses the relative information between the sequences. This complexity is measured by the number of steps required to generate a string given the prior knowledge of another string and a self-delimiting production process. This measure has a relation to measuring k-words in a sequence, as they can be easily used to generate the sequence. It is computational intensive method. Otu and Sayood (2003) used this method to construct five different distance measures for phylogenetic tree construction.

Context Modelling Compression

In the context modelling complexity the next-symbol predictions, of one or more statistical models, are combined or competing to yield a prediction that is based on events recorded in the past. The algorithmic information content derived from each symbol prediction can be used to compute algorithmic information profiles with a time proportional to the length of the sequence. The process has been applied to DNA sequence analysis.

Methods based on Graphical Representation

Iterated Maps

The use of iterated maps for sequence analysis was first introduced by HJ Jefferey in 1990 when he proposed to apply the Chaos Game to map genomic sequences into a unit square. That report coined the procedure as Chaos Game Representation (CGR). However, only 3 years later this approach was first dismissed as a projection of a Markov transition table by N Goldman. This objection was overruled by the end of that decade when the opposite was found to be the case – that CGR bijectively maps Markov transition is into a fractal, order-free (degree-free) representation. The realization that iterated maps provide a bijective map between the symbolic space and numeric space led to the identification of a variety of alignment-free approaches to sequence comparison and characterization. A number of web apps such as https://usm.github.com, are available to demonstrate how to encode and compare arbitrary symbolic sequences in a manner that takes full advantage of modern MapReduce distribution developed for cloud computing.

Comparison of Alignment based and Alignment-free Methods

Alignment-based Methods	Alignment-free Methods
These methods assume that homologous regions are contiguous (with gaps).	Does not assume such contiguity of homologous regions.
Computes all possible pairwise comparisons of sequences; hence computationally expensive.	Based on occurrences of sub-sequences; composition; computationally inexpensive, can be memory-intensive.
Well-established approach in phylogenomics.	Relatively recent and application in phylogenomics is limited; needs further testing for robustness and scalability.
Requires substitution/evolutionary models.	Less dependent on substitution/evolutionary models.
Sensitive to stochastic sequence variation, recombination, horizontal (or lateral) genetic transfer, rate heterogeneity and sequences of varied lengths, especially when similarity lies in the "twilight zone".	Less sensitive to stochastic sequence variation, recombination, horizontal (or lateral) genetic transfer, rate heterogeneity and sequences of varied lengths.
Best practice uses inference algorithms with complexity at least $O(n^2)$; less time-efficient.	Inference algorithms typically $O(n^2)$ or less; more time-efficient.
Heuristic in nature; statistical significance of how alignment scores relate to homology is difficult to assess.	Exact solutions; statistical significance of the sequence distances (and degree of similarity) can be readily assessed.
Relies on dynamic programming (computationally expensive) to find alignment that has optimal score.	side-steps computational expensive dynamic programming by indexing word counts or positions in fractal space.

Applications of Alignment-free Methods

- Genomic rearrangements.

- Molecular phylogenetics.

- Metagenomics.

- Next generation sequence data analysis.

- Epigenomics.

- Barcoding of species.

- Population genetics.

- Horizontal gene transfer.

- Sero/genotyping of viruses.

- Allergenicity prediction.

- SNP discovery.

- Recombination detection.

Gene Expression

Gene expression is the process by which information from a gene is used in the synthesis of a functional gene product. These products are often proteins, but in non-protein coding genes such as transfer RNA (tRNA) or small nuclear RNA (snRNA) genes, the product is a functional RNA.

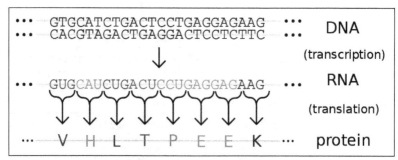

Genes are expressed by being transcribed into RNA, and this transcript may then be translated into protein.

The process of gene expression is used by all known life, eukaryotes (including multicellular organisms), prokaryotes (bacteria and archaea), and utilized by viruses to generate the macromolecular machinery for life.

Several steps in the gene expression process may be modulated, including the transcription, RNA splicing, translation, and post-translational modification of a protein. Gene regulation gives the cell control over structure and function, and is the basis for cellular differentiation, morphogenesis and the versatility and adaptability of any organism. Gene regulation may also serve as a substrate for evolutionary change, since control of the timing, location, and amount of gene expression can have a profound effect on the functions (actions) of the gene in a cell or in a multicellular organism.

In genetics, gene expression is the most fundamental level at which the genotype gives rise to the phenotype, i.e. observable trait. The genetic code stored in DNA is "interpreted" by gene expression, and the properties of the expression give rise to the organism's phenotype. Such phenotypes are often expressed by the synthesis of proteins that control the organism's shape, or that act as enzymes catalysing specific metabolic pathways characterising the organism. Regulation of gene expression is thus critical to an organism's development.

Mechanism

Transcription

A gene is a stretch of DNA that encodes information. Genomic DNA consists of two antiparallel and reverse complementary strands, each having 5' and 3' ends. With respect to a gene, the two strands may be labeled the "template strand," which serves as a blueprint for the production of an RNA transcript, and the "coding strand," which includes the DNA version of the transcript sequence. (Perhaps surprisingly, the "coding strand" is not physically involved in the coding process because it is the "template strand" that is read during transcription).

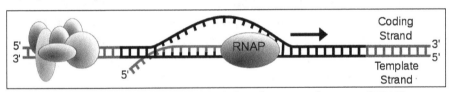

The process of transcription is carried out by RNA polymerase (RNAP), which uses DNA (black) as a template and produces RNA (blue).

The production of the RNA copy of the DNA is called transcription, and is performed in the nucleus by RNA polymerase, which adds one RNA nucleotide at a time to a growing RNA strand as per the complementarity law of the bases. This RNA is complementary to the template 3' → 5' DNA strand, which is itself complementary to the coding 5' → 3' DNA strand. Therefore, the resulting 5' → 3' RNA strand is identical to the coding DNA strand with the exception that thymines (T) are replaced with uracils (U) in the RNA. A coding DNA strand reading "ATG" is indirectly transcribed through the "TAC" in the non-coding template strand as "AUG" in the mRNA.

In prokaryotes, transcription is carried out by a single type of RNA polymerase, which needs a DNA sequence called a Pribnow box as well as a sigma factor (σ factor) to start transcription. In eukaryotes, transcription is performed by three types of RNA polymerases, each of which needs a special DNA sequence called the promoter and a set of DNA-binding proteins—transcription factors—to initiate the process. RNA polymerase I is responsible for transcription of ribosomal RNA (rRNA) genes. RNA polymerase II (Pol II) transcribes all protein-coding genes but also some non-coding RNAs (e.g., snRNAs, snoRNAs or long non-coding RNAs). Pol II includes a C-terminal domain (CTD) that is rich in serine residues. When these residues are phosphorylated, the CTD binds to various protein factors that promote transcript maturation and modification.

RNA polymerase III transcribes 5S rRNA, transfer RNA (tRNA) genes, and some small non-coding RNAs (e.g., 7SK). Transcription ends when the polymerase encounters a sequence called the terminator.

RNA Processing

While transcription of prokaryotic protein-coding genes creates messenger RNA (mRNA) that is ready for translation into protein, transcription of eukaryotic genes leaves a primary transcript of RNA (pre-mRNA), which first has to undergo a series of modifications to become a mature mRNA.

These include 5' *capping*, which is set of enzymatic reactions that add 7-methylguanosine (m^7G) to the 5' end of pre-mRNA and thus protect the RNA from degradation by exonucleases. The m^7G cap is then bound by cap binding complex heterodimer (CBC20/CBC80), which aids in mRNA export to cytoplasm and also protect the RNA from decapping.

Another modification is 3' *cleavage and polyadenylation*. They occur if polyadenylation signal sequence (5'- AAUAAA-3') is present in pre-mRNA, which is usually between protein-coding sequence and terminator. The pre-mRNA is first cleaved and then a series of ~200 adenines (A) are added to form poly(A) tail, which protects the RNA from degradation. Poly(A) tail is bound by multiple poly(A)-binding proteins (PABP) necessary for mRNA export and translation re-initiation.

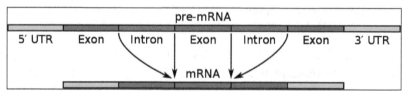

Simple illustration of exons and introns in pre-mRNA and the formation of mature mRNA by splicing. The UTRs are non-coding parts of exons at the ends of the mRNA.

A very important modification of eukaryotic pre-mRNA is *RNA splicing*. The majority of eukaryotic pre-mRNAs consist of alternating segments called exons and introns. During the process of splicing, an RNA-protein catalytical complex known as spliceosome catalyzes two transesterification reactions, which remove an intron and release it in form of lariat structure, and then splice neighbouring exons together. In certain cases, some introns or exons can be either removed or retained in mature mRNA. This so-called alternative splicing creates series of different transcripts originating from a single gene. Because these transcripts can be potentially translated into different proteins, splicing extends the complexity of eukaryotic gene expression.

Extensive RNA processing may be an evolutionary advantage made possible by the nucleus of eukaryotes. In prokaryotes, transcription and translation happen together, whilst in eukaryotes, the nuclear membrane separates the two processes, giving time for RNA processing to occur.

Non-coding RNA Maturation

In most organisms non-coding genes (ncRNA) are transcribed as precursors that undergo further processing. In the case of ribosomal RNAs (rRNA), they are often transcribed as a pre-rRNA that contains one or more rRNAs. The pre-rRNA is cleaved and modified (2'-O-methylation and pseudouridine formation) at specific sites by approximately 150 different small nucleolus-restricted RNA species, called snoRNAs. SnoRNAs associate with proteins, forming snoRNPs. While snoRNA part basepair with the target RNA and thus position the modification at a precise site, the protein part performs the catalytical reaction. In eukaryotes, in particular a snoRNP called RNase, MRP cleaves the 45S pre-rRNA into the 28S, 5.8S, and 18S rRNAs. The rRNA and RNA processing factors form large aggregates called the nucleolus.

In the case of transfer RNA (tRNA), for example, the 5' sequence is removed by RNase P, whereas the 3' end is removed by the tRNase Z enzyme and the non-templated 3' CCA tail is added by a nucleotidyl transferase. In the case of micro RNA (miRNA), miRNAs are first transcribed as primary transcripts or pri-miRNA with a cap and poly-A tail and processed to short, 70-nucleotide stem-loop structures known as pre-miRNA in the cell nucleus by the enzymes Drosha and Pasha. After being exported, it is then processed to mature miRNAs in the cytoplasm by interaction with the endonuclease Dicer, which also initiates the formation of the RNA-induced silencing complex (RISC), composed of the Argonaute protein.

Even snRNAs and snoRNAs themselves undergo series of modification before they become part of functional RNP complex. This is done either in the nucleoplasm or in the specialized compartments called Cajal bodies. Their bases are methylated or pseudouridinilated by a group of small Cajal body-specific RNAs (scaRNAs), which are structurally similar to snoRNAs.

RNA Export

In eukaryotes most mature RNA must be exported to the cytoplasm from the nucleus. While some RNAs function in the nucleus, many RNAs are transported through the nuclear pores and into the cytosol. Notably this includes all RNA types involved in protein synthesis. In some cases RNAs are additionally transported to a specific part of the cytoplasm, such as a synapse; they are then towed by motor proteins that bind through linker proteins to specific sequences (called "zipcodes") on the RNA.

Translation

For some RNA (non-coding RNA) the mature RNA is the final gene product. In the case of messenger RNA (mRNA) the RNA is an information carrier coding for the synthesis of one or more proteins. mRNA carrying a single protein sequence (common in eukaryotes) is monocistronic whilst mRNA carrying multiple protein sequences (common in prokaryotes) is known as polycistronic.

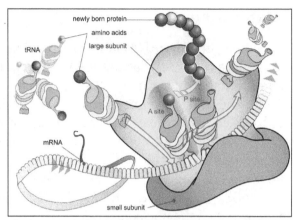

During the translation, tRNA charged with amino acid enters the ribosome and aligns with the correct mRNA triplet. Ribosome then adds amino acid to growing protein chain.

Every mRNA consists of three parts: a 5' untranslated region (5'UTR), a protein-coding region or open reading frame (ORF), and a 3' untranslated region (3'UTR). The coding region carries information for protein synthesis encoded by the genetic code to form triplets. Each triplet of nucleotides of the coding region is called a codon and corresponds to a binding site complementary to an anticodon triplet in transfer RNA. Transfer RNAs with the same anticodon sequence always carry an identical type of amino acid. Amino acids are then chained together by the ribosome according to the order of triplets in the coding region. The ribosome helps transfer RNA to bind to messenger RNA and takes the amino acid from each transfer RNA and makes a structure-less protein out of it. Each mRNA molecule is translated into many protein molecules, on average ~2800 in mammals.

In prokaryotes translation generally occurs at the point of transcription (co-transcriptionally), often using a messenger RNA that is still in the process of being created. In eukaryotes translation can occur in a variety of regions of the cell depending on where the protein being written is supposed to be. Major locations are the cytoplasm for soluble cytoplasmic proteins and the membrane of the endoplasmic reticulum for proteins that are for export from the cell or insertion into a cell membrane. Proteins that are supposed to be expressed at the endoplasmic reticulum are recognised part-way through the translation process. This is governed by the signal recognition particle—a protein that binds to the ribosome and directs it to the endoplasmic reticulum when it finds a signal peptide on the growing (nascent) amino acid chain.

Folding

Each protein exists as an unfolded polypeptide or random coil when translated from a sequence of mRNA into a linear chain of amino acids. This polypeptide lacks any developed three-dimensional structure (the left hand side of the neighboring figure). The polypeptide then folds into its characteristic and functional three-dimensional structure from a random coil. Amino acids interact with each other to produce a well-defined three-dimensional structure, the folded protein (the right hand side of the figure) known as the native state. The resulting three-dimensional structure is determined by the amino acid sequence (Anfinsen's dogma).

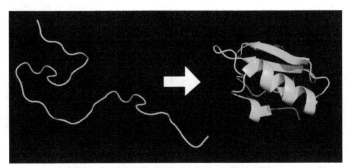

Protein before (left) and after (right) folding.

The correct three-dimensional structure is essential to function, although some parts of functional proteins may remain unfolded. Failure to fold into the intended shape usually produces inactive proteins with different properties including toxic prions. Several neurodegenerative and other diseases are believed to result from the accumulation of *misfolded* proteins. Many allergies are caused by the folding of the proteins, for the immune system does not produce antibodies for certain protein structures.

Enzymes called chaperones assist the newly formed protein to attain (fold into) the 3-dimensional structure it needs to function. Similarly, RNA chaperones help RNAs attain their functional shapes. Assisting protein folding is one of the main roles of the endoplasmic reticulum in eukaryotes.

Translocation

Secretory proteins of eukaryotes or prokaryotes must be translocated to enter the secretory pathway. Newly synthesized proteins are directed to the eukaryotic Sec61 or prokaryotic SecYEG translocation channel by signal peptides. The efficiency of protein secretion in eukaryotes is very dependent on the signal peptide which has been used.

Protein Transport

Many proteins are destined for other parts of the cell than the cytosol and a wide range of signalling sequences or (signal peptides) are used to direct proteins to where they are supposed to be. In prokaryotes this is normally a simple process due to limited compartmentalisation of the cell. However, in eukaryotes there is a great variety of different targeting processes to ensure the protein arrives at the correct organelle.

Not all proteins remain within the cell and many are exported, for example, digestive enzymes, hormones and extracellular matrix proteins. In eukaryotes the export pathway is well developed and the main mechanism for the export of these proteins is translocation to the endoplasmic reticulum, followed by transport via the Golgi apparatus.

Regulation of Gene Expression

Regulation of gene expression refers to the control of the amount and timing of appearance of the functional product of a gene. Control of expression is vital to allow a cell to produce the gene products it needs when it needs them; in turn, this gives cells the flexibility to adapt to a variable environment, external signals, damage to the cell, and other stimuli. More generally, gene regulation gives the cell control over all structure and function, and is the basis for cellular differentiation, morphogenesis and the versatility and adaptability of any organism.

The patchy colours of a tortoiseshell cat are the result of different levels of expression of pigmentation genes in different areas of the skin.

Numerous terms are used to describe types of genes depending on how they are regulated; these include:

- A constitutive gene is a gene that is transcribed continually as opposed to a facultative gene, which is only transcribed when needed.

- A *housekeeping gene* is a gene that is required to maintain basic cellular function and so is typically expressed in all cell types of an organism. Examples include actin, GAPDH and ubiquitin. Some housekeeping genes are transcribed at a relatively constant rate and these genes can be used as a reference point in experiments to measure the expression rates of other genes.

- A facultative gene is a gene only transcribed when needed as opposed to a constitutive gene.

- An inducible gene is a gene whose expression is either responsive to environmental change or dependent on the position in the cell cycle.

Any step of gene expression may be modulated, from the DNA-RNA transcription step to post-translational modification of a protein. The stability of the final gene product, whether it is RNA or protein, also contributes to the expression level of the gene—an unstable product results in a low expression level. In general gene expression is regulated through changes in the number and type of interactions between molecules that collectively influence transcription of DNA and translation of RNA.

Some simple examples of where gene expression is important are:

- Control of insulin expression so it gives a signal for blood glucose regulation.

- X chromosome inactivation in female mammals to prevent an "overdose" of the genes it contains.

- Cyclin expression levels control progression through the eukaryotic cell cycle.

Transcriptional Regulation

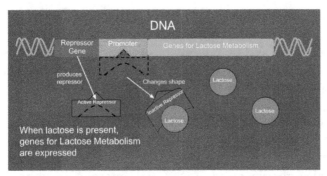

When lactose is present in a prokaryote, it acts as an inducer and inactivates the repressor so that the genes for lactose metabolism can be transcribed.

Regulation of transcription can be broken down into three main routes of influence; genetic (direct interaction of a control factor with the gene), modulation interaction of a control factor with the transcription machinery and epigenetic (non-sequence changes in DNA structure that influence transcription).

Direct interaction with DNA is the simplest and the most direct method by which a protein changes transcription levels. Genes often have several protein binding sites around the coding region with the specific function of regulating transcription. There are many classes of regulatory DNA binding sites known as enhancers, insulators and silencers. The mechanisms for regulating transcription are very varied, from blocking key binding sites on the DNA for RNA polymerase to acting as an activator and promoting transcription by assisting RNA polymerase binding.

The activity of transcription factors is further modulated by intracellular signals causing protein post-translational modification including phosphorylated, acetylated, or glycosylated. These changes influence a transcription factor's ability to bind, directly or indirectly, to promoter DNA, to recruit RNA polymerase, or to favor elongation of a newly synthesized RNA molecule.

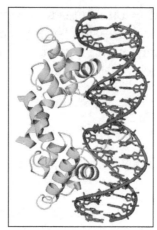

The lambda repressor transcription factor (green) binds as a dimer to major groove of
DNA target (red and blue) and disables initiation of transcription. From PDB: 1LMB.

The nuclear membrane in eukaryotes allows further regulation of transcription factors by the duration of their presence in the nucleus, which is regulated by reversible changes in their structure and by binding of other proteins. Environmental stimuli or endocrine signals may cause modification of regulatory proteins eliciting cascades of intracellular signals, which result in regulation of gene expression.

More recently it has become apparent that there is a significant influence of non-DNA-sequence specific effects on transcription. These effects are referred to as epigenetic and involve the higher order structure of DNA, non-sequence specific DNA binding proteins and chemical modification of DNA. In general epigenetic effects alter the accessibility of DNA to proteins and so modulate transcription.

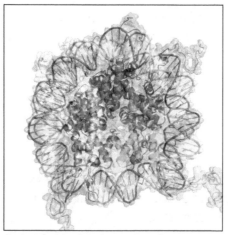

In eukaryotes, DNA is organized in form of nucleosomes. Note how the DNA
(blue and green) is tightly wrapped around the protein core made of histone octamer
(ribbon coils), restricting access to the DNA. From PDB: 1KX5.

DNA methylation is a widespread mechanism for epigenetic influence on gene expression and is seen in bacteria and eukaryotes and has roles in heritable transcription silencing and transcription regulation. In eukaryotes the structure of chromatin, controlled by the histone code, regulates access to DNA with significant impacts on the expression of genes in euchromatin and heterochromatin areas.

Transcriptional Regulation in Cancer

The majority of gene promoters contain a CpG island with numerous CpG sites. When many of a gene's promoter CpG sites are methylated the gene becomes silenced. Colorectal cancers typically have 3 to 6 driver mutations and 33 to 66 hitchhiker or passenger mutations. However, transcriptional silencing may be of more importance than mutation in causing progression to cancer. For example, in colorectal cancers about 600 to 800 genes are transcriptionally silenced by CpG island methylation. Transcriptional repression in cancer can also occur by other epigenetic mechanisms, such as altered expression of microRNAs. In breast cancer, transcriptional repression of BRCA1 may occur more frequently by over-expressed microRNA-182 than by hypermethylation of the BRCA1 promoter (see Low expression of BRCA1 in breast and ovarian cancers).

Post-transcriptional Regulation

In eukaryotes, where export of RNA is required before translation is possible, nuclear export is thought to provide additional control over gene expression. All transport in and out of the nucleus is via the nuclear pore and transport is controlled by a wide range of importin and exportin proteins.

Expression of a gene coding for a protein is only possible if the messenger RNA carrying the code survives long enough to be translated. In a typical cell, an RNA molecule is only stable if specifically protected from degradation. RNA degradation has particular importance in regulation of expression in eukaryotic cells where mRNA has to travel significant distances before being translated. In eukaryotes, RNA is stabilised by certain post-transcriptional modifications, particularly the 5' cap and poly-adenylated tail.

Intentional degradation of mRNA is used not just as a defence mechanism from foreign RNA (normally from viruses) but also as a route of mRNA *destabilisation*. If an mRNA molecule has a complementary sequence to a small interfering RNA then it is targeted for destruction via the RNA interference pathway.

Three Prime Untranslated Regions and MicroRNAs

Three prime untranslated regions (3'UTRs) of messenger RNAs (mRNAs) often contain regulatory sequences that post-transcriptionally influence gene expression. Such 3'-UTRs often contain both binding sites for microRNAs (miRNAs) as well as for regulatory proteins. By binding to specific sites within the 3'-UTR, miRNAs can decrease gene expression of various mRNAs by either inhibiting translation or directly causing degradation of the transcript. The 3'-UTR also may have silencer regions that bind repressor proteins that inhibit the expression of a mRNA.

The 3'-UTR often contains microRNA response elements (MREs). MREs are sequences to which miRNAs bind. These are prevalent motifs within 3'-UTRs. Among all regulatory motifs within the 3'-UTRs (e.g. including silencer regions), MREs make up about half of the motifs.

As of 2014, the miRBase web site, an archive of miRNA sequences and annotations, listed 28,645 entries in 233 biologic species. Of these, 1,881 miRNAs were in annotated human miRNA loci. miRNAs were predicted to have an average of about four hundred target mRNAs (affecting expression of several hundred genes). Friedman et al. estimate that >45,000 miRNA target sites within human mRNA 3'UTRs are conserved above background levels, and >60% of human protein-coding genes have been under selective pressure to maintain pairing to miRNAs.

Direct experiments show that a single miRNA can reduce the stability of hundreds of unique mRNAs. Other experiments show that a single miRNA may repress the production of hundreds of proteins, but that this repression often is relatively mild (less than 2-fold).

The effects of miRNA dysregulation of gene expression seem to be important in cancer. For instance, in gastrointestinal cancers, nine miRNAs have been identified as epigenetically altered and effective in down regulating DNA repair enzymes.

The effects of miRNA dysregulation of gene expression also seem to be important in neuropsychiatric disorders, such as schizophrenia, bipolar disorder, major depression, Parkinson's disease, Alzheimer's disease and autism spectrum disorders.

Translational Regulation

Neomycin	R¹	R²
B	CH_2NH_2	H
C	H	CH_2NH_2

Neomycin is an example of a small molecule that reduces expression of all protein genes inevitably leading to cell death; it thus acts as an antibiotic.

Direct regulation of translation is less prevalent than control of transcription or mRNA stability but is occasionally used. Inhibition of protein translation is a major target for toxins and antibiotics, so they can kill a cell by overriding its normal gene expression control. Protein synthesis inhibitors include the antibiotic neomycin and the toxin ricin.

Post-translational Modifications

Post-translational modifications (PTMs) are covalent modifications to proteins. Like RNA splicing, they help to significantly diversify the proteome. These modifications are usually catalyzed by enzymes. Additionally, processes like covalent additions to amino acid side chain residues can often be reversed by other enzymes. However, some, like the proteolytic cleavage of the protein backbone, are irreversible.

PTMs play many important roles in the cell. For example, phosphorylation is primarily involved in activating and deactivating proteins and in signaling pathways. PTMs are involved in transcriptional regulation: an important function of acetylation and methylation is histone tail modification, which alters how accessible DNA is for transcription. They can also be seen in the immune system, where glycosylation plays a key role. One type of PTM can initiate another type of PTM, as can be seen in how ubiquitination tags proteins for degradation through proteolysis. Proteolysis, other than being involved in breaking down proteins, is also important in activating and deactivating them, and in regulating biological processes such as DNA transcription and cell death.

Measurement

Measuring gene expression is an important part of many life sciences, as the ability to quantify the level at which a particular gene is expressed within a cell, tissue or organism can provide a lot of valuable information. For example, measuring gene expression can:

- Identify viral infection of a cell (viral protein expression).

- Determine an individual's susceptibility to cancer (oncoge ne expression).

- Find if a bacterium is resistant to penicillin (beta-lactamase expression).

Similarly, the analysis of the location of protein expression is a powerful tool, and this can be done on an organismal or cellular scale. Investigation of localization is particularly important for the study of development in multicellular organisms and as an indicator of protein function in single cells. Ideally, measurement of expression is done by detecting the final gene product (for many genes, this is the protein); however, it is often easier to detect one of the precursors, typically mRNA and to infer gene-expression levels from these measurements.

mRNA Quantification

Levels of mRNA can be quantitatively measured by northern blotting, which provides size and sequence information about the mRNA molecules. A sample of RNA is separated on an agarose gel and hybridized to a radioactively labeled RNA probe that is complementary to the target sequence. The radiolabeled RNA is then detected by an autoradiograph. Because the use of radioactive reagents makes the procedure time consuming and potentially dangerous, alternative labeling and detection methods, such as digoxigenin and biotin chemistries, have been developed. Perceived disadvantages of Northern blotting are that large quantities of RNA are required and that quantification may not be completely accurate, as it involves measuring band strength in an image of a gel. On the other hand, the additional mRNA size information from the Northern blot allows the discrimination of alternately spliced transcripts.

Another approach for measuring mRNA abundance is RT-qPCR. In this technique, reverse transcription is followed by quantitative PCR. Reverse transcription first generates a DNA template f rom the mRNA; this single-stranded template is called cDNA. The cDNA template is then amplified in the quantitative step, during which the fluorescence emitted by labeled hybridization probes or intercalating dyes changes as the DNA amplification process progresses. With a carefully constructed standard curve, qPCR can produce an absolute measurement of the number of copies of original mRNA, typically in units of copies per nanolitre of homogenized tissue or copies per cell. qPCR is very sensitive (detection of a single mRNA molecule is theoretically possible), but can be expensive depending on the type of reporter used; fluorescently labeled oligonucleotide probes are more expensive than non-specific intercalating fluorescent dyes.

For expression profiling, or high-throughput analysis of many genes within a sample, quantitative PCR may be performed for hundreds of genes simultaneously in the case of low-density arrays. A second approach is the hybridization microarray. A single array or "chip" may contain probes to determine transcript levels for every known gene in the genome of one or more organisms. Alternatively, "tag based" technologies like Serial analysis of gene expression (SAGE) and RNA-Seq, which can provide a relative measure of the cellular concentration of different mRNAs, can be used. An advantage of tag-based methods is the "open architecture", allowing for the exact measurement of any transcript, with a known or unknown sequence. Next-generation sequencing (NGS) such as RNA-Seq is another approach, producing vast quantities of sequence data that can be matched to a reference genome. Although NGS is comparatively time-consuming, expensive, and resource-intensive, it can identify single-nucleotide polymorphisms, splice-variants, and novel genes, and can also be used to profile expression in organisms for which little or no sequence information is available.

Protein Quantification

For genes encoding proteins, the expression level can be directly assessed by a number of methods with some clear analogies to the techniques for mRNA quantification.

The most commonly used method is to perform a Western blot against the protein of interest—this gives information on the size of the protein in addition to its identity. A sample (often cellular lysate) is separated on a polyacrylamide gel, transferred to a membrane and then probed with an antibody to the protein of interest. The antibody can either be conjugated to a fluorophore or to horseradish peroxidase for imaging and quantification. The gel-based nature of this assay makes quantification less accurate, but it has the advantage of being able to identify later modifications to the protein, for example proteolysis or ubiquitination, from changes in size.

mRNA-protein Correlation

Quantification of protein and mRNA permits a correlation of the two levels. The question of how well protein levels correlate with their corresponding transcript levels is highly debated and depends on multiple factors. Regulation on each step of gene expression can impact the correlation, as shown for regulation of translation or protein stability. Post-translational factors, such as protein transport in highly polar cells, can influence the measured mRNA-protein correlation as well.

Localisation

Analysis of expression is not limited to quantification; localisation can also be determined. mRNA can be detected with a suitably labelled complementary mRNA strand and protein can be detected via labelled antibodies. The probed sample is then observed by microscopy to identify where the mRNA or protein is.

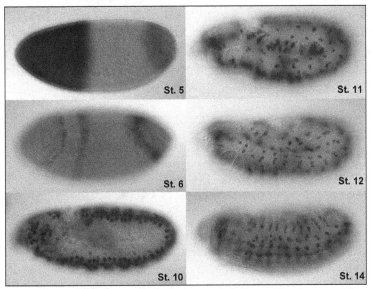

In situ-hybridization of Drosophila embryos at different developmental stages for the mRNA responsible for the expression of hunchback. High intensity of blue color marks places with high hunchback mRNA quantity.

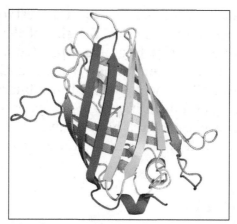

The three-dimensional structure of green fluorescent protein. The residues in the centre of the "barrel" are responsible for production of green light after exposing to higher energetic blue light. From PDB: 1EMA.

By replacing the gene with a new version fused to a green fluorescent protein (or similar) marker, expression may be directly quantified in live cells. This is done by imaging using a fluorescence microscope. It is very difficult to clone a GFP-fused protein into its native location in the genome without affecting expression levels so this method often cannot be used to measure endogenous gene expression. It is, however, widely used to measure the expression of a gene artificially introduced into the cell, for example via an expression vector. It is important to note that by fusing a target protein to a fluorescent reporter the protein's behavior, including its cellular localization and expression level, can be significantly changed.

The enzyme-linked immunosorbent assay works by using antibodies immobilised on a microtiter plate to capture proteins of interest from samples added to the well. Using a detection antibody conjugated to an enzyme or fluorophore the quantity of bound protein can be accurately measured by fluorometric or colourimetric detection. The detection process is very similar to that of a Western blot, but by avoiding the gel steps more accurate quantification can be achieved.

Expression System

An expression system is a system specifically designed for the production of a gene product of choice. This is normally a protein although may also be RNA, such as tRNA or a ribozyme. An expression system consists of a gene, normally encoded by DNA, and the molecular machinery required to transcribe the DNA into mRNA and translate the mRNA into protein using the reagents provided. In the broadest sense this includes every living cell but the term is more normally used to refer to expression as a laboratory tool. An expression system is therefore often artificial in some manner. Expression systems are, however, a fundamentally natural process. Viruses are an excellent example where they replicate by using the host cell as an expression system for the viral proteins and genome.

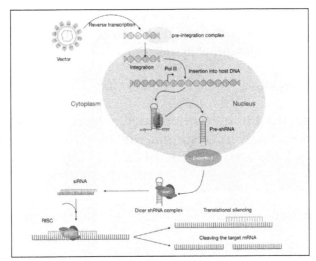

Tet-ON inducible shRNA system.

Inducible Expression

Doxycycline is also used in "Tet-on" and "Tet-off" tetracycline controlled transcriptional activation to regulate transgene expression in organisms and cell cultures.

In Nature

In addition to these biological tools, certain naturally observed configurations of DNA (genes, promoters, enhancers, repressors) and the associated machinery itself are referred to as an expression system. This term is normally used in the case where a gene or set of genes is switched on under well defined conditions, for example, the simple repressor switch expression system in Lambda phage and the lac operator system in bacteria. Several natural expression systems are directly used or modified and used for artificial expression systems such as the Tet-on and Tet-off expression system.

Gene Networks

Genes have sometimes been regarded as nodes in a network, with inputs being proteins such as transcription factors, and outputs being the level of gene expression. The node itself performs a function, and the operation of these functions have been interpreted as performing a kind of information processing within cells and determines cellular behavior.

Gene networks can also be constructed without formulating an explicit causal model. This is often the case when assembling networks from large expression data sets. Co-variation and correlation of expression is computed across a large sample of cases and measurements (often transcriptome or proteome data). The source of variation can be either experimental or natural (observational). There are several ways to construct gene expression networks, but one common approach is to compute a matrix of all pair-wise correlations of expression across conditions, time points, or individuals and convert the matrix (after thresholding at some cut-off value) into a graphical representation in which nodes represent genes, transcripts, or proteins and edges connecting these nodes represent the strength of association.

Techniques and Tools

The following experimental techniques are used to measure gene expression and are listed in roughly chronological order, starting with the older, more established technologies. They are divided into two groups based on their degree of multiplexity.

- Low-to-mid-plex techniques:

    ◦ Reporter gene.

    ◦ Northern blot.

    ◦ Western blot.

    ◦ Fluorescent in situ hybridization.

    ◦ Reverse transcription PCR.

- Higher-plex techniques:

    ◦ SAGE.

    ◦ DNA microarray.

    ◦ Tiling array.

    ◦ RNA-Seq.

Protein Expression

Proteins are synthesized and regulated depending upon the functional need in the cell. The blueprints for proteins are stored in DNA and decoded by highly regulated transcriptional processes to produce messenger RNA (mRNA). The message coded by an mRNA is then translated into a protein. Transcription is the transfer of information from DNA to mRNA, and translation is the synthesis of protein based on a sequence specified by mRNA.

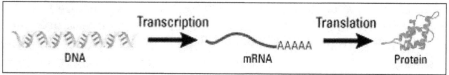

Simple diagram of transcription and translation. This describes the general flow of information from DNA base-pair sequence (gene) to amino acid polypeptide sequence (protein).

In prokaryotes, the process of transcription and translation occur simultaneously. The translation of mRNA starts even before a mature mRNA transcript is fully synthesized. This simultaneous transcription and translation of a gene is termed coupled transcription and translation. In eukaryotes, the processes are spatially separated and occur sequentially with transcription happening in the nucleus and translation, or protein synthesis, occurring in the cytoplasm.

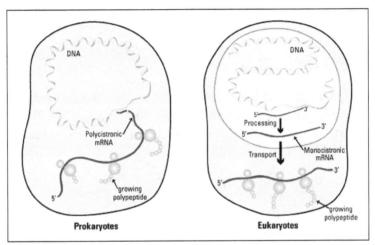

Comparison of transcription and translation in prokaryotes vs. eukaryotes.

Transcription and Translation

Transcription occurs in three steps in both prokaryotes and eukaryotes: initiation, elongation and termination. Transcription begins when the double-stranded DNA is unwound to allow the binding of RNA polymerase. Once transcription is initiated, RNA polymerase is released from the DNA. Transcription is regulated at various levels by activators and repressors and also by chromatin structure in eukaryotes. In prokaryotes, no special modification of mRNA is required and translation of the message starts even before the transcription is complete. In eukaryotes, however, mRNA is further processed to remove introns (splicing), addition of a cap at the 5' end and multiple adenines at the mRNA 3' end to generate a polyA tail. The modified mRNA is then exported to the cytoplasm where it is translated.

Translation or protein synthesis is a multi-step process that requires macromolecules like ribosomes, transfer RNAs (tRNA), mRNA and protein factors as well as small molecules like amino acids, ATP, GTP and other cofactors. There are specific protein factors for each step of translation. The overall process is similar in both prokaryotes and eukaryotes, although particular differences exist.

During initiation, the small subunit of the ribosome bound to initiator t-RNA scans the mRNA starting at the 5' end to identify and bind the initiation codon (AUG). The large subunit of the ribosome joins the small ribosomal subunit to generate the initiation complex at the initiation codon. Protein factors as well as sequences in mRNA are involved in the recognition of the initiation codon and formation of the initiation complex. During elongation, tRNAs bind to their designated amino acids (known as tRNA charging) and shuttle them to the ribosome where they are polymerized to form a peptide. The sequence of amino acids added to the growing peptide is dependent on the mRNA sequence of the transcript. Finally, the nascent polypeptide is released in the termination step when the ribosome reaches the termination codon. At this point, the ribosome is released from the mRNA and is ready to initiate another round of translation.

Post-translational Modification

After translation, polypeptides are modified in various ways to complete their structure, designate their location or regulate their activity within the cell. Post-translational modifications (PTMs) are various additions or alterations to the chemical structure and are critical features of the overall cell biology.

Types of post-translational modifications include:

- Polypeptide folding into a globular protein with the help of chaperone proteins to arrive at the lowest energy state.

- Modifications of the amino acids present, such as removal of the first methionine residue.

- Disulfide bridge formation or reduction.

- Protein modifications that facilitate binding functions:

  ○ Glycosylation.

  ○ Prenylation of proteins for membrane localization.

  ○ Acetylation of histones to modify DNA–histone interactions.

- Addition of functional groups that regulate protein activity:

  ○ Phosphorylation.

  ○ Nitrosylation.

  ○ GTP binding.

Mammalian Protein Expression

Mammalian expression systems can be used to produce mammalian proteins that have the most native structure and activity due to its physiologically relevant environment. This results in high levels of post-translational processing and functional activity. Mammalian expression systems are the preferred system for the expression of mammalian proteins and can be used for the production of antibodies, complex proteins and proteins for use in functional cell-based assays. However, these benefits are coupled with more demanding culture conditions.

Mammalian expression systems can be used to produce proteins transiently or through stable cell lines, where the expression construct is integrated into the host genome. While stable cell lines can be used over several experiments, transient production can generate large amounts of protein in one to two weeks. These transient, high-yield mammalian expression systems utilize suspension cultures and can produce gram-per-liter yields. Furthermore, these proteins have more native folding and post-translational modifications, such as glycosylation, as compared to other expression systems. In the example that follows, 3 different mammalian expression systems were used to express recombinant proteins.

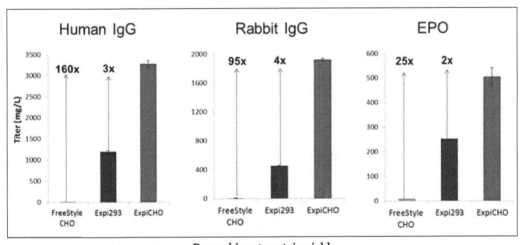

Recombinant protein yield.

The Gibco FreeStyle CHO, Expi293 and ExpiCHO Expression Systems were used to transiently expresses human IgG, rabbit IgG and EPO (erythropoietin) using the pcDNA 3.4 expression vector. The Max Titer protocol was used for ExpiCHO and proteins were harvested at day 10–12. For FreeStyleCHO and Expi293, the proteins were harvested at day 6 or 7. All proteins were quantitated by ForteBio Octet or ELISA. Use of ExpiCHO results in higher protein titers as compared to FreeStyle CHO and Expi293.

Insect Protein Expression

Insect cells can be used for high level protein expression with modifications similar to mammalian systems. There are several systems that can be used to produce recombinant baculovirus, which can then be utilized to express the protein of interest in insect cells. These systems can be easily scaled up and adapted to high-density suspension culture for large-scale expression of protein that is more functionally similar to native mammalian protein. Though yields can be up to 500 mg/L, recombinant baculovirus production can be time consuming and culture conditions more challenging than prokaryotic systems.

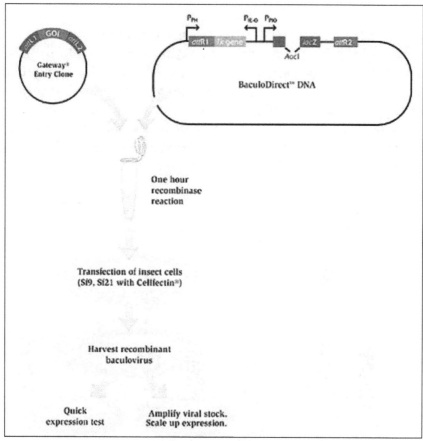

Baculovirus Expression System Protocol Summary.

The Invitrogen BaculoDirect Baculovirus Expression System utilizes Invitrogen Gateway technology for cloning. After a 1-hour recombinase reaction and transfection in insect cells, baculovirus containing the gene of interest is produced. A quick expression test can then be performed before amplifying the viral stock and scaling up expression. Use of this system allows for baculovirus expression in insect cells.

Bacterial Protein Expression

Bacterial protein expression systems are popular because bacteria are easy to culture, grow fast and produce high yields of recombinant protein. However, multi-domain eukaryotic proteins expressed in bacteria often are non-functional because the cells are not equipped to accomplish the required post-translational modifications or molecular folding. Also, many proteins become insoluble as inclusion bodies that are very difficult to recover without harsh denaturants and subsequent cumbersome protein-refolding procedures. In the example that follows, a bacterial cell-based system was used to express 8 different recombinant proteins.

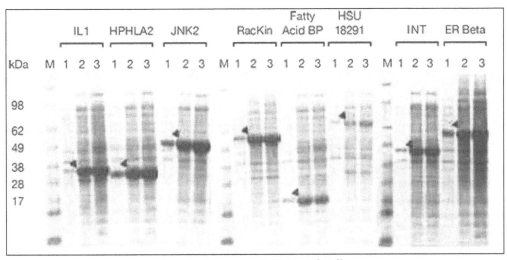

Protein Expression in Bacterial Cells.

Gateway cloning was used to clone 8 human proteins into the Invitrogen Champion pET300/NT-DEST vector. BL21(DE3) *E. coli* were utilized to express positive clones in either LB + IPTG (1), ready-to-use Invitrogen MagicMedia medium (2), or MagicMedia medium prepared from powder (3). Samples were lysed and analyzed on a Coomassie blue dye–stained Invitrogen NuPAGE 4-12% Bis-Tris Protein Gel. M = Invitrogen See-Blue Protein Standard. Use of MagicMedia *E. coli* medium results in higher protein yield across different samples.

Cell-free Protein Expression

Cell-free protein expression is the *in vitro* synthesis of a protein using translation-compatible extracts of whole cells. In principle, whole cell extracts contain all the macromolecules and components needed for transcription, translation and even post-translational modification. These components include RNA polymerase, regulatory protein factors, transcription factors, ribosomes and tRNA. When supplemented with cofactors, nucleotides and the specific gene template, these extracts can synthesize proteins of interest in a few hours.

Although not sustainable for large scale production, cell-free, or *in vitro* translation (IVT) protein expression systems, have several advantages over traditional *in vivo* systems. Cell-free expression allows for fast synthesis of recombinant proteins without the hassle of cell culture. Cell-free systems enable protein labeling with modified amino acids, as well as expression of proteins that undergo rapid proteolytic degradation by intracellular proteases. Also, with the cell-free method, it is simpler to express many different proteins simultaneously (e.g., testing protein mutations by expression on a small scale from many different recombinant DNA templates). In this representative experiment, an IVT system was used to express human caspase 3 protein.

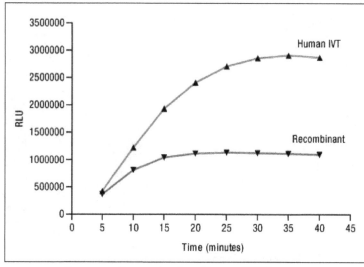

Caspase-3 Expression in a Human IVT System.

Caspase-3 was expressed using the Thermo Scientific 1-Step Human High-Yield IVT Kit (Human IVT) and in *E. coli* (Recombinant). Active caspase-3 activity was assayed using equal amounts of protein. Caspase-3 protein expressed using the IVT system was more active as compared to a protein expressed in bacteria.

Chemical Protein Synthesis

Chemical synthesis of proteins can be used for applications requiring proteins labeled with unnatural amino acids, proteins labeled at specific sites or proteins that are toxic to biological expression systems. Chemical synthesis produces highly pure protein but works well only for small proteins and peptides. Yield is often quite low with chemical synthesis, and the method is prohibitively expensive for longer polypeptides.

Gene Prediction

In computational biology, gene prediction or gene finding refers to the process of identifying the regions of genomic DNA that encode genes. This includes protein-coding genes as well as RNA genes, but may also include prediction of other functional elements such as regulatory regions. Gene finding is one of the first and most important steps in understanding the genome of a species once it has been sequenced.

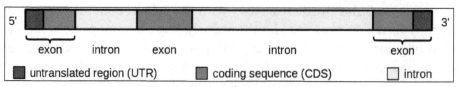

Structure of a eukaryotic gene.

In its earliest days, "gene finding" was based on painstaking experimentation on living cells and organisms. Statistical analysis of the rates of homologous recombination of several different genes could determine their order on a certain chromosome, and information from many such experiments could be combined to create a genetic map specifying the rough location of known genes relative to each other. Today, with comprehensive genome sequence and powerful computational resources at the disposal of the research community, gene finding has been redefined as a largely computational problem.

Determining that a sequence is functional should be distinguished from determining the function of the gene or its product. Predicting the function of a gene and confirming that the gene prediction is accurate still demands *in vivo* experimentation through gene knockout and other assays, although frontiers of bioinformatics research are making it increasingly possible to predict the function of a gene based on its sequence alone.

Gene prediction is one of the key steps in genome annotation, following sequence assembly, the filtering of non-coding regions and repeat masking.

Gene prediction is closely related to the so-called 'target search problem' investigating how DNA-binding proteins (transcription factors) locate specific binding sites within the genome. Many aspects of structural gene prediction are based on current understanding of underlying biochemical processes in the cell such as gene transcription, translation, protein–protein interactions and regulation processes, which are subject of active research in the various omics fields such as transcriptomics, proteomics, metabolomics, and more generally structural and functional genomics.

Empirical Methods

In empirical (similarity, homology or evidence-based) gene finding systems, the target genome is searched for sequences that are similar to extrinsic evidence in the form of the known expressed sequence tags, messenger RNA (mRNA), protein products, and homologous or orthologous sequences. Given an mRNA sequence, it is trivial to derive a unique genomic DNA sequence from which it had to have been transcribed. Given a protein sequence, a family of possible coding DNA sequences can be derived by reverse translation of the genetic code. Once candidate DNA sequences have been determined, it is a relatively straightforward algorithmic problem to efficiently search a target genome for matches, complete or partial, and exact or inexact. Given a sequence, local alignment algorithms such as BLAST, FASTA and Smith-Waterman look for regions of similarity between the target sequence and possible candidate matches. Matches can be complete or partial, and exact or inexact. The success of this approach is limited by the contents and accuracy of the sequence database.

A high degree of similarity to a known messenger RNA or protein product is strong evidence that a region of a target genome is a protein-coding gene. However, to apply this approach systemically requires extensive sequencing of mRNA and protein products. Not only is this expensive, but in complex organisms, only a subset of all genes in the organism's genome are expressed at any given time, meaning that extrinsic evidence for many genes is not readily accessible in any single cell culture. Thus, to collect extrinsic evidence for most or all of the genes in a complex organism requires the study of many hundreds or thousands of cell types, which presents further difficulties. For example, some human genes may be expressed only during development as an embryo or fetus, which might be difficult to study for ethical reasons.

Despite these difficulties, extensive transcript and protein sequence databases have been generated for human as well as other important model organisms in biology, such as mice and yeast. For example, the RefSeq database contains transcript and protein sequence from many different species, and the Ensembl system comprehensively maps this evidence to human and several other genomes. It is, however, likely that these databases are both incomplete and contain small but significant amounts of erroneous data.

New high-throughput transcriptome sequencing technologies such as RNA-Seq and ChIP-sequencing open opportunities for incorporating additional extrinsic evidence into gene prediction and validation, and allow structurally rich and more accurate alternative to previous methods of measuring gene expression such as expressed sequence tag or DNA microarray.

Major challenges involved in gene prediction involve dealing with sequencing errors in raw DNA data, dependence on the quality of the sequence assembly, handling short reads, frameshift mutations, overlapping genes and incomplete genes.

In prokaryotes it's essential to consider horizontal gene transfer when searching for gene sequence homology. An additional important factor underused in current gene detection tools is existence of gene clusters—operons(is a functioning unit of DNA containing a cluster of genes under the control of a single promoter) in both prokaryotes and eukaryotes. Most popular gene detectors treat each gene in isolation, independent of others, which is not biologically accurate.

Ab Initio Methods

Ab Initio gene prediction is an intrinsic method based on gene content and signal detection. Because of the inherent expense and difficulty in obtaining extrinsic evidence for many genes, it is also necessary to resort to *ab initio* gene finding, in which the genomic DNA sequence alone is systematically searched for certain tell-tale signs of protein-coding genes. These signs can be broadly categorized as either *signals*, specific sequences that indicate the presence of a gene nearby, or *content*, statistical properties of the protein-coding sequence itself. *Ab initio* gene finding might be more accurately characterized as gene *prediction*, since extrinsic evidence is generally required to conclusively establish that a putative gene is functional.

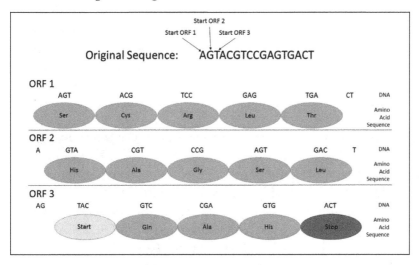

This picture shows how Open Reading Frames (ORFs) can be used for gene prediction. Gene prediction is the process of determining where a coding gene might be in a genomic sequence. Functional proteins must begin with a Start codon (where DNA transcription begins), and end with a Stop codon (where transcription ends). By looking at where those codons might fall in a DNA sequence, one can see where a functional protein might be located. This is important in gene prediction because it can reveal where coding genes are in an entire genomic sequence. In this example, a functional protein can be discovered using ORF3 because it begins with a Start codon, has multiple amino acids, and then ends with a Stop codon, all within the same reading frame.

In the genomes of prokaryotes, genes have specific and relatively well-understood promoter sequences (signals), such as the Pribnow box and transcription factor binding sites, which are easy to systematically identify. Also, the sequence coding for a protein occurs as one contiguous open reading frame (ORF), which is typically many hundred or thousands of base pairs long. The statistics of stop codons are such that even finding an open reading frame of this length is a fairly informative sign. (Since 3 of the 64 possible codons in the genetic code are stop codons, one would expect a stop codon approximately every 20–25 codons, or 60–75 base pairs, in a random sequence.) Furthermore, protein-coding DNA has certain periodicities and other statistical properties that are easy to detect in sequence of this length. These characteristics make prokaryotic gene finding relatively straightforward, and well-designed systems are able to achieve high levels of accuracy.

Ab initio gene finding in eukaryotes, especially complex organisms like humans, is considerably more challenging for several reasons. First, the promoter and other regulatory signals in these genomes are more complex and less well-understood than in prokaryotes, making them more difficult to reliably recognize. Two classic examples of signals identified by eukaryotic gene finders are CpG islands and binding sites for a poly(A) tail.

Second, splicing mechanisms employed by eukaryotic cells mean that a particular protein-coding sequence in the genome is divided into several parts (exons), separated by non-coding sequences (introns). (Splice sites are themselves another signal that eukaryotic gene finders are often designed to identify.) A typical protein-coding gene in humans might be divided into a dozen exons, each less than two hundred base pairs in length, and some as short as twenty to thirty. It is therefore much more difficult to detect periodicities and other known content properties of protein-coding DNA in eukaryotes.

Advanced gene finders for both prokaryotic and eukaryotic genomes typically use complex probabilistic models, such as hidden Markov models (HMMs) to combine information from a variety of different signal and content measurements. The GLIMMER system is a widely used and highly accurate gene finder for prokaryotes. GeneMark is another popular approach. Eukaryotic *ab initio* gene finders, by comparison, have achieved only limited success; notable examples are the GENSCAN and geneid programs. The SNAP gene finder is HMM-based like Genscan, and attempts to be more adaptable to different organisms, addressing problems related to using a gene finder on a genome sequence that it was not trained against. A few recent approaches like mSplicer, CONTRAST, or mGene also use machine learning techniques like support vector machines for successful gene prediction. They build a discriminative model using hidden Markov support vector machines or conditional random fields to learn an accurate gene prediction scoring function.

Ab Initio methods have been benchmarked, with some approaching 100% sensitivity, however as the sensitivity increases, accuracy suffers as a result of increased false positives.

Other Signals

Among the derived signals used for prediction are statistics resulting from the sub-sequence statistics like k-mer statistics, Isochore (genetics) or Compositional domain GC composition/uniformity/entropy, sequence and frame length, Intron/Exon/Donor/Acceptor/Promoter and Ribosomal binding site vocabulary, Fractal dimension, Fourier transform of a pseudo-number-coded DNA, Z-curve parameters and certain run features.

It has been suggested that signals other than those directly detectable in sequences may improve gene prediction. For example, the role of secondary structure in the identification of regulatory motifs has been reported. In addition, it has been suggested that RNA secondary structure prediction helps splice site prediction.

Neural Networks

Artificial neural networks are computational models that excel at machine learning and pattern recognition. Neural networks must be trained with example data before being able to generalise for experimental data, and tested against benchmark data. Neural networks are able to come up with approximate solutions to problems that are hard to solve algorithmically, provided there is sufficient training data. When applied to gene prediction, neural networks can be used alongside other *ab initio* methods to predict or identify biological features such as splice sites. One approach involves using a sliding window, which traverses the sequence data in an overlapping manner. The output at each position is a score based on whether the network thinks the window contains a donor splice site or an acceptor splice site. Larger windows offer more accuracy but also require more computational power. A neural network is an example of a signal sensor as its goal is to identify a functional site in the genome.

Combined Approaches

Programs such as Maker combine extrinsic and *ab initio* approaches by mapping protein and EST data to the genome to validate *ab initio* predictions. Augustus, which may be used as part of the Maker pipeline, can also incorporate hints in the form of EST alignments or protein profiles to increase the accuracy of the gene prediction.

Comparative Genomics Approaches

As the entire genomes of many different species are sequenced, a promising direction in current research on gene finding is a comparative genomics approach.

This is based on the principle that the forces of natural selection cause genes and other functional elements to undergo mutation at a slower rate than the rest of the genome, since mutations in functional elements are more likely to negatively impact the organism than mutations elsewhere. Genes can thus be detected by comparing the genomes of related species to detect this evolutionary pressure for conservation. This approach was first applied to the mouse and human genomes, using programs such as SLAM, SGP and TWINSCAN/N-SCAN and CONTRAST.

Multiple Informants

TWINSCAN examined only human-mouse synteny to look for orthologous genes. Programs such as N-SCAN and CONTRAST allowed the incorporation of alignments from multiple organisms, or in the case of N-SCAN, a single alternate organism from the target. The use of multiple informants can lead to significant improvements in accuracy.

CONTRAST is composed of two elements. The first is a smaller classifier, identifying donor splice sites and acceptor splice sites as well as start and stop codons. The second element involves constructing a full model using machine learning. Breaking the problem into two means that smaller targeted data sets can be used to train the classifiers, and that classifier can operate independently and be trained with smaller windows. The full model can use the independent classifier, and not have to waste computational time or model complexity re-classifying intron-exon boundaries. The paper in which

CONTRAST is introduced proposes that their method (and those of TWINSCAN, etc.) be classified as *de novo* gene assembly, using alternate genomes, and identifying it as distinct from *ab initio*, which uses a target 'informant' genomes.

Comparative gene finding can also be used to project high quality annotations from one genome to another. Notable examples include Projector, GeneWise, GeneMapper and GeMoMa. Such techniques now play a central role in the annotation of all genomes.

Pseudogene Prediction

Pseudogenes are close relatives of genes, sharing very high sequence homology, but being unable to code for the same protein product. Whilst once relegated as byproducts of gene sequencing, increasingly, as regulatory roles are being uncovered, they are becoming predictive targets in their own right. Pseudogene prediction utilises existing sequence similarity and ab initio methods, whilst adding additional filtering and methods of identifying pseudogene characteristics.

Sequence similarity methods can be customised for pseudogene prediction using additional filtering to find candidate pseudogenes. This could use disablement detection, which looks for nonsense or frameshift mutations that would truncate or collapse an otherwise functional coding sequence. Additionally, translating DNA into proteins sequences can be more effective than just straight DNA homology.

Content sensors can be filtered according to the differences in statistical properties between pseudogenes and genes, such as a reduced count of CpG islands in pseudogenes, or the differences in G-C content between pseudogenes and their neighbours. Signal sensors also can be honed to pseudogenes, looking for the absence of introns or polyadenine tails.

Metagenomic Gene Prediction

Metagenomics is the study of genetic material recovered from the environment, resulting in sequence information from a pool of organisms. Predicting genes is useful for comparative metagenomics.

Metagenomics tools also fall into the basic categories of using either sequence similarity approaches (MEGAN4) and ab initio techniques (GLIMMER-MG).

Glimmer-MG is an extension to GLIMMER that relies mostly on an ab initio approach for gene finding and by using training sets from related organisms. The prediction strategy is augmented by classification and clustering gene data sets prior to applying ab initio gene prediction methods. The data is clustered by species. This classification method leverages techniques from metagenomic phylogenetic classification. An example of software for this purpose is, Phymm, which uses interpolated markov models—and PhymmBL, which integrates BLAST into the classification routines.

MEGAN4 uses a sequence similarity approach, using local alignment against databases of known sequences, but also attempts to classify using additional information on functional roles, biological pathways and enzymes. As in single organism gene prediction, sequence similarity approaches are limited by the size of the database.

FragGeneScan and MetaGeneAnnotator are popular gene prediction programs based on Hidden Markov model. These predictors account for sequencing errors, partial genes and work for short reads.

Another fast and accurate tool for gene prediction in metagenomes is MetaGeneMark. This tool is used by the DOE Joint Genome Institute to annotate IMG/M, the largest metagenome collection to date.

BLAST Biotechnology

In bioinformatics, BLAST (basic local alignment search tool) is an algorithm for comparing primary biological sequence information, such as the amino-acid sequences of proteins or the nucleotides of DNA and RNA sequences. A BLAST search enables a researcher to compare a subject protein or nucleotide sequence (called a query) with a library or database of sequences, and identify library sequences that resemble the query sequence above a certain threshold.

Different types of BLASTs are available according to the query sequences. For example, following the discovery of a previously unknown gene in the mouse, a scientist will typically perform a BLAST search of the human genome to see if humans carry a similar gene; BLAST will identify sequences in the human genome that resemble the mouse gene based on similarity of sequence.

BLAST is one of the most widely used bioinformatics programs for sequence searching. It addresses a fundamental problem in bioinformatics research. The heuristic algorithm it uses is much faster than other approaches, such as calculating an optimal alignment. This emphasis on speed is vital to making the algorithm practical on the huge genome databases currently available, although subsequent algorithms can be even faster.

Before BLAST, FASTA was developed by David J. Lipman and William R. Pearson in 1985.

Before fast algorithms such as BLAST and FASTA were developed, searching databases for protein or nucleic sequences was very time consuming because a full alignment procedure (e.g., the Smith–Waterman algorithm) was used.

BLAST came from the 1990 stochastic model of Samuel Karlin and Stephen Altschul They "proposed a method for estimating similarities between the known DNA sequence of one organism with that of another," and their work has been described as "the statistical foundation for BLAST". Subsequently, Altschul, along with Warren Gish, Webb Miller, Eugene Myers, and David J. Lipman at the National Institutes of Health designed the BLAST algorithm, which was published in the *Journal of Molecular Biology* in 1990 and cited over 75,000 times.

While BLAST is faster than any Smith-Waterman implementation for most cases, it cannot "guarantee the optimal alignments of the query and database sequences" as Smith-Waterman algorithm does. The optimality of Smith-Waterman "ensured the best performance on accuracy and the most precise results" at the expense of time and computer power.

BLAST is more time-efficient than FASTA by searching only for the more significant patterns in the sequences, yet with comparative sensitivity. This could be further realized by understanding the algorithm of BLAST introduced below.

Examples of other questions that researchers use BLAST to answer are:

- Which bacterial species have a protein that is related in lineage to a certain protein with known amino-acid sequence.

- What other genes encode proteins that exhibit structures or motifs such as ones that have just been determined.

BLAST is also often used as part of other algorithms that require approximate sequence matching.

BLAST is available on the web on the NCBI website. Alternative implementations include AB-BLAST (formerly known as WU-BLAST), FSA-BLAST (last updated in 2006), and ScalaBLAST.

Input

Input sequences (in FASTA or Genbank format) and weight matrix.

Output

BLAST output can be delivered in a variety of formats. These formats include HTML, plain text, and XML formatting. For NCBI's web-page, the default format for output is HTML. When performing a BLAST on NCBI, the results are given in a graphical format showing the hits found, a table showing sequence identifiers for the hits with scoring related data, as well as alignments for the sequence of interest and the hits received with corresponding BLAST scores for these. The easiest to read and most informative of these is probably the table.

If one is attempting to search for a proprietary sequence or simply one that is unavailable in databases available to the general public through sources such as NCBI, there is a

BLAST program available for download to any computer, at no cost. This can be found at BLAST+ executables. There are also commercial programs available for purchase. Databases can be found from the NCBI site, as well as from Index of BLAST databases (FTP).

Process

Using a heuristic method, BLAST finds similar sequences, by locating short matches between the two sequences. This process of finding similar sequences is called seeding. It is after this first match that BLAST begins to make local alignments. While attempting to find similarity in sequences, sets of common letters, known as words, are very important. For example, suppose that the sequence contains the following stretch of letters, GLK-FA. If a BLAST was being conducted under normal conditions, the word size would be 3 letters. In this case, using the given stretch of letters, the searched words would be GLK, LKF, KFA. The heuristic algorithm of BLAST locates all common three-letter words between the sequence of interest and the hit sequence or sequences from the database. This result will then be used to build an alignment. After making words for the sequence of interest, the rest of the words are also assembled. These words must satisfy a requirement of having a score of at least the threshold T, when compared by using a scoring matrix.

One commonly used scoring matrix for BLAST searches is BLOSUM62, although the optimal scoring matrix depends on sequence similarity. Once both words and neighborhood words are assembled and compiled, they are compared to the sequences in the database in order to find matches. The threshold score T determines whether or not a particular word will be included in the alignment. Once seeding has been conducted, the alignment which is only 3 residues long, is extended in both directions by the algorithm used by BLAST. Each extension impacts the score of the alignment by either increasing or decreasing it. If this score is higher than a pre-determined T, the alignment will be included in the results given by BLAST. However, if this score is lower than this pre-determined T, the alignment will cease to extend, preventing the areas of poor alignment from being included in the BLAST results. Note that increasing the T score limits the amount of space available to search, decreasing the number of neighborhood words, while at the same time speeding up the process of BLAST

Algorithm

To run the software, BLAST requires a query sequence to search for, and a sequence to search against (also called the target sequence) or a sequence database containing multiple such sequences. BLAST will find sub-sequences in the database which are similar to sub sequences in the query. In typical usage, the query sequence is much smaller than the database, e.g., the query may be one thousand nucleotides while the database is several billion nucleotides.

The main idea of BLAST is that there are often High-scoring Segment Pairs (HSP) contained in a statistically significant alignment. BLAST searches for high scoring sequence alignments between the query sequence and the existing sequences in the database using a heuristic approach that approximates the Smith-Waterman algorithm. However, the exhaustive Smith-Waterman approach is too slow for searching large genomic databases such as GenBank. Therefore, the BLAST algorithm uses a heuristic approach that is less accurate than the Smith-Waterman algorithm but over 50 times faster. The speed and relatively good accuracy of BLAST are among the key technical innovations of the BLAST programs.

An overview of the BLAST algorithm (a protein to protein search) is as follows:

1. Remove low-complexity region or sequence repeats in the query sequence: "Low-complexity region" means a region of a sequence composed of few kinds of elements. These regions might give high scores that confuse the program to find the actual significant sequences in the database, so they should be filtered out. The regions will be marked with an X (protein sequences) or N (nucleic acid sequences) and then be ignored by the BLAST program. To filter out the low-complexity regions, the SEG program is used for protein sequences and the program DUST is used for DNA sequences. On the other hand, the program XNU is used to mask off the tandem repeats in protein sequences.

2. Make a k-letter word list of the query sequence: Take $k=3$ for example, we list the words of length 3 in the query protein sequence (k is usually 11 for a DNA sequence) "sequentially", until the last letter of the query sequence is included. The method is illustrated in figure.

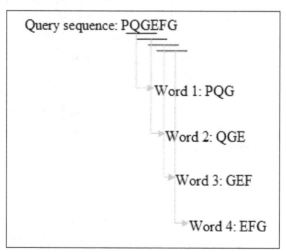

The method to establish the k-letter query word list.

3. List the possible matching words: This step is one of the main differences between BLAST and FASTA. FASTA cares about all of the common words in the database and query sequences that are listed in step 2; however, BLAST only cares about the high-scoring words. The scores are created by comparing the word in the list in step 2 with all the 3-letter words. By using the scoring matrix (substitution matrix)

to score the comparison of each residue pair, there are 20^3 possible match scores for a 3-letter word. For example, the score obtained by comparing PQG with PEG and PQA is respectively 15 and 12 with the BLOSUM62 weighting scheme. For DNA words, a match is scored as +5 and a mismatch as -4, or as +2 and -3. After that, a neighborhood word score threshold T is used to reduce the number of possible matching words. The words whose scores are greater than the threshold T will remain in the possible matching words list, while those with lower scores will be discarded. For example, PEG is kept, but PQA is abandoned when T is 13.

4. Organize the remaining high-scoring words into an efficient search tree: This allows the program to rapidly compare the high-scoring words to the database sequences.

5. Repeat step 3 to 4 for each k-letter word in the query sequence.

6. Scan the database sequences for exact matches with the remaining high-scoring words: The BLAST program scans the database sequences for the remaining high-scoring word, such as PEG, of each position. If an exact match is found, this match is used to seed a possible un-gapped alignment between the query and database sequences.

7. Extend the exact matches to high-scoring segment pair: The original version of BLAST stretches a longer alignment between the query and the database sequence in the left and right directions, from the position where the exact match occurred. The extension does not stop until the accumulated total score of the HSP begins to decrease. A simplified example is presented in figure. To save more time, a newer version of BLAST, called BLAST2 or gapped BLAST, has been developed. BLAST2 adopts a lower neighborhood word score threshold to maintain the same level of sensitivity for detecting sequence similarity. Therefore, the possible matching words list in step 3 becomes longer. Next, the exact matched regions, within distance A from each other on the same diagonal in figure, will be joined as a longer new region. Finally, the new regions are then extended by the same method as in the original version of BLAST, and the HSPs' (High-scoring segment pair) scores of the extended regions are then created by using a substitution matrix as before.

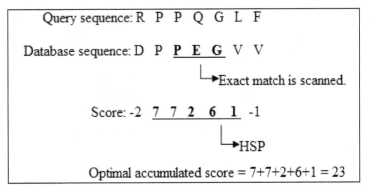

The process to extend the exact match. Adapted from Biological Sequence Analysis I, Current Topics in Genome Analysis.

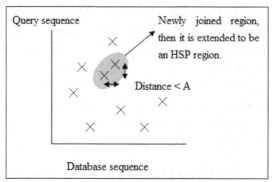

The positions of the exact matches.

8. List all of the HSPs in the database whose score is high enough to be considered: We list the HSPs whose scores are greater than the empirically determined cutoff score S. By examining the distribution of the alignment scores modeled by comparing random sequences, a cutoff score S can be determined such that its value is large enough to guarantee the significance of the remaining HSPs.

9. Evaluate the significance of the HSP score: BLAST next assesses the statistical significance of each HSP score by exploiting the Gumbel extreme value distribution (EVD). (It is proved that the distribution of Smith-Waterman local alignment scores between two random sequences follows the Gumbel EVD. For local alignments containing gaps it is not proved.). In accordance with the Gumbel EVD, the probability p of observing a score S equal to or greater than x is given by the equation:

$$p(S \geq x) = 1 - \exp\left(-e^{-\lambda(x-\mu)}\right)$$

where, $\mu = \dfrac{\log\left(Km'n'\right)}{\lambda}$

The statistical parameters λ and K are estimated by fitting the distribution of the un-gapped local alignment scores, of the query sequence and a lot of shuffled versions (Global or local shuffling) of a database sequence, to the Gumbel extreme value distribution. Note that λ and K depend upon the substitution matrix, gap penalties, and sequence composition (the letter frequencies). m' and n' are the effective lengths of the query and database sequences, respectively. The original sequence length is shortened to the effective length to compensate for the edge effect (an alignment start near the end of one of the query or database sequence is likely not to have enough sequence to build an optimal alignment). They can be calculated as:

$$m' \approx m - \frac{\ln Kmn}{H}$$

$$n' \approx n - \frac{\ln Kmn}{H}$$

where His the average expected score per aligned pair of residues in an alignment of two random sequences. Altschul and Gish gave the typical values, $\lambda = 0.318\,K = 0.13$, and $H = 0.40$, for un-gapped local alignment using BLOSUM62 as the substitution matrix. Using the typical values for assessing the significance is called the lookup table method; it is not accurate. The expect score E of a database match is the number of times that an unrelated database sequence would obtain a score S higher than x by chance. The expectation E obtained in a search for a database of D sequences is given by:

$$E \approx 1 - e^{-p(s>x)D}$$

Furthermore, when $p < 0.1$, , E could be approximated by the Poisson distribution as:

$$E \approx pD$$

This expectation or expect value "E" (often called an E score or E-value or e-value) assessing the significance of the HSP score for un-gapped local alignment is reported in the BLAST results. The calculation shown here is modified if individual HSPs are combined, such as when producing gapped alignments, due to the variation of the statistical parameters.

10. Make two or more HSP regions into a longer alignment: Sometimes, we find two or more HSP regions in one database sequence that can be made into a longer alignment. This provides additional evidence of the relation between the query and database sequence. There are two methods, the Poisson method and the sum-of-scores method, to compare the significance of the newly combined HSP regions. Suppose that there are two combined HSP regions with the pairs of scores (65, 40) and (52, 45), respectively. The Poisson method gives more significance to the set with the maximal lower score (45>40). However, the sum-of-scores method prefers the first set, because 65+40 (105) is greater than 52+45(97). The original BLAST uses the Poisson method; gapped BLAST and the WU-BLAST uses the sum-of scores method.

11. Show the gapped Smith-Waterman local alignments of the query and each of the matched database sequences: The original BLAST only generates un-gapped alignments including the initially found HSPs individually, even when there is more than one HSP found in one database sequence. BLAST2 produces a single alignment with gaps that can include all of the initially found HSP regions. Note

that the computation of the score and its corresponding E-value involves use of adequate gap penalties.

12. Report every match whose expect score is lower than a threshold parameter E.

Parallel BLAST

Parallel BLAST versions of split databases are implemented using MPI and Pthreads, and have been ported to various platforms including Windows, Linux, Solaris, Mac OS X, and AIX. Popular approaches to parallelize BLAST include query distribution, hash table segmentation, computation parallelization, and database segmentation (partition). Databases are split into equal sized pieces and stored locally on each node. Each query is run on all nodes in parallel and the resultant BLAST output files from all nodes merged to yield the final output. Specific implementations include MPIblast, ScalaBLAST, DCBLAST and so on.

Program

The BLAST program can either be downloaded and run as a command-line utility "blastall" or accessed for free over the web. The BLAST web server, hosted by the NCBI, allows anyone with a web browser to perform similarity searches against constantly updated databases of proteins and DNA that include most of the newly sequenced organisms.

The BLAST program is based on an open-source format, giving everyone access to it and enabling them to have the ability to change the program code. This has led to the creation of several BLAST "spin-offs".

There are now a handful of different BLAST programs available, which can be used depending on what one is attempting to do and what they are working with. These different programs vary in query sequence input, the database being searched, and what is being compared. These programs and their details are listed below:

BLAST is actually a family of programs (all included in the blastall executable). These include:

1. Nucleotide-nucleotide BLAST (blastn): This program, given a DNA query, returns the most similar DNA sequences from the DNA database that the user specifies.

2. Protein-protein BLAST (blastp): This program, given a protein query, returns the most similar protein sequences from the protein database that the user specifies.

3. Position-Specific Iterative BLAST (PSI-BLAST) (blastpgp): This program is used to find distant relatives of a protein. First, a list of all closely related proteins is created. These proteins are combined into a general "profile" sequence,

which summarises significant features present in these sequences. A query against the protein database is then run using this profile, and a larger group of proteins is found. This larger group is used to construct another profile, and the process is repeated. By including related proteins in the search, PSI-BLAST is much more sensitive in picking up distant evolutionary relationships than a standard protein-protein BLAST.

4. Nucleotide 6-frame translation-protein (blastx): This program compares the six-frame conceptual translation products of a nucleotide query sequence (both strands) against a protein sequence database.

5. Nucleotide 6-frame translation-nucleotide 6-frame translation (tblastx): This program is the slowest of the BLAST family. It translates the query nucleotide sequence in all six possible frames and compares it against the six-frame translations of a nucleotide sequence database. The purpose of tblastx is to find very distant relationships between nucleotide sequences.

6. Protein-nucleotide 6-frame translation (tblastn): This program compares a protein query against the all six reading frames of a nucleotide sequence database.

7. Large numbers of query sequences (megablast): When comparing large numbers of input sequences via the command-line BLAST, "megablast" is much faster than running BLAST multiple times. It concatenates many input sequences together to form a large sequence before searching the BLAST database, then post-analyzes the search results to glean individual alignments and statistical values.

Of these programs, BLASTn and BLASTp are the most commonly used because they use direct comparisons, and do not require translations. However, since protein sequences are better conserved evolutionarily than nucleotide sequences, tBLASTn, tBLASTx, and BLASTx, produce more reliable and accurate results when dealing with coding DNA. They also enable one to be able to directly see the function of the protein sequence, since by translating the sequence of interest before searching often gives you annotated protein hits.

Alternative Versions

A version designed for comparing large genomes or DNA is BLASTZ.

CS-BLAST (Context-Specific BLAST) is an extended version of BLAST for searching protein sequences that finds twice as many remotely related sequences as BLAST at the same speed and error rate. In CS-BLAST, the mutation probabilities between amino acids depend not only on the single amino acid, as in BLAST, but also on its local sequence context. Washington University produced an alternative version of NCBI BLAST, called WU-BLAST. The rights have since been acquired to Advanced Biocomputing, LLC.

In 2009, NCBI has released a new set of BLAST executables, the C++ based BLAST+, and has released C versions until 2.2.26. Starting with version 2.2.27 (April 2013), only BLAST+ executables are available. Among the changes is the replacement of the blastall executable with separate executables for the different BLAST programs, and changes in option handling. The formatdb utility (C based) has been replaced by makeblastdb (C++ based) and databases formatted by either one should be compatible for identical blast releases. The algorithms remain similar, however, the number of hits found and their order can vary significantly between the older and the newer version. BLAST+ since

Accelerated Versions

TimeLogic offers an FPGA-accelerated implementation of the BLAST algorithm called Tera-BLAST that is hundreds of times faster.

Other formerly supported versions include:

- FPGA-accelerated:

  ◦ Prior to their acquisition by Qiagen, CLC bio collaborated with SciEngines GmbH on an FPGA accelerator they claimed will give 188x acceleration of BLAST.

  ◦ The Mitrion-C Open Bio Project was an effort to port BLAST to run on Mitrion FPGAs.

- GPU-accelerated:

  ◦ GPU-Blast is an accelerated version of NCBI BLASTP for CUDA which is 3x~4x faster than NCBI Blast.

  ◦ CUDA-BLASTP is a version of BLASTP that is GPU-accelerated and is claimed to run up to 10x faster than NCBI BLAST.

  ◦ G-BLASTN is an accelerated version of NCBI blastn and megablast, whose speedup varies from 4x to 14x (compared to the same runs with 4 CPU threads). Its current limitation is that the database must fit into the GPU memory.

- CPU-accelerated:

  ◦ MPIBlast is a parallel implementation of NCBI BLAST using Message Passing Interface. By efficiently utilizing distributed computational resources through database fragmentation, query segmentation, intelligent scheduling, and parallel I/O, mpiBLAST improves NCBI BLAST performance by several orders of magnitude while scaling to hundreds of processors.

- ◦ CaBLAST makes search on large databases orders of magnitude faster by exploiting redundancy in data.

- ◦ Paracel BLAST was a commercial parallel implementation of NCBI BLAST, supporting hundreds of processors.

- ◦ QuickBLAST (kblastp) from NCBI is an implementation accelerated by prefiltering based on Jaccard index estimates with hashed pentameric fragments. The filtering slightly reduces sensitivity, but increases performance by an order of magnitude. NCBI only makes the search available on their non-redundant (nr) protein collection, and does not offer downloads.

Alternatives to BLAST

The predecessor to BLAST, FASTA, can also be used for protein and DNA similarity searching. FASTA provides a similar set of programs for comparing proteins to protein and DNA databases, DNA to DNA and protein databases, and includes additional programs for working with unordered short peptides and DNA sequences. In addition, the FASTA package provides SSEARCH, a vectorized implementation of the rigorous Smith-Waterman algorithm. FASTA is slower than BLAST, but provides a much wider range of scoring matrices, making it easier to tailor a search to a specific evolutionary distance.

An extremely fast but considerably less sensitive alternative to BLAST is BLAT (*B*last *L*ike *A*lignment *T*ool). While BLAST does a linear search, BLAT relies on k-mer indexing the database, and can thus often find seeds faster. Another software alternative similar to BLAT is PatternHunter.

Advances in sequencing technology in the late 2000s has made searching for very similar nucleotide matches an important problem. New alignment programs tailored for this use typically use BWT-indexing of the target database (typically a genome). Input sequences can then be mapped very quickly, and output is typically in the form of a BAM file. Example alignment programs are BWA, SOAP, and Bowtie.

For protein identification, searching for known domains (for instance from Pfam) by matching with Hidden Markov Models is a popular alternative, such as HMMER.

An alternative to BLAST for comparing two banks of sequences is PLAST. PLAST provides a high-performance general purpose bank to bank sequence similarity search tool relying on the PLAST and ORIS algorithms. Results of PLAST are very similar to BLAST, but PLAST is significantly faster and capable of comparing large sets of sequences with a small memory (i.e. RAM) footprint.

For applications in metagenomics, where the task is to compare billions of short DNA reads against tens of millions of protein references, DIAMOND runs at up to 20,000 times as fast as BLASTX, while maintaining a high level of sensitivity.

The open-source software MMseqs is an alternative to BLAST/PSI-BLAST, which improves on current search tools over the full range of speed-sensitivity trade-off, achieving sensitivities better than PSI-BLAST at more than 400 times its speed.

Optical computing approaches have been suggested as promising alternatives to the current electrical implementations. OptCAM is an example of such approaches and is shown to be faster than BLAST.

Comparing BLAST and the Smith-Waterman Process

While both Smith-Waterman and BLAST are used to find homologous sequences by searching and comparing a query sequence with those in the databases, they do have their differences.

Due to the fact that BLAST is based on a heuristic algorithm, the results received through BLAST, in terms of the hits found, may not be the best possible results, as it will not provide you with all the hits within the database. BLAST misses hard to find matches.

A better alternative in order to find the best possible results would be to use the Smith-Waterman algorithm. This method varies from the BLAST method in two areas, accuracy and speed. The Smith-Waterman option provides better accuracy, in that it finds matches that BLAST cannot, because it does not miss any information. Therefore, it is necessary for remote homology. However, when compared to BLAST, it is more time consuming, not to mention that it requires large amounts of computer usage and space. However, technologies to speed up the Smith-Waterman process have been found to improve the time necessary to perform a search dramatically. These technologies include FPGA chips and SIMD technology.

In order to receive better results from BLAST, the settings can be changed from their default settings. However, there is no given or set way of changing these settings in order to receive the best results for a given sequence. The settings available for change are E-Value, gap costs, filters, word size, and substitution matrix. Note, that the algorithm used for BLAST was developed from the algorithm used for Smith-Waterman. BLAST employs an alignment which finds "local alignments between sequences by finding short matches and from these initial matches (local) alignments are created".

BLAST Output Visualization

To help users interpreting BLAST results, different software is available. According to installation and use, analysis features and technology, here are some available tools:

- NCBI BLAST service.

- General BLAST output interpreters, GUI-based: JAMBLAST, Blast Viewer, BLASTGrabber.

- Integrated BLAST environments: PLAN, BlastStation-Free.

- BLAST output parsers: MuSeqBox, Zerg, BioParser, BLAST-Explorer.

- Specialized BLAST-related tools: MEGAN, BLAST2GENE, BOV, Circoletto.

Uses of BLAST

BLAST can be used for several purposes. These include identifying species, locating domains, establishing phylogeny, DNA mapping, and comparison.

- Identifying species: With the use of BLAST, you can possibly correctly identify a species or find homologous species. This can be useful, for example, when you are working with a DNA sequence from an unknown species.

- Locating domains: When working with a protein sequence you can input it into BLAST, to locate known domains within the sequence of interest.

- Establishing phylogeny: Using the results received through BLAST you can create a phylogenetic tree using the BLAST web-page. Phylogenies based on BLAST alone are less reliable than other purpose-built computational phylogenetic methods, so should only be relied upon for "first pass" phylogenetic analyses.

- DNA mapping: When working with a known species, and looking to sequence a gene at an unknown location, BLAST can compare the chromosomal position of the sequence of interest, to relevant sequences in the database(s). NCBI has a "Magic-BLAST" tool built around BLAST for this purpose.

- Comparison: When working with genes, BLAST can locate common genes in two related species, and can be used to map annotations from one organism to another.

Role of Bioinformatics in Biotechnology

Bioinformatics is the short form for 'Biological Informatics'. This is considered to be an amalgam of biological sciences and computer science and now a days, many scientists prefer to use the term, computational biology. This branch of science became more popular when human genome project came into existence. Bioinformatics merges biology, computer science and information technology to form a single discipline. It covers many areas of biological science especially of modern biology viz. genomics, transcriptomics, proteomics, genetics, and evolution. The ultimate goal of the field is to enable the discovery of new biological insights as well as to create a global perspective from which unifying principles in biology can be recognized.

Bioinformatics is a fascinating subject having input of engineering art as well as of science. Bioinformaticians are mostly engaged in designing new algorithms, software, developing updated databases which all help in solving many biological problems. A number of bioinformatics tools, software and databases are available for better understanding of biological complexity and analyze and store the biological data. Thus, the bioinformatics research is used to avoid time, cost and wet lab practice. Scientists realized the importance of sequence databases in 1950s and that's why, first protein sequence database was created in 1956 just after insulin peptides sequences became available. The human genome sequence data is so huge that if compiled in books, the data would run into 200 volumes of 1000 pages each and reading alone would require 26 years working around the clock. This challenge of handling such a huge data can only be possible because of bioinformatics.

The growth of the biotechnology industry in recent years is unprecedented, and advancements in molecular modelling, disease characterization, pharmaceutical discovery, clinical healthcare, forensics, and agriculture fundamentally impact economic and social issues worldwide. As a result, with people confidence and development of biotechnology, bioinformatics also reached to new heights among all the biological sciences. There exists a number of applications of bioinformatics for accelerating research in the area of biotechnology that include automatic genome sequencing, gene identification, prediction of gene function, prediction of protein structure, phylogeny, drug designing and development, identification of organisms, vaccine designing, understanding the gene and genome complexity, understanding protein structure, functionality and folding. By using bioinformatics in research, many long term projects are turned up so fast like genome mapping of human and other organisms. Similarly, it is expected that bioinformatics innovation in future will also meet the demands of biotechnology.

Genomics

The study of genes and their expression is called as Genomics. This field generates a vast amount of data from gene sequences, their interrelation and functions. To manage this vast enormous data, bioinformatics plays a very important role. With the complete genome sequences for an increasing number of organisms, bioinformatics is beginning to provide both conceptua l bases and practical methods for detecting systemic functional behaviours of the cell and the organism. Bioinformatics plays a vital role in the areas of structural genomics, functional genomics and nutritional genomics.

Proteomics

The study of protein structure, function, and interactions produced by a particular cell, tissue, or organism is called as proteomics. It deals with techniques of genetics, biochemistry and molecular biology. Advanced techniques in biology led to accumulate enormous data of protein-protein interactions, protein profiles, protein activity pattern and organelles compositions. This vast data can be managed and access easily by using bioinformatics tools, software and databases. Till now, many algorithms in the field of proteomics viz. image analysis of 2D gels, peptide mass fingerprinting and peptide fragmentation fingerprinting have been developed.

Transcriptomics

The study of sets of all messenger RNA molecules in the cell is called as transcriptomics. This can also be called as Expression Profiling where DNA microarray is used to determine the expression level of mRNA in a given cell population. The microarray technique generates vast amount of data, single run generates thousands of data value and one experiment requires hundreds of runs. Analysis of such vast data is done by numerous software packages. In this way, bioinformatics is used for transcriptome analysis where mRNA expression levels can be determined. RNA sequencing (RNAseq) also has been included under transcriptomics. It is carried out using next generation sequencing to determine the presence and quantity of RNA in a sample at a given time. It is used to analyze the continuously changing cellular transcriptome.

Cheminformatics

Cheminformatics (chemical informatics) focuses on storing, indexing, searching, retrieving, and applying information about chemical compounds. It involves organization of chemical data in a logical form to facilitate the retrieval of chemical properties, structures and their relationships. Using bioinformatics, it is possible through computer algorithm to identify and structurally modify a natural product, to design a compound with the desired properties and to assess its therapeutic effects, theoretically. Cheminformatics analysis includes analyses such as similarity searching, clustering, QSAR modelling, virtual screening, etc.

Drug Discovery

Bioinformatics is playing an increasingly important role in nearly all aspects of drug discovery, drug assessment and drug development. This growing importance is not because bioinformatics handles large volumes of data but also in the utility of bioinformatics tools to predict, analyze and help interpretation in clinical and preclinical findings. Traditionally, pharmacology and chemistry-based drug discovery approaches face various difficulties in finding new drugs. The increasing pressure to generate more and more drugs in a short period of time with low risk has resulted in remarkable interest in bioinformatics. In fact, now there is an existence of new separate field known as computer-aided drug design (CADD). Bioinformatics provides a huge support to overcome the cost and time context in various ways. It provides wide range of drug-related databases and softwares which can be used for various purposes related to drug designing and development process.

Evolutionary Studies

The study of evolutionary relationship among individuals or group of organisms is defined as phylogenetics. Taxonomists find the evolutionary relationship using various anatomical methods that takes too much time. Using Bioinformatics, phylogenetic trees are constructed based on the sequence alignment using various methods. Various algorithmic methods are developed for the construction of phylogenetic tree that are used depending on the various evolutionary lineages.

Crop Improvement

Sustainable agricultural production is an urgent issue in response to global climate change and population increase. Innovations in omics based research improve the plant based research. The integrated 'omics' strategies clarify the molecular system of the plant which are used to improve the plant productivity. Genomics strategy, especially comparative genomics helps in understanding the genes and their functions, and also the biological properties of each species. Bioinformatics databases are also used in designing new techniques and experiments for increased plant production.

Veterinary Science

Food production from livestock can meet demand of human population for food. For better bio-economy, there is a need of efficient animal production and reproduction. This is achieved with better understanding of livestock species. Current and new methods in livestock species using data from experimental or field studies with bioinformatics are helping in understanding the systems genetics of complex traits and provide biologically meaningful and accurate predictions. Finally, almost all of the next generations-omics tools and methods that are used in other fields of biological sciences, can also be used in veterinary sciences.

Forensic Science

Forensic science includes the study regarding identification and relatedness of individuals. It is inherently interdisciplinary with bioinformatics as both are dependent on computer science and statistics. This field is based on the molecular data and many databases are being developed to store the DNA profiles of known offenders. This field is being pushed due to technological and statistical advances in microarray, Bayesian networks, machine learning algorithms, TFT biosensors and others. This provides the effective way of evidence organization and inference.

Biodefense

Biodefense includes measures to restore biosecurity to a group of organisms who are subjected to biological threats or infectious diseases (in context of bio-war or bioterrorism). Today, bioinformatics has a limited impact on forensic and intelligence operations. There is a need of more algorithms in bioinformatics for biodefense so that the developed databases may show interoperability with each other. In order to use next generation genome sequencing for forensic operation, bio-threat awareness, mitigation and medical intelligence, there is a need for development of more computational applications.

Waste Cleanup

Today, the major concern all over the Globe is environmental pollutants. The main concern of the environmentalists is waste generated from the industries. These pollutants progressively deteriorate the environment which in turn affects human health. There are few microorganisms that are considered to remediate the pollutants into the natural biogeochemical cycle. Bioremediation is the recent technology which explores the microbial potentiality for biodegradation. This technology can be further improved by using bioinformatics. Genomic and bioinformatics data provide a wealth of information that would be greatly enhanced by structural characterisation of some protein. Bioinformatics provides data of microbial genomics, proteomics, systems biology, computational biology, and bioinformatics tools for understanding of the mechanisms of biodegradative pathways.

Climate Change Studies

Another Global concern is the Climate change because of loss of sea ice, accelerated sea level rise and longer and more intense heat waves. To solve this issue, bioinformatics may help by way of sequencing microbial genome which can reduce levels of carbon dioxide and other greenhouse gases. This plays an important role in stabilizing the global climate change. Not much work has been done in this area in bioinformatics domain, and more region-specific work must be conducted considering microbes of that region and their capability in CO_2 reduction.

Bioenergy/Biofuels

Biofuels offer great promise in contributing to the growing global demand for alternative sources of renewable energy. Bioinformatics is important in understanding and analysis of biofuel producing pathways. Recent progress in algal genomics, in conjunction with other "omics" approaches, has accelerated the ability to identify metabolic pathways and genes that are potential targets in the development of genetically engineered micro-algal strains with optimum lipid content.

References

- Leontis NB, Westhof E (2001). "Geometric nomenclature and classification of RNA base pairs". RNA. 7 (4): 499–512. Doi:10.1017/S1355838201002515. PMC 1370104. PMID 11345429

- Bioinformatics, science: britannica.com, Retrieved 21 January, 2019

- Peitsch, M.C., and Schwede, T. (2008) Computational Structural Biology: Methods and Applications World Scientific, ISBN 978-9812778772

- Overview-protein-expression-systems, pierce-protein-methods, protein-biology-resource-library, protein-biology-learning-center, protein-biology, life-science: thermofisher.com, Retrieved 22 February, 2019

- Wooley, JC; Godzik, A; Friedberg, I (Feb 26, 2010). "A primer on metagenomics". Plos Comput Biol. 6 (2): e1000667. Bibcode:2010PLSCB...6E0667W. Doi:10.1371/journal.pcbi.1000667. PMC 2829047. PMID 20195499

- Role-of-bioinformatics-in-biotechnology: tsijournals.com, Retrieved 23 March, 2019

- Camacho, C.; Coulouris, G.; Avagyan, V.; Ma, N.; Papadopoulos, J.; Bealer, K.; Madden, T. L. (2009). "BLAST+: Architecture and applications". BMC Bioinformatics. 10: 421. Doi:10.1186/1471-2105-10-421. PMC 2803857. PMID 20003500

Phylogenetics Analysis 4

- **Phylogenetic Tree**
- **Tree Alignment**
- **Distance Matrices in Phylogeny**
- **Treefinder**
- **Bayesian Inference in Phylogeny**

The application of computational algorithms, methods, and programs to phylogenetic analysis is referred to as computational phylogenetics. The fundamental concepts that come under this field are phylogenetic tree, tree alignment, treefinder, etc. This chapter closely examines these key concepts related to computational phylogenetics to provide an extensive understanding of the subject.

Computational phylogenetics is the application of computational algorithms, methods, and programs to phylogenetic analyses. The goal is to assemble a phylogenetic tree representing a hypothesis about the evolutionary ancestry of a set of genes, species, or other taxa. For example, these techniques have been used to explore the family tree of hominid species and the relationships between specific genes shared by many types of organisms. Traditional phylogenetics relies on morphological data obtained by measuring and quantifying the phenotypic properties of representative organisms, while the more recent field of molecular phylogenetics uses nucleotide sequences encoding genes or amino acid sequences encoding proteins as the basis for classification. Many forms of molecular phylogenetics are closely related to and make extensive use of sequence alignment in constructing and refining phylogenetic trees, which are used to classify the evolutionary relationships between homologous genes represented in the genomes of divergent species. The phylogenetic trees constructed by computational methods are unlikely to perfectly reproduce the evolutionary tree that represents the historical relationships between the species being analyzed. The historical species tree may also differ from the historical tree of an individual homologous gene shared by those species.

Producing a phylogenetic tree requires a measure of homology among the characteristics shared by the taxa being compared. In morphological studies, this requires explicit decisions about which physical characteristics to measure and how to use them to encode distinct states corresponding to the input taxa. In molecular studies, a primary problem is in producing a multiple sequence alignment (MSA) between the genes or amino acid sequences of interest. Progressive sequence alignment methods produce a phylogenetic tree by necessity because they incorporate new sequences into the calculated alignment in order of genetic distance.

Types of Phylogenetic Trees and Networks

Phylogenetic trees generated by computational phylogenetics can be either rooted or unrooted depending on the input data and the algorithm used. A rooted tree is a directed graph that explicitly identifies a most recent common ancestor (MRCA), usually an imputed sequence that is not represented in the input. Genetic distance measures can be used to plot a tree with the input sequences as leaf nodes and their distances from the root proportional to their genetic distance from the hypothesized MRCA. Identification of a root usually requires the inclusion in the input data of at least one "outgroup" known to be only distantly related to the sequences of interest.

By contrast, unrooted trees plot the distances and relationships between input sequences without making assumptions regarding their descent. An unrooted tree can always be produced from a rooted tree, but a root cannot usually be placed on an unrooted tree without additional data on divergence rates, such as the assumption of the molecular clock hypothesis.

The set of all possible phylogenetic trees for a given group of input sequences can be conceptualized as a discretely defined multidimensional "tree space" through which search paths can be traced by optimization algorithms. Although counting the total number of trees for a nontrivial number of input sequences can be complicated by variations in the definition of a tree topology, it is always true that there are more rooted than unrooted trees for a given number of inputs and choice of parameters.

Both rooted and unrooted phylogenetic trees can be further generalized to rooted or unrooted phylogenetic networks, which allow for the modelling of evolutionary phenomena such as hybridization or horizontal gene transfer.

Coding Characters and Defining Homology

Morphological Analysis

The basic problem in morphological phylogenetics is the assembly of a matrix representing a mapping from each of the taxa being compared to representative measurements for each of the phenotypic characteristics being used as a classifier. The types of phenotypic data used to construct this matrix depend on the taxa being compared; for individual species, they may involve measurements of average body size, lengths or sizes of particular bones or other physical features, or even behavioral manifestations.

Of course, since not every possible phenotypic characteristic could be measured and encoded for analysis, the selection of which features to measure is a major inherent obstacle to the method. The decision of which traits to use as a basis for the matrix necessarily represents a hypothesis about which traits of a species or higher taxon are evolutionarily relevant. Morphological studies can be confounded by examples of convergent evolution of phenotypes. A major challenge in constructing useful classes is the high likelihood of inter-taxon overlap in the distribution of the phenotype's variation. The inclusion of extinct taxa in morphological analysis is often difficult due to absence of or incomplete fossil records, but has been shown to have a significant effect on the trees produced; in one study only the inclusion of extinct species of apes produced a morphologically derived tree that was consistent with that produced from molecular data.

Some phenotypic classifications, particularly those used when analyzing very diverse groups of taxa, are discrete and unambiguous; classifying organisms as possessing or lacking a tail, for example, is straightforward in the majority of cases, as is counting features such as eyes or vertebrae. However, the most appropriate representation of continuously varying phenotypic measurements is a controversial problem without a general solution. A common method is simply to sort the measurements of interest into two or more classes, rendering continuous observed variation as discretely classifiable (e.g., all examples with humerus bones longer than a given cutoff are scored as members of one state, and all members whose humerus bones are shorter than the cutoff are scored as members of a second state). This results in an easily manipulated data set but has been criticized for poor reporting of the basis for the class definitions and for sacrificing information compared to methods that use a continuous weighted distribution of measurements.

Because morphological data is extremely labor-intensive to collect, whether from literature sources or from field observations, reuse of previously compiled data matrices is not uncommon, although this may propagate flaws in the original matrix into multiple derivative analyses.

Molecular Analysis

The problem of character coding is very different in molecular analyses, as the characters in biological sequence data are immediate and discretely defined - distinct nucleotides in DNA or RNA sequences and distinct amino acids in protein sequences. However, defining homology can be challenging due to the inherent difficulties of multiple sequence alignment. For a given gapped MSA, several rooted phylogenetic trees can be constructed that vary in their interpretations of which changes are "mutations" versus ancestral characters, and which events are insertion mutations or deletion mutations. For example, given only a pairwise alignment with a gap region, it is impossible to determine whether one sequence bears an insertion mutation or the other carries a deletion. The problem is magnified in MSAs with unaligned and nonoverlapping gaps.

In practice, sizable regions of a calculated alignment may be discounted in phylogenetic tree construction to avoid integrating noisy data into the tree calculation.

Distance-matrix Methods

Distance-matrix methods of phylogenetic analysis explicitly rely on a measure of "genetic distance" between the sequences being classified, and therefore they require an MSA as an input. Distance is often defined as the fraction of mismatches at aligned positions, with gaps either ignored or counted as mismatches. Distance methods attempt to construct an all-to-all matrix from the sequence query set describing the distance between each sequence pair. From this is constructed a phylogenetic tree that places closely related sequences under the same interior node and whose branch lengths closely reproduce the observed distances between sequences. Distance-matrix methods may produce either rooted or unrooted trees, depending on the algorithm used to calculate them. They are frequently used as the basis for progressive and iterative types of multiple sequence alignments. The main disadvantage of distance-matrix methods is their inability to efficiently use information about local highvariation regions that appear across multiple subtrees.

Neighbor-joining

Neighbor-joining methods apply general data clustering techniques to sequence analysis using genetic distance as a clustering metric. The simple neighborjoining method produces unrooted trees, but it does not assume a constant rate of evolution (i.e., a molecular clock) across lineages. Its relative, UPGMA (Unweighted Pair Group Method with Arithmetic mean) produces rooted trees and requires a constant-rate assumption - that is, it assumes an ultrametric tree in which the distances from the root to every branch tip are equal.

Fitch-Margoliash Method

The Fitch-Margoliash method uses a weighted least squares method for clustering based on genetic distance. Closely related sequences are given more weight in the tree construction process to correct for the increased inaccuracy in measuring distances between distantly related sequences. The distances used as input to the algorithm must be normalized to prevent large artifacts in computing relationships between closely related and distantly related groups. The distances calculated by this method must be linear; the linearity criterion for distances requires that the expected values of the branch lengths for two individual branches must equal the expected value of the sum of the two branch distances - a property that applies to biological sequences only when they have been corrected for the possibility of back mutations at individual sites. This correction is done through the use of a substitution matrix such as that derived from the Jukes-Cantor model of DNA evolution. The distance correction is only necessary in practice when the evolution rates differ among branches. Another modification of the algorithm can be helpful, especially in case of concentrated distances (please report to concentration of measure phenomenon and curse of dimensionality): that modification, described in, has been shown to improve the efficiency of the algorithm and its robustness.

The least-squares criterion applied to these distances is more accurate but less efficient than the neighbor-joining methods. An additional improvement that corrects for correlations between distances that arise from many closely related sequences in the data set can also be applied at increased computational cost. Finding the optimal least-squares tree with any correction factor is NPcomplete, so heuristic search methods like those used in maximum-parsimony analysis are applied to the search through tree space.

Using Outgroups

Independent information about the relationship between sequences or groups can be used to help reduce the tree search space and root unrooted trees. Standard usage of distance-matrix methods involves the inclusion of at least one outgroup sequence known to be only distantly related to the sequences of interest in the query set. This usage can be seen as a type of experimental control. If the outgroup has been appropriately chosen, it will have a much greater genetic distance and thus a longer branch length than any other sequence, and it will appear near the root of a rooted tree. Choosing an appropriate outgroup requires the selection of a sequence that is moderately related to the sequences of interest; too close a relationship defeats the purpose of the outgroup and too distant adds noise to the analysis. Care should also be taken to avoid situations in which the species from which the sequences were taken are distantly related, but the gene encoded by the sequences is highly conserved across lineages. Horizontal gene transfer, especially between otherwise divergent bacteria, can also confound outgroup usage.

Phylogenetic Tree

A phylogenetic tree or evolutionary tree is a branching diagram or "tree" showing the evolutionary relationships among various biological species or other entities—their phylogeny based upon similarities and differences in their physical or genetic characteristics. All life on Earth is part of a single phylogenetic tree, indicating common ancestry.

In a *rooted* phylogenetic tree, each node with descendants represents the inferred most recent common ancestor of those descendants, and the edge lengths in some trees may be interpreted as time estimates. Each node is called a taxonomic unit. Internal nodes are generally called hypothetical taxonomic units, as they cannot be directly observed.

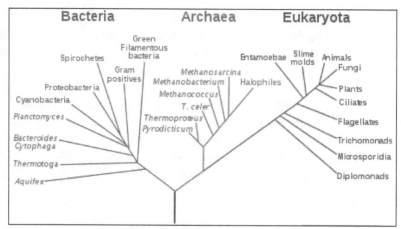

A speculatively rooted tree for rRNA genes, showing the three life domains: bacteria, archaea, and eukaryota. The black trunk at the bottom of the tree links the three branches of living organisms to the last universal common ancestor.

Trees are useful in fields of biology such as bioinformatics, systematics, and phylogenetics. Unrooted trees illustrate only the relatedness of the leaf nodes and do not require the ancestral root to be known or inferred.

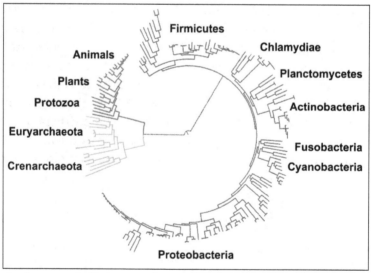

A highly resolved, automatically generated tree of life, based on completely sequenced genomes.

The idea of a "tree of life" arose from ancient notions of a ladder-like progression from lower into higher forms of life (such as in the Great Chain of Being). Early representations of "branching" phylogenetic trees include a "paleontological chart" showing the geological relationships among plants and animals in the book *Elementary Geology*, by Edward Hitchcock.

Charles Darwin also produced one of the first illustrations and crucially popularized the notion of an evolutionary "tree" in his seminal book *The Origin of Species*. Over a century later, evolutionary biologists still use tree diagrams to depict evolution because such diagrams effectively convey the concept that speciation occurs through the adaptive and semirandom splitting of lineages. Over time, species classification has become less static and more dynamic.

Properties

Rooted Tree

A rooted phylogenetic tree is a directed tree with a unique node — the root — corresponding to the (usually imputed) most recent common ancestor of all the entities at the leaves of the tree. The root node does not have a parent node, but serves as the parent of all other nodes in the tree. The root is therefore a node of degree 2 while other internal nodes have a minimum degree of 3 (where "degree" here refers to the total number of incoming and outgoing edges).

The most common method for rooting trees is the use of an uncontroversial outgroup— close enough to allow inference from trait data or molecular sequencing, but far enough to be a clear outgroup.

Unrooted Tree

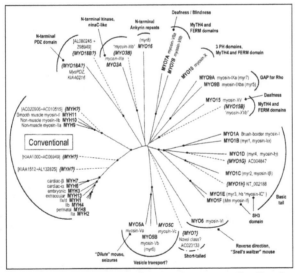

An unrooted phylogenetic tree for myosin, a superfamily of proteins.

Unrooted trees illustrate the relatedness of the leaf nodes without making assumptions about ancestry. They do not require the ancestral root to be known or inferred. Unrooted trees can always be generated from rooted ones by simply omitting the root. By contrast, inferring the root of an unrooted tree requires some means of identifying ancestry. This is normally done by including an outgroup in the input data so that the root is necessarily between the outgroup and the rest of the taxa in the tree, or by introducing additional assumptions about the relative rates of evolution on each branch, such as an application of the molecular clock hypothesis.

Bifurcating versus Multifurcating

Both rooted and unrooted trees can be either bifurcating or multifurcating. A rooted bifurcating tree has exactly two descendants arising from each interior node (that is, it forms a binary tree), and an unrooted bifurcating tree takes the form of an unrooted binary tree, a free tree with exactly three neighbors at each internal node. In contrast, a rooted multifurcating tree may have more than two children at some nodes and an unrooted multifurcating tree may have more than three neighbors at some nodes.

Labeled versus Unlabeled

Both rooted and unrooted trees can be either labeled or unlabeled. A labeled tree has specific values assigned to its leaves, while an unlabeled tree, sometimes called a tree shape, defines a topology only.

Enumerating Trees

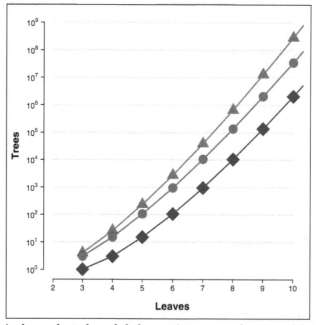

Increase in the total number of phylogenetic trees as a function of the number of labeled leaves: unrooted binary trees (blue diamonds), rooted binary trees (red circles), and rooted multifurcating or binary trees (green: triangles). The Y-axis scale is logarithmic.

The number of possible trees for a given number of leaf nodes depends on the specific type of tree, but there are always more labeled than unlabeled trees, more multifurcating than bifurcating trees, and more rooted than unrooted trees. The last distinction is the most biologically relevant; it arises because there are many places on an unrooted tree to put the root. For bifurcating labeled trees, the total number of rooted trees is,

$$2n-3)!! = \frac{(2n-3)!}{2^{n-2}(n-2)!} \text{ for } n \geq 2, ,$$

where n represents the number of leaf nodes.

For bifurcating labeled trees, the total number of unrooted trees is:

$$(2n-5)!! = \frac{(2n-5)!}{2^{n-3}(n-3)!} \text{ for } n \geq 3.$$

Among labeled bifurcating trees, the number of unrooted trees with n leaves is equal to the number of rooted trees with $n-1$ leaves.

The number of rooted trees grows quickly as a function of the number of tips. For 10 tips, there are more than 34×10^6 possible bifurcating trees, and the number of multi-furcating trees rises faster, with ca. 7 times as many of the latter as of the former.

Counting trees.				
Labeled leaves	Binary unrooted Trees	Binary rooted Trees	Multifurcating rooted Trees	All Possible rooted Trees
1	1	1	0	1
2	1	1	0	1
3	1	3	1	4
4	3	15	11	26
5	15	105	131	236
6	105	945	1,807	2,752
7	945	10,395	28,813	39,208
8	10,395	135,135	524,897	660,032
9	135,135	2,027,025	10,791,887	12,818,912
10	2,027,025	34,459,425	247,678,399	282,137,824

Special Tree Types

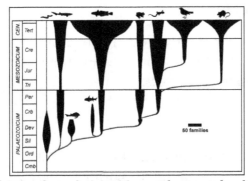

A spindle diagram, showing the evolution of the vertebrates at class level, width of spindles indicating number of families. Spindle diagrams are often used in evolutionary taxonomy.

Dendrogram

A dendrogram is a general name for a tree, whether phylogenetic or not, and hence also for the diagrammatic representation of a phylogenetic tree.

Cladogram

A cladogram only represents a branching pattern; i.e., its branch spans do not represent time or relative amount of character change, and its internal nodes do not represent ancestors.

Phylogram

A phylogram is a phylogenetic tree that has branch spans proportional to the amount of character change.

Chronogram

A chronogram is a phylogenetic tree that explicitly represents time through its branch spans.

Spindle Diagram

A spindle diagram (often called a Romerogram after the American palaeontologist Alfred Romer) is the representation of the evolution and abundance of the various taxa through time, but is not an evolutionary tree.

Dahlgrenogram

A Dahlgrenogram is a diagram representing a cross section of a phylogenetic tree.

Phylogenetic Network

A phylogenetic network is not strictly speaking a tree, but rather a more general graph, or a directed acyclic graph in the case of rooted networks. They are used to overcome some of the limitations inherent to trees.

Coral of Life

Darwin also mentioned that the *coral* may be a more suitable metaphor than the *tree*. Indeed, phylogenetic corals are useful for portraying past and present life, and they have some advantages over trees (anastomoses allowed, etc).

The coral of life.

Construction

Phylogenetic trees composed with a nontrivial number of input sequences are constructed using computational phylogenetics methods. Distance-matrix methods such as neighbor-joining or UPGMA, which calculate genetic distance from multiple sequence alignments, are simplest to implement, but do not invoke an evolutionary model. Many sequence alignment methods such as ClustalW also create trees by using the simpler algorithms (i.e. those based on distance) of tree construction. Maximum parsimony is another simple method of estimating phylogenetic trees, but implies an implicit model of evolution (i.e. parsimony). More advanced methods use the optimality criterion of maximum likelihood, often within a Bayesian framework, and apply an explicit model of evolution to phylogenetic tree estimation. Identifying the optimal tree using many of these techniques is NP-hard, so heuristic search and optimization methods are used in combination with tree-scoring functions to identify a reasonably good tree that fits the data.

Tree-building methods can be assessed on the basis of several criteria:

- Efficiency: How long does it take to compute the answer, how much memory does it need?

- Power: Does it make good use of the data, or is information being wasted?

- Consistency: Will it converge on the same answer repeatedly, if each time given different data for the same model problem?

- Robustness: Does it cope well with violations of the assumptions of the underlying model?

- Falsifiability: Does it alert us when it is not good to use, i.e. when assumptions are violated?

Tree-building techniques have also gained the attention of mathematicians. Trees can also be built using T-theory.

Limitations of Phylogenetic Analysis

Although phylogenetic trees produced on the basis of sequenced genes or genomic data in different species can provide evolutionary insight, these analyses have important limitations. Most importantly, the trees that they generate are not necessarily correct – they do not necessarily accurately represent the evolutionary history of the included taxa. As with any scientific result, they are subject to falsification by further study (e.g., gathering of additional data, analyzing the existing data with improved methods). The data on which they are based may be noisy; the analysis can be confounded by genetic recombination, horizontal gene transfer, hybridisation between species that were not nearest neighbors on the tree before hybridisation takes place, convergent evolution, and conserved sequences.

Also, there are problems in basing an analysis on a single type of character, such as a single gene or protein or only on morphological analysis, because such trees constructed from another unrelated data source often differ from the first, and therefore great care is needed in inferring phylogenetic relationships among species. This is most true of genetic material that is subject to lateral gene transfer and recombination, where different haplotype blocks can have different histories. In these types of analysis, the output tree of a phylogenetic analysis of a single gene is an estimate of the gene's phylogeny (i.e. a gene tree) and not the phylogeny of the taxa (i.e. species tree) from which these characters were sampled, though ideally, both should be very close. For this reason, serious phylogenetic studies generally use a combination of genes that come from different genomic sources (e.g., from mitochondrial or plastid vs. nuclear genomes), or genes that would be expected to evolve under different selective regimes, so that homoplasy (false homology) would be unlikely to result from natural selection.

When extinct species are included as terminal nodes in an analysis (rather than, for example, to constrain internal nodes), they are considered not to represent direct ancestors of any extant species. Extinct species do not typically contain high-quality DNA.

The range of useful DNA materials has expanded with advances in extraction and sequencing technologies. Development of technologies able to infer sequences from smaller fragments, or from spatial patterns of DNA degradation products, would further expand the range of DNA considered useful.

Phylogenetic trees can also be inferred from a range of other data types, including morphology, the presence or absence of particular types of genes, insertion and deletion events – and any other observation thought to contain an evolutionary signal.

Phylogenetic networks are used when bifurcating trees are not suitable, due to these complications which suggest a more reticulate evolutionary history of the organisms sampled.

Tree Alignment

In computational phylogenetics, tree alignment is a computational problem concerned with producing multiple sequence alignments, or alignments of three or more sequences of DNA, RNA, or protein. Sequences are arranged into a phylogenetic tree, modelling the evolutionary relationships between species or taxa. The edit distances between sequences are calculated for each of the tree's internal vertices, such that the sum of all edit distances within the tree is minimized. Tree alignment can be accomplished using one of several algorithms with various trade-offs between manageable tree size and computational effort.

Input: A set S of sequences, a phylogenetic tree T leaf-labeled by S and an edit distance function d between sequences.

Output: A labeling of the internal vertices of T such that $\Sigma_{e \in T} d(e)$ is minimized, where $d(e)$ is the edit distance between the endpoints of the task is NP-hard.

Sequence Alignment

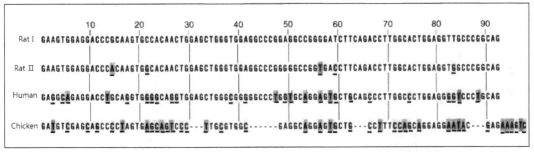

This is a simple Sequence Alignment of Insulin gene between rat, human and chicken. The labeled nucleotides are the different nucleotides with rats I and means the missing nucleotides.

In bioinformatics, the basic method of information processing is to contrast the sequence data. Biologists use it to discover the function, structure, and evolutionary information in biological sequences. The following analyses are based on the sequence assembly: the phylogenetic analysis, the haplotype comparison, and the prediction of RNA structure. Therefore, the efficiency of sequence alignment will directly affect the efficacy of solving these problems. In order to design a rational and efficient sequence alignment, the algorithm derivation becomes an important branch of research in the field of bioinformatics.

Generally, sequence alignment means constructing a string from two or more given strings with the greatest similarity by adding letters, deleting letters, or adding a space for each string. The multiple sequence alignment problem is generally based on pairwise sequence alignment and currently, for a pairwise sequence alignment problem, biologists can use a dynamic programming approach to obtain its optimal solution.

However, the multiple sequence alignment problem is still one of the more challenging problems in bioinformatics. This is because finding the optimal solution for multiple sequence alignment has been proven as an NP-complete problem and only an approximate optimal solution can be obtained.

Distance Matrix Method

Distance method measures the minimum operation number of character insertions, deletions, and substitutions that are required to transform one sequence u to the other sequence v when being operated on a pair of strings. The calculation of edit distance can be based on dynamic programming, and the equation is in $O(|u| \times |v|)$ time, where $|u|$ and $|v|$ are the lengths of u and v. The efficient estimation of edit distance is essential as Distance method is a basic principle in computational biology For functions of hereditary properties "symmetrization" can be used. Due to a series of functions being used to calculate edit distance, different functions may result in different results. Finding an optimal edit distance function is essential for the tree alignment problem.

The Problem of Tree Alignment

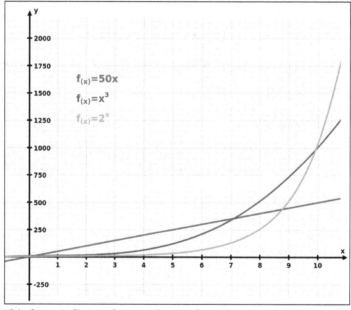

This figure indicates the growth rate about the exponential time, the polynomial time and the linear time.

Tree alignment results in a NP-hard problem, where scoring modes and alphabet sizes are restricted. It can be found as an algorithm, which is used to find the optimized solution. However, there is an exponential relationship between its efficiency and the number sequences, which means that when the length of the sequence is very large, the computation time required to get results is enormously long. Using star alignment to get the approximate optimized solution is faster than using tree alignment. However, whatever the degree of multiple-sequence similarity is, the time complexity of star alignment has a proportional relationship with the square of the sequence number and the square of the sequence average length. As usual, the sequence in MSA is so long that it is also inefficient or even unacceptable. Therefore, the challenge of reducing the time complexity to linear is one of the core issues in tree alignment.

Combinatorial Optimization Strategy

Combinatorial optimization is a good strategy to solve MSA problems. The idea of combinatorial optimization strategy is to transform the multiple sequence alignment into pair sequence alignment to solve this problem. Depending on its transformation strategy, the combinatorial optimization strategy can be divided into the tree alignment algorithm and the star alignment algorithm. For a given multi-sequence set $S = \{s_1, ..., s_n\}$ find an evolutionary tree which has n leaf nodes and establishing one to one relationship between this evolutionary tree and the set S. By assigning the sequence to the internal nodes of the evolutionary tree, we calculate the total score of each edge, and the sum of all edges' scores is the score of the evolutionary tree. The aim of tree alignment is to find an assigned sequence, which can obtain a maximum score, and get the final matching result from the evolutionary tree and its nodes' assigned sequence. Star alignment can be seen as a special case of the tree alignment. When we use star alignment, the evolutionary tree has only one internal node and n leaf nodes. The sequence, which is assigned to the internal node, is called the core sequence.

The Keyword Tree Theory and The Aho-Corasick Search Algorithm

When the combinatorial optimization strategy is used to transform the multiple sequence alignment into pair sequence alignment, the main problem is changed from "How to improve the efficiency of multiple sequence alignment" to "How to improve the efficiency of pairwise sequence alignment". The Keyword Tree Theory and the Aho-Corasick search algorithm is an efficient approach to solve the pairwise sequence alignment problem. The aim of combining the keyword tree theory and the Aho-Corasick search algorithm is to solve this kind of problem: for a given long string T and a set of short strings $P = \{p_1, p_2, ..., p_z\}$ ($z \in N, z > 1$), find the location of all P_i. in T. The keyword tree produced by set P is used, and then searched for in T with this keyword tree through the Aho-Corasick search algorithm. The total time complexity of using this method to find all P_i.'s location in the T is O $(m + n + k)$, where $m = |T|$ (the length of T), $n = \sum |P_i|$ (the sum of all 's P_i. lengths) and k means the sum of occurrence for all P_i. in T.

Keyword Tree Theory

The keyword tree of the setm $P = \{p_1, p_2, ..., p_2\}$ (z∈N,z>1) mis a rooted tree, whose root denoted by K, and this keyword tree satisfies:

1. Each edge clearly demarcates one letter.

2. Any two edges separated from the same node are to correspond to different letters.

3. Each pattern P_i. (i=1,2,...,z) corresponds to a node v, and the path from the root K to the node v can exactly correctly spell the string P_i.

For each leaf node of this K tree, it corresponds to one of the certain patterns of set P. $L(v)$ is used to represent the STRING which is connected from the root node to the node v. $Lp(v)$ will then be used to represent the length of the longest suffix (also, this suffix is the prefix of one of patterns in the set P). Searching this prefix from the root node in the keyword tree, and the last node denoted by n_v when the search is over.

For example, the set $P = \{potato, tattoo, theater, other\}$, and the keyword tree is shown on the right. In that example, if $L(v) = potat$, then $Lp(v) = |tat| = 3$, and the failure link of the node v is shown in that figure.

Establishing a failure link is the key to improve the time complexity of the Aho-Corasick algorithm. It can be used to reduce the original polynomial time to the linear time for searching. Therefore, the core of keyword tree theory is to find all failure links (which also means finding all n_v s) of a keyword tree in the linear time. It is assumed that every n_v of all nodes v, whose distance from the root node is less than or equal k, can be found. The n_v of the node v whose distance from the root node is $k+1$ can then be sought for. Its parent node is v', and the letter represented by the node v and v', is x.

1. If the next letter of the node $n_{v'}$ is x, the other node of this edge can be set as:

   w, and $n_v = w$

2. If all letters are not x by searching all edges between $n_{v'}$ and its child nodes, $L(n_v)$ is a suffix of $L(n_{v'})$ plus x. Because this suffix matches the STRING beginning with the root node (similar to prefix), the x after $n_{v'}$ can be detected or not. If not, this process can be continued until x or the root node is found.

Aho-Corasick Search Algorithm

After establishing all failure links in the keyword tree, the Aho-Corasick search algorithm is used to find the locations of all P_i (i=1,2,...,z) in the linear time. In this step, the time complexity is O(m+k).

Other Strategies

In MSA, DNA, RNA, and proteins, sequences are usually generated and they are assumed to have an evolutionary relationship. By comparing generated maps of RNA, DNA, and sequences from evolutionary families, people can assess conservation of proteins and find functional gene domains by comparing differences between evolutionary sequences. Generally, heuristic algorithms and tree alignment graphs are also adopted to solve multiple sequence alignment problems.

Heuristic Algorithm

Generally, heuristic algorithms rely on the iterative strategy, which is to say that based on a comparison method, optimizing the results of multiple sequence alignment by the iterative process. Davie M. proposed using the particle swarm optimization algorithm to solve the multiple sequence alignment problem; Ikeda Takahiro proposed a heuristic algorithm which is based on the A* search algorithm; E. Birney first proposed using the hidden Markov model to solve the multiple sequence alignment problem; and many other biologists use the genetic algorithm to solve it. All these algorithms generally are robust and insensitive to the number of sequences, but they also have shortcomings. For example, the results from the particle swarm optimization algorithm are unstable and its merits depend on the selection of random numbers, the runtime of the A* search algorithm is too long, and the genetic algorithm is easy to fall into local excellent.

Tree Alignment Graph

Roughly, tree alignment graph aims to align trees into a graph and finally synthesize them to develop statistics. In biology, tree alignment graphs (TAGs) are used to remove the evolutionary conflicts or overlapping taxa from sets of trees and can then be queried to explore uncertainty and conflict. By integrating methods of aligning, synthesizing and analyzing, the TAG aims to solve the conflicting relationships and partial overlapping taxon sets obtained from a wide range of sequences. Also, the tree alignment graph serves as a fundamental approach for supertree and grafting exercises, which have been successfully tested to construct supertrees by Berry. Because the transformation from trees to a graph contain similar nodes and edges from their source trees, TAGs can also provide extraction of original source trees for further analysis. TAG is a combination of a set of aligning trees. It can store conflicting hypotheses evolutionary relationship and synthesize the source trees to develop evolutionary hypotheses. Therefore, it is a basic method to solve other alignment problems.

Distance Matrices in Phylogeny

Distance matrices are used in phylogeny as non-parametric distance methods and were originally applied to phenetic data using a matrix of pairwise distances. These distances are then reconciled to produce a tree (a phylogram, with informative branch lengths). The distance matrix can come from a number of different sources, including measured distance (for example from immunological studies) or morphometric analysis, various pairwise distance formulae (such as euclidean distance) applied to discrete morphological characters, or genetic distance from sequence, restriction fragment, or allozyme data. For phylogenetic character data, raw distance values can be calculated by simply counting the number of pairwise differences in character states (Hamming distance).

Distance-matrix Methods

Distance-matrix methods of phylogenetic analysis explicitly rely on a measure of "genetic distance" between the sequences being classified, and therefore they require an MSA (multiple sequence alignment) as an input. Distance is often defined as the fraction of mismatches at aligned positions, with gaps either ignored or counted as mismatches. Distance methods attempt to construct an all-to-all matrix from the sequence query set describing the distance between each sequence pair. From this is constructed a phylogenetic tree that places closely related sequences under the same interior node and whose branch lengths closely reproduce the observed distances between sequences. Distance-matrix methods may produce either rooted or unrooted trees, depending on the algorithm used to calculate them. They are frequently used as the basis for progressive and iterative types of multiple sequence alignment. The main disadvantage of distance-matrix methods is their inability to efficiently use information about local high-variation regions that appear across multiple subtrees.

Neighbor-joining

Neighbor-joining methods apply general data clustering techniques to sequence analysis using genetic distance as a clustering metric. The simple neighbor-joining method produces unrooted trees, but it does not assume a constant rate of evolution (i.e., a molecular clock) across lineages.

UPGMA and WPGMA

The UPGMA (Unweighted Pair Group Method with Arithmetic mean) and WPGMA (Weighted Pair Group Method with Arithmetic mean) methods produce rooted trees and require a constant-rate assumption – that is, it assumes an ultrametric tree in which the distances from the root to every branch tip are equal.

Fitch–Margoliash Method

The Fitch–Margoliash method uses a weighted least squares method for clustering based on genetic distance. Closely related sequences are given more weight in the tree construction process to correct for the increased inaccuracy in measuring distances between distantly related sequences. In practice, the distance correction is only necessary when the evolution rates differ among branches. The distances used as input to the algorithm must be normalized to prevent large artifacts in computing relationships between closely related and distantly related groups. The distances calculated by this method must be linear; the linearity criterion for distances requires that the expected values of the branch lengths for two individual branches must equal the expected value of the sum of the two branch distances – a property that applies to biological sequences only when they have been corrected for the possibility of back mutations at individual sites. This correction is done through the use of a substitution matrix such as that derived from the Jukes–Cantor model of DNA evolution.

The least-squares criterion applied to these distances is more accurate but less efficient than the neighbor-joining methods. An additional improvement that corrects for correlations between distances that arise from many closely related sequences in the data set can also be applied at increased computational cost. Finding the optimal least-squares tree with any correction factor is NP-complete, so heuristic search methods like those used in maximum-parsimony analysis are applied to the search through tree space.

Using Outgroups

Independent information about the relationship between sequences or groups can be used to help reduce the tree search space and root unrooted trees. Standard usage of distance-matrix methods involves the inclusion of at least one outgroup sequence known to be only distantly related to the sequences of interest in the query set. This usage can be seen as a type of experimental control. If the outgroup has been appropriately chosen, it will have a much greater genetic distance and thus a longer branch length than any other sequence, and it will appear near the root of a rooted tree. Choosing an appropriate outgroup requires the selection of a sequence that is moderately related to the sequences of interest; too close a relationship defeats the purpose of the outgroup and too distant adds noise to the analysis. Care should also be taken to avoid situations in which the species from which the sequences were taken are distantly related, but the gene encoded by the sequences is highly conserved across lineages. Horizontal gene transfer, especially between otherwise divergent bacteria, can also confound outgroup usage.

Weaknesses of Different Methods

In general, pairwise distance data are an underestimate of the path-distance between taxa on a phylogram. Pairwise distances effectively "cut corners" in a manner analogous to geographic distance: the distance between two cities may be 100 miles "as the crow flies," but a traveler may actually be obligated to travel 120 miles because of the layout of roads, the terrain, stops along the way, etc. Between pairs of taxa, some character changes that took place in ancestral lineages will be undetectable, because later changes have erased the evidence (often called multiple hits and back mutations in sequence data). This problem is common to all phylogenetic estimation, but it is particularly acute for distance methods, because only two samples are used for each distance calculation; other methods benefit from evidence of these hidden changes found in other taxa not considered in pairwise comparisons. For nucleotide and amino acid sequence data, the same stochastic models of nucleotide change used in maximum likelihood analysis can be employed to "correct" distances, rendering the analysis "semi-parametric".

Several simple algorithms exist to construct a tree directly from pairwise distances, including UPGMA and neighbor joining (NJ), but these will not necessarily produce the best tree for the data. To counter potential complications noted above, and to find the best tree for the data, distance analysis can also incorporate a tree-search protocol that seeks to satisfy an explicit optimality criterion. Two optimality criteria are commonly applied to distance data, minimum evolution (ME) and least squares inference. Least squares is part of a broader class of regression-based methods lumped together here for simplicity. These regression formulae minimize the residual differences between path-distances along the tree and pairwise distances in the data matrix, effectively "fitting" the tree to the empirical distances. In contrast, ME accepts the tree with the shortest sum of branch lengths, and thus minimizes the total amount of evolution assumed. ME is closely akin to parsimony, and under certain conditions, ME analysis of distances based on a discrete character dataset will favor the same tree as conventional parsimony analysis of the same data.

Phylogeny estimation using distance methods has produced a number of controversies. UPGMA assumes an ultrametric tree (a tree where all the path-lengths from the root to the tips are equal). If the rate of evolution were equal in all sampled lineages (a molecular clock), and if the tree were completely balanced (equal numbers of taxa on both sides of any split, to counter the node density effect), UPGMA should not produce a biased result. These expectations are not met by most datasets, and although UPGMA is somewhat robust to their violation, it is not commonly used for phylogeny estimation. The advantage of UPGMA is that it is fast and can handle many sequences.

Neighbor-joining is a form of star decomposition and, as a heuristic method, is generally the least computationally intensive of these methods. It is very often used on its own, and in fact quite frequently produces reasonable trees. However, it lacks any sort of tree search and optimality criterion, and so there is no guarantee that the recovered tree is the one that best fits the data. A more appropriate analytical procedure would be to use NJ to produce a starting tree, then employ a tree search using an optimality criterion, to ensure that the best tree is recovered.

Many scientists eschew distance methods, for various reasons. A commonly cited reason is that distances are inherently phenetic rather than phylogenetic, in that they do not distinguish between ancestral similarity (symplesiomorphy) and derived similarity (synapomorphy). This criticism is not entirely fair: most currently implementations of parsimony, likelihood, and Bayesian phylogenetic inference use time-reversible character models, and thus accord no special status to derived or ancestral character states. Under these models, the tree is estimated unrooted; rooting, and consequently determination of polarity, is performed after the analysis. The primary difference between these methods and distances is that parsimony, likelihood, and Bayesian methods fit individual characters to the tree, whereas distance methods fit all the characters at once. There is nothing inherently less phylogenetic about this approach.

More practically, distance methods are avoided because the relationship between individual characters and the tree is lost in the process of reducing characters to distances. These methods do not use character data directly, and information locked in the distribution of character states can be lost in the pairwise comparisons. Also, some complex phylogenetic relationships may produce biased distances. On any phylogram, branch lengths will be underestimated because some changes cannot be discovered at all due to failure to sample some species due to either experimental design or extinction (a phenomenon called the node density effect). However, even if pairwise distances from genetic data are "corrected" using stochastic models of evolution as mentioned above, they may more easily sum to a different tree than one produced from analysis of the same data and model using maximum likelihood. This is because pairwise distances are not independent; each branch on a tree is represented in the distance measurements of all taxa it separates. Error resulting from any characteristic of that branch that might confound phylogeny (stochastic variability, change in evolutionary parameters, an abnormally long or short branch length) will be propagated through all of the relevant distance measurements. The resulting distance matrix may then better fit an alternate (presumably less optimal) tree.

Despite these potential problems, distance methods are extremely fast, and they often produce a reasonable estimate of phylogeny. They also have certain benefits over the methods that use characters directly. Notably, distance methods allow use of data that may not be easily converted to character data, such as DNA-DNA hybridization assays. They also permit analyses that account for the possibility that the rate at which particular nucleotides are incorporated into sequences may vary over the tree, using LogDet distances. For some network-estimation methods (notably NeighborNet), the abstraction of information about individual characters in distance data are an advantage. When considered character-by character, conflict between character and a tree due to reticulation cannot be told from conflict due either to homoplasy or error. However, pronounced conflict in distance data, which represents an amalgamation of many characters, is less likely due to error or homoplasy unless the data are strongly biased, and is thus more likely to be a result of reticulation.

Distance methods are popular among molecular systematists, a substantial number of whom use NJ without an optimization stage almost exclusively. With the increasing speed of character-based analyses, some of the advantages of distance methods will probably wane. However, the nearly instantaneous NJ implementations, the ability to incorporate an evolutionary model in a speedy analysis, LogDet distances, network estimation methods, and the occasional need to summarize relationships with a single number all mean that distance methods will probably stay in the mainstream for a long time to come.

Treefinder

Treefinder is a computer program for the likelihood-based reconstruction of phylogenetic trees from molecular sequences. It was written by Gangolf Jobb, a Treefinder is free of charge, though the most recent license prohibits its use in the USA and eight European countries.

A platform-independent graphical environment integrates a standard suite of analyses: phylogeny reconstruction, bootstrap analysis, model selection, hypothesis testing, tree calibration, manipulation of trees and sequence data. Treefinder is scriptable through a proprietary scripting language called TL.

Treefinder has an efficient tree search algorithm that can infer trees with thousands of species within a short time. Result trees are displayed and can then be saved as a reconstruction report, which may serve as an input for further analysis, for example hypothesis testing. The report contains all information about the tree and the models used. Treefinder also supports exporting results as NEWICK or NEXUS files.

The software supports a broad collection of models of sequence evolution. The June 2008 release implements 7 models of nucleotide substitution (HKY, TN, J1, J2, J3 (= TIM), TVM, GTR), 14 empirical models of amino acid substitution (BLOSUM, cpREV, Dayhoff, JTT, LG, mtArt, mtMam, mtREV, PMB, rtREV, betHIV, witHIV, VT, WAG), 4 substitution models of structured rRNA (bactRNA, eukRNA, euk23RNA, mitoRNA), the 6-state "Dayhoff Groups" protein model (DG), 2-state and 3-state models of DNA (GTR3, GTR2), a parametric mixed model (MIX) mixing the empirical models of proteins or rRNA, and also a user-definable GTR-type model (MAP) mapping characters to states as needed. Three models of among-site rate heterogeneity are available (Gamma, Gamma+I, I), which can be combined with any of the substitution models. One can assume different models for different partitions of a sequence alignment, and partitions may be assumed to evolve at different speeds. All parameters of the models can be estimated from the data by maximization of likelihood. Certain TL expressions, the "model expressions", allow the concise notation of complex models, together with their parameters and optimization modes.

Treefinder's original publication from 2004 has been cited more than a thousand times in the scientific literature.

Bayesian Inference in Phylogeny

A Bayesian analysis combines ones prior beliefs about the probability of a hypothesis with the likelihood. The likelihood is the vehicle that carries the information about the hypothesis contained in the observations. In this case, the likelihood is simply the probability of observing a four and a six given that the die is biased or fair. Assuming independence of the tosses, the probability of observing a four and a six is:

$$Pr\left[4,6|Fair\right] = \frac{1}{6} \times \frac{1}{6} = \frac{1}{36}$$

for a fair die and,

$$Pr\left[4,6|Biased\right] = \frac{4}{21} \times \frac{6}{21} = \frac{24}{441}$$

for a biased die. The probability of observing the data is 1.96 times greater under the hypothesis that the die is biased. In other words, the ratio of the likelihoods under the two hypotheses suggests that the die is biased.

Bayesian inferences are based upon the posterior probability of a hypothesis. The posterior probability that the die is biased can be obtained using Bayes' (1) formula:

$$Pr\left[Biased \mid 4,6\right] = \frac{Pr\left[4,6\mid Biased\right] \times Pr\left[Biased\right]}{Pr\left[4,6\mid Biased\right] \times Pr\left[Biased\right] + Pr\left[4,6\mid Fair\right] \times Pr\left[Fair\right]}$$

where Pr[Biased] and Pr[Fair] are the prior probabilities that the die is biased or fair, respectively, a reasonable prior probability that the die is biased would be the proportion of the dice in the box that were biased. The posterior probability is then:

$$Pr\left[Biased|4,6\right] = \frac{\frac{24}{441} \times \frac{1}{10}}{\frac{24}{441} \times \frac{1}{10} + \frac{1}{36} \times \frac{9}{10}} = 0.179$$

This means that our opinion that the die is biased changed from 0.1 to 0.179 after observing the four and six.

Depending upon one's viewpoint, the incorporation of prior beliefs about a parameter is either a strength or a weakness of Bayesian inference. It is a strength in as much as the method explicitly incorporates prior information in inferences about a hypothesis. However, it can often be difficult to specify a prior. For the dice example, it is easy to specify the prior as we provided information on the number of fair and biased dice in the box and also specify that a die was randomly selected. However, if we were to simply state that the die is either fair or biased, but did not specify a physical description of how the die was chosen, it would have been much more difficult to specify a prior specifying the probability that the die is biased. For example, one could have taken the two hypotheses to have been a priori equally probable or given much more weight to the hypothesis that had the die fair as severely biased dice are rarely encountered (or manufactured) in the real world.

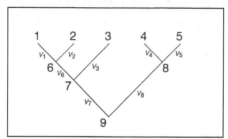

An example of a phylogenetic tree for s = 5 species. The branch lengths are denoted v $_i$.

Bayesian Inference of Phylogeny

Bayesian inference of phylogeny is based upon the posterior probability of a phylogenetic tree, τ. The posterior probability of the i th phylogenetic tree, τ i, conditioned on the observed matrix of aligned DNA sequences (X) is obtained using Bayes formula:

$$f(\tau_i \mid X) = \frac{f(X \mid \tau i) f(\tau i)}{\sum_{j=1}^{B(s)} f(X \mid \tau_j) f(\tau_j)}$$

[throughout, It denote conditional probabilities a $f(\cdot \mid \cdot)$]. Here, $f(\tau_i \mid X)$ is the posterior probability of the i th phylogeny and can be interpreted as the probability that τ $_i$ is the correct tree given the DNA sequence data. The likelihood of the i th tree is $f(X \mid \tau_i)$ and the prior probability of the i th tree is $f(\tau_i)$. The summation in the denominator is over all $B(s)$ trees that are possible for s species. This number is $B(s) = \dfrac{(2s-3)!}{2^{s-2}(s-2)!}$ for rooted trees, $B(s) = \dfrac{(2s-5)!}{2^{s-3}(s-3)!}$ for unrooted trees, and

$B(s) = \dfrac{s!(s-1)!}{2^{s-1}}$ for labelled histories. Typically, an uninformative prior is used for

trees, such that f(τi) = 1 B(s).

DNA sequence data.— We consider an aligned matrix of s DNA sequences:

$$X = \{x_{ij}\} = \begin{matrix} \text{Species 1} \\ \text{Species 2} \\ \text{Species 3} \\ \vdots \\ \text{Species } s \end{matrix} \begin{bmatrix} A & A & C & C & T \\ A & A & C & G & G \\ A & C & C & C & T \\ \vdots & \vdots & \vdots & \vdots & \vdots \\ A & C & C & C & T \end{bmatrix}$$

The data matrix consists of the sequences for s species for $c = 5$ sites from a gene (c is the length of the aligned DNA sequences). The observations at the first site are $x_1 = \{A, A, A,..., A\}'$. In general, the information at the ith site in the matrix is denoted x_i.

Phylogenetic models.—What is the probability of observing the data at the ith site? To calculate this probability, we assume a phylogenetic model. A phylogenetic model consists of a tree (τ_i) with branch lengths specified on the tree (v_i) and a stochastic model of DNA substitution.

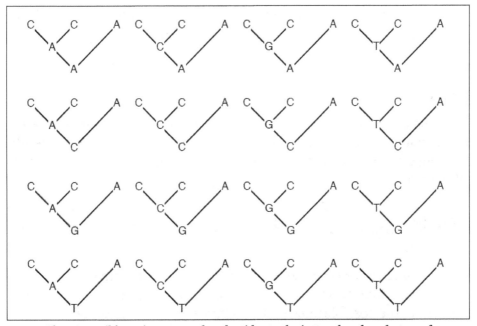

The 16 possible assignments of nucleotides to the internal nodes of a tree of $s = 3$ species. The observations at the site are $x_i = \{C, C, A\}$ and the unobserved nucleotides at the internal nodes of the tree are denoted y.

Figure shows an example of a phylogenetic tree of $s = 5$ species. The tips of the tree are labeled 1, 2,...,s and the internal nodes of the tree are labeled $s + 1, s + 2,..., 2s - 1$; the root of the tree is always labeled $2s - 1$. The lengths of the branches are denoted v_i and are in terms of the number of substitutions expected to occur along the ith branch. In general, the ancestor of node k will be denoted σ(k); the ancestor of node 4 is σ(4) = 8. The ancestor of the root is σ(2s − 1) = ∅.

The second part of the phylogenetic model consists of a stochastic model of DNA substitution. Here, the typical assumption is that DNA substitution follows a time-homogeneous Poisson process. The heart of the model is a matrix specifying the instantaneous rate of substitution from one nucleotide state to another:

$$Q = \{q_{ij}\} = \begin{pmatrix} \cdot & \pi_C r_{AC} & \pi_G r_{AG} & \pi_T r_{AT} \\ \pi_A r_{AC} & \cdot & \pi_G r_{CG} & \pi_T r_{CT} \\ \pi_A r_{AG} & \pi_C r_{CG} & \cdot & \pi_T r_{GT} \\ \pi_A r_{AT} & \pi_C r_{CT} & \pi_G r_{CT} & \cdot \end{pmatrix}$$

where the matrix specifies the rate of change from nucleotide i (row) to nucleotide j (column). The nucleotides are in the order A, C, G, T. The diagonals of the matrix are specified such that the rows each sum to 0. The equilibrium (or stationary) frequencies of the four nucleotides are denoted πi ($\pi = \{\pi_A, \pi_C, \pi_G, \pi_T\}$). This matrix specifies the most general time-reversible model of DNA substitution and is referred to as the GTR model. Because the rate of substitution and time are confounded, the Q matrix is rescaled such that $-\sum \pi_i q_{ii} = 1$ for all i (making the average rate of substitution 1). Over a branch of length v the transition probabilities are calculated as $P(v, \theta) = \{p_{ij}(v, \theta)\} = e^{Qv}$. The parameters of the substitution model are contained in a vector θ.

The likelihood of a phylogeny.—The phylogenetic model consists of a tree (τ_i) with branch lengths (vi) and a stochastic model of DNA substitution that is specified by a matrix of instantaneous rates. The probability of observing the data at the ith site in the aligned matrix is a sum over all possible assignments of nucleotides to the internal nodes of the tree:

$$f(x_i \mid \tau_j, v_j, \theta) = \sum_y \left[\pi_{y_{2s-1}} \left(\prod_{k=1}^{s} p_{y_{i\sigma(k)}, x_{ik}}(v_k, \theta) \right) \left(\prod_{k=s+1}^{ss-2} p_{y_{i\sigma(k)}, y_{ik}}(v_k, \theta) \right) \right]$$

Here, y_{ij} is the (unobserved) nucleotide at the jth node for the ith site. The summation is over all 4^{s-1} ways that nucleotides can be assigned to the internal nodes of the tree. Figure illustrates the possible nucleotide assignments for a simple tree of s = 3 species. Felsenstein introduced a pruning algorithm that efficiently calculates the summation. Often, the rate at the site is assumed to be drawn from a gamma distribution. This allows one to relax the assumption that the rate of substitution is equal across all sites. If gamma-distributed rate variation is assumed, then the probability of observing the data at the ith site becomes:

$$f(x_i \mid \tau_j, v_j, \theta, \alpha) \int_0^{\infty} \left\{ \sum_y \left[\pi_{y_{2s-1}} \left(\prod_{k=1}^{s} p_{y_{i\sigma(k)}, x_{ik}}(v_k r, \theta) \right) \left(\prod_{k=s+1}^{2s-2} p_{y_{i\sigma(k)}, y_{ik}}(v_k r, \theta) \right) \right] \right\} f(r \mid \alpha) dr$$

where $f(r|\alpha)$ is the density of the rate r under the gamma model. The parameter α is the shape parameter of the gamma distribution (here, the shape and the scale parameters of the gamma distribution are both set to α). Typically, this integral is impossible to evaluate. Hence, an approximation first suggested by Yang is used in which the continuous gamma distribution is broken into K categories, each with equal weight. The mean rate from each category represents the rate for the entire category. The probability of observing the data at the ith site then becomes:

$$f\left(x_i \mid \tau_j, v_j, \theta, \alpha\right)\sum_{n=1}^{K}\left\{\sum_{y}\left[\pi_{y_{2s-1}}\left(\prod_{k=1}^{s}p_{y_{i\sigma(k)},x_{ik}}\left(v_k r_n, \theta\right)\right)\left(\prod_{k=s+1}^{2s-2}p_{y_{i\sigma(k)},y_{ik}}\left(v_k r_n, \theta\right)\right)\right]\right\}\frac{1}{K}$$

Assuming independence of the substitutions across sites, the probability of observing the aligned matrix of DNA sequences is:

$$f\left(x_i \mid \tau_j, v_j, \theta, \alpha\right)\prod_{i=1}^{c}f\left(x_i \mid \tau_j, v_j, \theta, \alpha\right)$$

Importantly, the likelihood can be calculated under a number of different models of character change. For example, the codon model describes the substitution process over triplets of sites (a codon) and allows the estimation of the nonsynonymous/synonymous rate ratio. Similarly, models of DNA substitution have been described that allow nonindenpendent substitutions to occur in stem regions of rRNA genes. Finally, one can calculate likelihoods for amino acid, restriction site, and, more recently, morphological data.

The likelihood depends upon several unknown parameters; generally, the phylogeny, branch lengths, and substitution parameters are unknown. The method of maximum likelihood estimates these parameters by finding the values of the parameters which maximize the likelihood function. Currently, programs such as PAUP*, PAML, and PHYLIP estimate phylogeny using the method of maximum likelihood:

$$f\left(\tau_j \mid X\right)=\frac{f\left(\tau_j \mid X\right)f\left(\tau_i\right)}{\sum_{j=1}^{B(s)}f\left(X \mid \tau_j\right)f(\tau_j)}$$

where the likelihood function is integrated over all possible values for the branch lengths and substitution parameters:

$$f\left(X \mid \tau i\right)=\int_{v_i}\int_{\theta}\int_{\alpha}f\left(x_i \mid \tau_j, v_j, \theta, \alpha\right)f\left(v_i\right)f\left(\theta\right)f\left(\alpha\right)\,dv_i\,d\theta\,d\alpha$$

Markov chain Monte Carlo.—Typically, the posterior probability cannot be calculated analytically. However, the posterior probability of phylogenies can be approximated by sampling trees from the posterior probability distribution. Markov chain Monte Carlo

(MCMC) can be used to sample phylogenies according to their posterior probabilities. The Metropolis-Hastings-Green (MHG) algorithm is an MCMC algorithm that has been used successfully to approximate the posterior probabilities of trees.

The MHG algorithm works as follows. Let $\Psi = \{\tau, v, \theta, \alpha\}$ be a specific tree, combination of branch lengths, substitution parameters, and gamma shape parameter. The MHG algorithm constructs a Markov chain that has as its stationary frequency the posterior probability of interest (in this case, the joint posterior probability of τ, v, θ, and α). The current state of the chain is denoted Ψ. If this is the first generation of the chain, then the chain is initialized (perhaps by randomly picking a state from the prior). A new state is then proposed, Ψ'. The probability of proposing the new state given the old state is $f\left(\Psi'|\Psi\right)$ and the probability of making the reverse move (which is never actually made) is $f\left(\Psi|\Psi'\right)$. The new state is accepted with probability:

$$
\begin{aligned}
R &= \min\left(1, \frac{f\left(\Psi'|X\right)}{f\left(\Psi|X\right)} \times \frac{f\left(\Psi|\Psi'|\right)}{f\left(\Psi'|\Psi\right)}\right) \\[1em]
&= \min\left(1, \frac{f\left(X|\Psi'\right)f\left(\Psi'\right)/f\left(X\right)}{f\left(X|\Psi\right)f\left(\Psi'\right)/f\left(X\right)} \times \frac{f\left(\Psi|\Psi'|\right)}{f\left(\Psi'|\Psi\right)}\right) \\[1em]
&= \min\left(1, \underbrace{\frac{f\left(X|\Psi'\right)}{f\left(X|\Psi\right)}}_{\text{Likelihood Ratio}} \times \underbrace{\frac{f\left(\Psi'\right)}{f\left(\Psi\right)}}_{\text{Prior Ratio}} \times \underbrace{\frac{f\left(\Psi|\Psi'|\right)}{f\left(\Psi'|\Psi\right)}}_{\text{Proposal Ratio}}\right)
\end{aligned}
$$

A uniform random variable between 0 and 1 is drawn. If this number is less than R, then the proposed state is accepted and $\Psi = \Psi'$. Otherwise, the chain remains in the original state. This process of proposing a new state, calculating the acceptance probability, and either accepting or rejecting the proposed move is repeated many thousands of times. The sequence of states visited forms a Markov chain. This chain is sampled (either every step, or the chain is "thinned" and samples are taken every so often). The samples from the Markov chain form a valid, albeit dependent, sample from the posterior probability distribution. As described here, the Markov chain samples from the joint probability density of trees, branch lengths, and substitution parameters. The marginal probability of trees can be calculated by simply printing to a file the trees that are visited during the course of the MCMC analysis. The proportion of the time any single tree is found in this sample is an approximation of the posterior probability of the tree.

An example of Bayesian inference of phylogeny.—Here we will demonstrate Bayesian inference of phylogeny for a simple example of five species. The DNA sequences are albumin and c-myc sequences sampled from a fish, frog, bird, rodent, and human (albumin: Actinoptergyii, Salmo salar, X52397; Amphibia, Xenopus laevis, M18350; Aves, Gallus gallus, X60688; Rodentia, Rattus norvegicus, J00698; Primates, Homo sapiens, L00132; c-myc: Actinoptergyii, Salmo gairdneri, M13048; Amphibia, Xenopus laevis, M14455; Aves, Gallus gallus, M20006; Rodentia, Rattus norvegicus, Y00396; Primates, Homo sapiens, V00568). There are a total of B(5) = 15 unrooted trees possible for the five sequences. The prior probability of any single tree, then, is $\frac{1}{15}=0.067$.

We first analyzed the c-myc DNA sequences using a program written by J.P.H. The HKY85+Γ model of DNA substitution was assumed. This model allows there to be a different rate of transitions and transversions, different stationary nucleotide frequencies, and among-site rate variation (as described by a discrete gamma distribution). The Markov chain was run for 100,000 generations and sampled every 100 generations. The first 10,000 generations of the chain were discarded; the chain was started from a random tree and branch lengths and it took some time for the chain to reach apparent stationarity. Hence, inferences were based upon a sample of 900 trees. Figure summarizes the results of the analysis. The tree with the largest posterior probability was (Fish,Frog,(Bird,(Rodent,Human))) and the posterior probability of this tree was 0.964. Figure shows the posterior probability of the clades on the tree with the maximum posterior probability.

One of the advantages of Bayesian inference of phylogeny is that the results are easy to interpret. For example, the sum of the posterior probabilities of all trees will sum to 1. Moreover, the posterior probability of any single clade is simply the sum of the posterior probabilities of all trees that contain that clade.

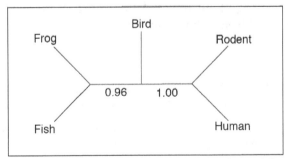

The tree with the maximum posterior probability for the analysis of the c-myc sequences. The numbers at the internal branches represent the posterior probability that the clade is correct.

a credible set of trees can be formed by ordering all of the trees from largest to smallest posterior probability and then adding those trees with the highest posterior probability to a set until the cumulative posterior probability is 0.95. A 95% credible set of trees for the c-myc gene would contain only one tree.

The posterior probability of trees can form the prior for any subsequent analysis of the species. For example, let us imagine that the albumin sequences were analyzed after the c-myc sequences. The posterior probabilities of phylogenies from the analysis of the c-myc sequences is the prior for the analysis of the albumin sequences. The posterior probability of the trees after analysis of the albumin sequences is shown in the table. The posterior probability of τ_1 is now 0.996. Our beliefs about the phylogeny of the five species have changed throughout the analysis. For example, our initial belief about the the phylogeny τ_1 was 0.067. After observing the c-myc sequences, our belief that this is the true phylogeny increased from 0.067 to 0.964. The albumin sequences strengthened our beliefs about this phylogeny. The final posterior probability of this phylogeny was 0.996. This probability could form the prior probability for tree 1 for any subsequent analysis.

One modification of the analysis of the vertebrate sequences would be to modify the prior probabilities of trees. There is overwhelming morphological and paleontological evidence that the correct phylogeny for fish, frogs, birds, rodents, and humans is tree τ_1. Hence, a systematist might reflect this prior information as a different prior probability on the trees. For example, he or she may decide to put almost all of the prior probability on τ_1 and very little prior probability on the other trees.

Programs for Bayesian inference of phylogeny. There are a few programs for the Bayesian analysis of phylogenetic trees. BAMBE approximates the posterior probability of phylogenies using MCMC (specifically, BAMBE uses the MHG algorithm). BAMBE assumes uniform priors on phylogenies and branch lengths. The program uses an improved method for calculating likelihoods that is very fast. Another program, MCMCTREE in the PAML package of programs calculates posterior probabilities of trees using a combination of Monte Carlo and MCMC integration. The program works for up to $s = 11$ species. Besides the algorithm for approximating posterior probabilities, the program differs from BAMBE in assuming a birth-death process prior on phylogenies. This prior places equal weight on labelled histories(where a labelled history differs from a rooted tree in considering the relative speciation times).

References

- Mayr, Ernst (2009)"Cladistic analysis or cladistic classification?". Journal of Zoological Systematics and Evolutionary Research. 12: 94–128. Doi:10.1111/j.1439-0469.1974.tb00160.x

- Fox, Emily. "The dendrogram". Coursea. Coursea. Archived from the original on 28 September 2017. Retrieved 28 September 2017

- Townsend JP, Su Z, Tekle Y (2012). "Phylogenetic Signal and Noise: Predicting the Power of a Data Set to Resolve Phylogeny". Genetics. 61 (5): 835–849. Doi:10.1093/sysbio/sys036. PMID 22389443

- "Retraction Note: TREEFINDER: a powerful graphical analysis environment for molecular phylogenetics. BMC Evolutionary Biology". 2015-11-11. Retrieved 2015-11-11

- Ostrovsky, Rafail; Rabani, Yuval (2007-10-01). "Low distortion embeddings for edit distance". Journal of the ACM. Association for Computing Machinery (ACM). 54 (5): 23–es. Doi:10.1145/1284320.1284322. ISSN 0004-5411

Systems Biology: An Integrated Study | 5

- **Biochemical Systems Theory**

- **Biological Network Inference**

- **BioPAX**

- **Cellular Model**

- **Cancer Systems Biology**

The mathematical and computational models that are used for the analysis of complex biological systems are referred to as systems biology. Biochemical systems theory, biological network inference, BioPAX, cellular model and cancer systems biology are a few concepts that come under systems biology. The topics elaborated in this chapter will help in gaining a better perspective about systems biology.

Systems biology seeks to study biological systems as a whole, contrary to the reductionist approach that has dominated biology.

Biological systems are enormously complex, organised across several levels of hierarchy. At the core of this organisation is the genome that contains information in a digital form to make thousands of different molecules and drive various biological processes. This genomic view of biology has been primarily ushered in by the human genome project. The development of sequencing and other high-throughput technologies that generate vast amounts of biological data has fuelled the development of new ways of hypothesis-driven research. Development of computational techniques for analysis of the large data, as well as for the modelling and simulation of the complex biological systems have followed as a logical consequence. Simulatable computational models of biological systems and processes form the cornerstone of the emerging science of systems biology.

Traditionally, biology has focused on identifying individual genes, proteins and cells, and studying their specific functions. Each of these is indeed extremely important in understanding the individual molecules, but as individual isolated pieces of information, they are insufficient to provide insights about complex phenomena such as human health and disease. As an analogy, More importantly, it would not provide any understanding of what component influences what other component in what manner and to what extent, an understanding which is very important to effectively set things right when something malfunctions. In the same way, since diseases occur when there is some malfunction in the form or function of one or more of the cellular components, we need an understanding how various molecules in a cell influence each other in health, in order to attempt curing or correcting it to the extent possible.

The scale at which various molecular level studies can now be carried out is providing us systematic data on many fronts enabling us to reconstruct holistic models of larger systems. Systems biology seeks to study biochemical and biological systems from a holistic perspective, promising to transform how biology is done. The goal is for a comprehensive understanding of the system's influence on its individual components, leading to the appearance of complex properties such as robustness, emergence, adaptation, regulation and synchronisation, seen so very often in biological systems. Essentially, systems biology advocates a departure from the reductionist viewpoint, emphasising on the importance of a holistic view of biological systems. It also aims at a departure from the "spherical cow" 1, in trying to encapsulate the enormous complexity of biological systems in greater detail. Systems biology adopts an integrated approach to study and understand the function of biological systems, particularly, the response of such systems to perturbations such as the inhibition of a reaction in a pathway, or the administration of a drug. It can of course be argued that systems biology is just a new name for the conventional disciplines such as physiology and pharmacology, which are well established for several decades now. Undoubtedly, these disciplines emphasise the need for considering whole systems. Yet, systems biology emerges as a new discipline, since it differs from the conventional disciplines in a fundamental way: the latter treat much of the whole system as a 'black-box', giving us only an idea of the end picture but not enabling us to ask 'why' or 'how' a particular outcome is seen. Systems biology on the other hand aims to reconstruct systems by a bottom-up approach, with detailed knowledge about the individual components that make up the system and how these components interact with each other. Modelling and simulation of complex biological networks form the cornerstone of systems biology; the coupling of in silico models with in vivo and in vitro experimentation, with modelling guiding experimentation and experimentation aiding in model refinement, can provide impetus to improve the understanding of biological systems. Effects and influences of one component on the other are deciphered, providing a greater understanding of how genotypes relate to phenotypes.

Elements of Systems Biology

Systems biology, being a holistic approach involves modelling and analysis of metabolic pathways, regulatory and signal transduction networks for understanding cellular behaviour. There are also various levels of abstraction at which these systems are modelled, with a wide variety of techniques that can be employed based on the quality and quantity of data available.

The critical step in the modelling and analysis of these pathways is their reconstruction, involving the integration of diverse sources of data to create a representation of the chemical events underlying biological networks. A variety of high-throughput experiments have been developed to provide extensive data on the proteome, metabolome, transcriptome and the reactome in a cell. Some of these techniques include microarray analyses of the transcriptome and mass spectrometry analyses that generate proteomics data. It is important to understand that these experiments generate genome-scale 'omics' data, which cover a majority of the components such as metabolites, transcripts and proteins, in a cell. Another major feature of systems biology is the strong integration of experiment with theory; it is quite common that a model is used to generate one or more hypotheses, which are then tested experimentally, and iteratively contribute to model refinement. In essence, the various parts of a systems biology study are (a) define a model system, (b) identify a choice of attributes/parameters to study the system that is appropriate for the problem being addressed, (c) comprehensive experimental measurements, (d) appropriate mathematical abstraction of the system that is computationally tractable and (e) computational simulations that can generate and test various hypotheses, (f) that can later be verified by experimental approaches.

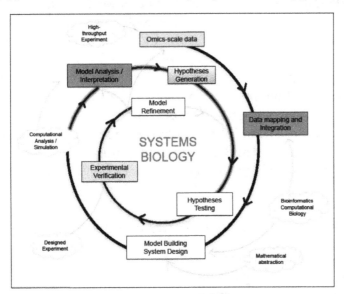

Systems biology process. This process relies on an iterative procedure of model building, experimental verification, model analysis and model refinement. The concepts that underlie these processes have been shown as clouds.

Systems biology experiments are often characterised by a synergy between theory and experiment. As in traditional biological experiments, the chosen model system must be suitable for experimental investigations, and should also be complex enough to capture the biological phenomenon of interest. Simple bacteria such as E. coli are often used as model organisms to understand the organisation and behaviour of prokaryotic systems. Saccharomyces cerevisiae is the de facto standard model organism for understanding eukaryotic systems. Similarly, the fruitfly Drosophila and the worm

Caenorhabditis elegans are used as models to incrementally understand more and more complex multi-cellular organisms. It is important to note that, although some of these systems are significantly less complex than mammalian systems, several processes are conserved, leading to the possibility of very useful predictions of the behaviour of mammalian systems from the modelling of simpler systems. Very often, it is impractical to consider whole organisms or whole cells, especially to address questions pertaining to the mechanism of a given process. Pathways or sets of pathways function as modules of the larger systems, which provide a practical framework to study the biological processes/phenomena.

Metabolic pathways, signal transduction pathways and regulatory pathways have been studied from a variety of organisms from which a wide range of biological insights have been obtained. Such pathways have also been combined into the larger context of networks, where the abstraction is often a bit less quantitative, again for practical reasons. Studies on transcriptional network of yeast, metabolic network of E. coli, serve as examples of studies at this level. Thus, the scale of the system can vary from tens of components to several thousands. The resolution of information can also vary from detailed atomistic information to broad cellular views. For example, a defined model could contain thermodynamic data of the metabolic reactions in a given pathway, that in turn have sound correlations with the three-dimensional structures of the involved enzymes. On the other hand the defined system could simply contain logical connections between different cellular states implying functional correlations without any further details on the cells themselves. A systems biology approach is characterised by a series of iterative experimentation and model refinement, often using perturbations to the system as a handle to affirm roles of known components as well as to discriminate between alternative models. Another important feature is that most of these components, from computation to high-throughput laboratory experiments are amenable to automation.

Modelling in Systems Biology: Model Abstraction

Conceptual and theoretical modelling constructs are expressed as sets of algorithms and implemented as software packages.For example, in drug discovery, a model can refer to the relationship of the structure of a target molecule to its ability to bind a certain type of ligand at one end of the spectrum, while at the other end, it can refer to a statistically derived relationship of a set of ligands to a particular biological activity, with no explicit consideration of the mechanism or the basis of such activities. Conceptual modelling is an integral part of problem solving in general and in fact an essential component of any activity that attempts to achieve a goal in a systematic way.

The advantages of having a model are manifold: (a) it gives the precise definition of the components of a given system (or the genotype), (b) it allows performing simulations and monitoring the end-effect, which may be the given phenotype in this context, (c) it helps in dissecting the role of every component in the system through the analysis of perturbations, (d) it helps us to interpret complex hard-to-understand problems, (e) it helps in studying systems that are impractical to study through conventional experiments, (f) it helps both in designing minimal systems that can result in a particular phenotype, as well as analysing the effect of the addition of newer components into the framework, and (g) it is highly amenable for high-throughput simulations and highly cost-effective, useful especially in applications such as drug discovery.

Thus, models not only provide significant insights into the underlying biology and application opportunities, but also enable the efficient study of what may be highly impractical, or even impossible through biochemical and molecular biology experiments. It must however be emphasised that a model is only as good as our understanding of what constitutes a system and how it has been built. Model building is thus a critical step in in silico analysis and is often iterated and refined with validation steps.

Given that biological systems and processes are understood at many different levels and in many different aspects, it is no wonder that many different kinds of models should exist in practice. Figure illustrates that models span a wide range, emanating from the organisational hierarchy in which biological systems are understood.

On one hand, there are structural models at atomic levels implying certain functions, whereas on the other hand, there are whole genome-based mathematical models of either pathways or entire organisms implying functions at very different levels.

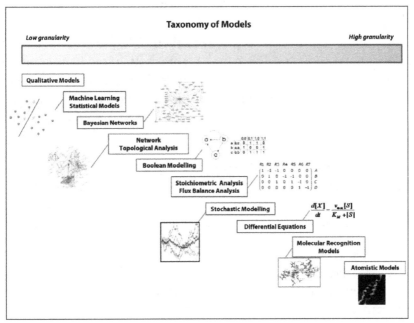

Modelling techniques in systems biology. The various methods have been represented alongside an axis that details the granularity (or resolution) typical for each method.

It is important to understand the abstraction levels of the models, so that conclusions are drawn at appropriate levels from the analyses. The choice of the method depends upon the type and extent of data available, as well as the objective of the modelling exercise in terms of the level at which the system is desired to be understood.

Model validation is a critical quality control step that endorses the results obtained through simulation of the model. Typical model validation involves the comparison of model predictions against known biochemical and genetic evidences obtained by various experiments, particularly when experimental data has not been used for tuning the models.

Key Properties of Biological Systems

Biological systems are characterised by several key properties, which distinguish them from models in other disciplines. Knowledge of these fundamental principles, which characterise biological systems, is important both for understanding their function and for modelling them. Some of these interesting properties are discussed.

Irreducibility

Irreducibility is an important concept that makes systems thinking important. We may undoubtedly gain significant insight into each of the components of the system by studying them individually, but we will require to study the system as a whole in order to gain a holistic perspective of what these components do when they are all put together in an appropriate manner. An analogy to a book is often drawn, where one cannot understand a book by reading one word at a time. In other words, knowing the meaning of every word in a book does not tell us what the book is about. They have to be placed in context to grasp the story in the book. It is this context that is sought out in systems biology; thus it is not only the form and function of individual molecules, but rather their functional orchestration in a 'context' in a complex manner that makes a living species.

Emergence

Systems are composed of individual elements or 'parts' that interact in various ways. As Anderson put it as early as 1972, in his classic paper by the same title, "More is different" it is not possible to reliably predict the behaviour of a complex system, despite a good knowledge of the fundamental laws governing the individual components.

The ability to reduce everything to simple fundamental laws does not imply the ability to start from those laws and reconstruct the universe. The constructionist hypothesis breaks down when confronted with the twin difficulties of scale and complexity. At each level of complexity entirely new properties appear. Psychology is not applied biology, nor is biology applied chemistry. We can now see that the whole becomes not merely more, but very different from the sum of its parts.

This reinforces the need to develop methods to study biological systems at the systems level, rather than at the level of individual components.

Complexity

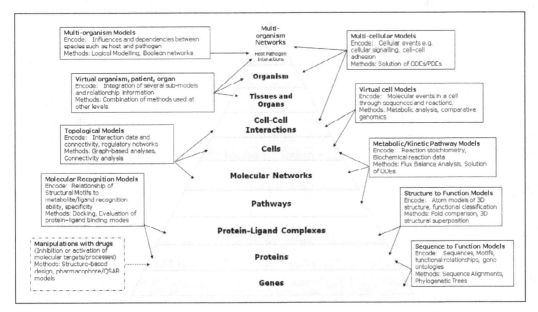

Levels of hierarchies for understanding and modelling biological systems. The figure illustrates different types of models that are appropriate at a given level of hierarchy. Theinformationthey encode (abstraction level) are listed for each of them as also the methods that are in current practice to design, build and analyse the models.

The term complexity, a concept linked to the concept of systems itself, is often used in a variety of disciplines to characterise a system with a number of components intricately linked to each other, giving rise to behaviours that may not be described by simple models. Emergent behaviour is one of the most fundamental features of complex systems. Health or disease are examples of complex systems. These cannot be predicted simply by analyzing the individual ligands or proteins that comprise the cells. A more complete picture of their context would be necessary to achieve it. Biological systems, needless to say, are extraordinarily complex, which is evident in individual prokaryotic cells, let alone multi-cellular organisms. For example an E. coli cell has about 4500 genes coding for at least as many proteins. At the outset, trying to understand how these many proteins embedded in less than femtolitre (10–15 L) of volume, perform together to enable the many functions of the E. coli cell appears to be a daunting task. However, we can understand many aspects of the cell if we divide complexity in hierarchies and then focus on understanding each individual level in a stepwise manner and then re-assimilate them in an appropriate context. In other words, understanding how, at the bottom of the hierarchy, DNA, proteins and metabolites function in individual cells, helps us to understand how different proteins give rise to pathways, how pathways come together to form processes, and how these are organised in a functional cell. In higher organisms, we would extend this to understanding how different cell types are formed and organised in tissues, how tissues make complex organs, and finally, how many different organs are orchestrated in the top hierarchical level, the organism. However, amidst this complexity, there is modularity with many common mechanisms for a range of biological events. Different cell types and functions use recurrent basic mechanisms of organisation and communication; thus common patterns underlie diverse expressions of life. Understanding single cell types, even when the organisms containing them are evolutionarily distant, such as bacteria and humans, would inevitably provide enormous amount of information to understand other cell types. Complexity has important implications for modelling; the complexity of large systems often makes them intractable for analyses. Therefore, large systems are often broken down into their constituent modules, or sub-systems, which are more amenable for analyses.

Modularity

Modules constitute semi-autonomous entities with dense internal functional connections and relatively looser external connections with their environment. Modularity or the encapsulation of functions, can contribute to both robustness (by confinement of damage) and to evolvability (by rewiring of modules for new functionality). An obvious example of a module is a cell in a multi-cellular organism, which interacts with both the environment and other cells. Modules are also commonly organised in a hierarchical fashion: a cell is composed of organelles, while also being a part of higher structures such as tissues and organs. At a different level, a signal transduction systemis an extended module that achieves isolation on account of the specificity of the binding of chemical signals to receptor proteins as well as the specificity of the interactions between the signalling proteins within the cell.

Robustness and Fragility

internal or external. No system can be robust to all kinds of perturbations. Robustness in biological systems is achieved using several complex mechanisms involvingfeedback, alternative (fail-safe) mechanisms featuring redundancy and diversity (heterogeneity), structuring of complex systems into semi-autonomous functional units (modularity), and their reliable co-ordination via establishment of hierarchies and protocols. Sensitivity or fragility, however, characterises the ability of organisms to respond adequately to a stimulus. Robustness and fragility have been described in the literature as inseparable; the 'robust, yet fragile' nature of complex systems is thought to exhibit 'highly optimised tolerance'.

Complex engineered systems (and biological systems) are often quite resistant to designed-for uncertainties, but quite susceptible to other perturbations. For example, modern aeroplanes, vis-à-vis the Wright brothers' aeroplane, are quite stable to atmospheric perturbations, but are fundamentally sensitive to complete electrical failure, due to the tight dependence of the control on a wide variety of electrical systems. Several biological systems are quite sensitive to what may be quantitatively small perturbations. There are several examples of networks which exhibit high insensitivity to attacks on nodes in random, but high sensitivity showing high disruption when there is a targeted attack on a few highly connected (hub) nodes.

Practice of Systems Biology

A variety of modelling techniques encompassing a wide spectrum of resolution and accuracy are used. Figure shows some of these methods, also indicating the level of detail that the method usually deals with. The levels of biological organisational hierarchy at which such methods can be used have already been illustrated in figure.

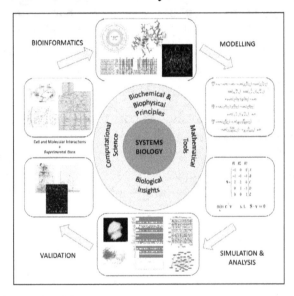

An overview of modelling in systems biology. This figure illustrates the various components of the systems biology modelling cycle, of how various types of experimental data are translated to a mathematical model, followed by simulation. The simulation results are then used to infer predictions (system behaviour), which are often compared against experimental results, leading to further improvements to the mathematical model.

At the highest level of resolution, there are atomistic models, followed by molecular recognition models, incorporating details at the lowest atomic level. These are followed by mechanistic models of molecular networks, which are usually realised using differential equations detailing kinetic parameters and stochastic modelling, to account for inherent noise in biochemical systems. At a lower level of resolution are the constraint-based modelling techniques such as flux balance analysis (FBA) and stoichiometric analyses, which rely more on global properties of networks, such as stoichiometry and mass conservation, rather than the intricate kinetic parameters.

Boolean networks thrive with lesser data, where interactions between network components are represented by means of Boolean functions such as 'OR', 'AND', 'AND NOT' and so on. Such discrete modelling techniques have applications in several areas.

Topological analyses of networks, which are constructed predominantly based on knowledge of association or causality, can also provide interesting insights into the organisation and properties of biological systems. At a further lower level of resolution are Bayesian networks and other statistical learning models, as well as qualitative models of biological systems.

The choice of methods for modelling and simulation is predominantly determined by the quality and quantity of data that are available, as well as the desired objective of the modelling exercise. When well-characterised kinetic parameters are available for a set of reactions in a given pathway, a kinetic model consisting of differential equations describing the rate of change of concentration of each of the metabolites can be constructed. Such a system of equations can then be solved to obtain insights about the essentiality of each component. For example, a mathematical model of glycolysis in T. brucei has been built, based on in vitro enzyme kinetic data.

When kinetic parameters are not available, constraint-based models of reaction networks can be constructed and analysed, obtaining insights into the metabolic capabilities of systems as well as gene essentiality. At a lower level of resolution, interaction networks of metabolites or more importantly, proteins, can be constructed and analysed, obtaining fundamental insights into centrality, and consequently lethality (or essentiality).

Kinetic Modelling

Typically, ordinary differential equations (ODEs) are used for this purpose. ODE-based simulations involve a mechanistic representation of the reaction network, with all the involved association/dissociation constants, rate constants and affinities or appropriate approximations. Since such data is not always available, this method has limited applicability. Biochemical reactions are regularly represented by differential equations that indicate the rate of consumption and production of various species involved in the reactions. The system of differential equations so generated can be solved and the system can be simulated. An important caveat is that even where kinetic parameters are available, they have often been determined in vitro, rather than in vivo, which again significantly impacts the accuracy of simulations.

Constraint-based Modelling

Kinetic data available for the simulation of networks are quite scarce, rendering the kinetic modelling of metabolic networks a challenging task. An approach used often to overcome the limitation of data, is to add appropriate 'constraints' on the systems, so as to make it feasible to find meaningful solutions. Constraints are generally in the form of rules, which define the upper and lower limits of the acceptable values for a given variable or in the form of some well-known laws of chemistry that must be upheld while solving for the system. Constraint-based analyses of reconstructed metabolic networks have proved to be quite effective in various applications such as metabolic engineering, prediction of outcomes of gene deletions, and in the elucidation of cellular regulatory networks.

One specific example of metabolic modelling using a constraint-based approach is Flux-Balance Analysis (FBA), which uses linear optimisation to determine the steady-state reaction flux distribution in a metabolic network by maximising an objective function, such as ATP production or growth rate. FBA involves carrying out a steady state analysis, using the stoichiometric matrix for the system in question. An important assumption is that the cell performs optimally with respect to a metabolic function, such as maximisation of biomass production or minimisation of nutrient utilisation, on the premise that selection pressures during evolution, guide systems towards optimality. Once an objective function is fixed, the system of equations can be solved to obtain a steady state flux distribution. This flux distribution is then used to interpret the metabolic capabilities of the system.

FBA has the capabilities to address the effects of gene deletions and other types of perturbations on the system. Gene deletion studies can be performed by constraining the reaction flux(es) corresponding to the gene(s) (and therefore, of their corresponding proteins(s)), to zero. Effects of inhibitors of particular proteins can also be studied in a similar way, by constraining the upper bounds of their fluxes to any defined fraction of the normal flux, corresponding to the extents of inhibition. FBA gives a general idea of the metabolic capabilities of an organism; gene deletion studies using FBA yield information on the criticality of genes for the growth/survival of an organism. The analysis of perturbations using flux balance models of metabolic networks provides a handle to analyse the lethality of individual gene deletions, as well as double knock-outs, to identify pairs of genes that are indispensable, as well as to determine and analyse synthetic genetic interactions.

Pathway Models

A pathway model is the lowest level of abstraction in systembased models. It looks at only the reactions in the metabolome of an organism and accounts for several of the interactions between the gene products of an organism and its metabolites. However, this is a significant improvement on the mere sequence data that is often employed for modelling and analysis. Several paradigms exist for pathway modelling and they are reviewed in the literature. Based on the availability of data, a suitable paradigm can be chosen for modelling; this affects the accuracy of the simulations performed on the systems. Some examples of the use of pathway models are illustrated in later sections.

Network-based Analysis

Barabási and Oltvai have shown that tools from network theory may be adapted to biology, providing profound insights into cellular organisation and evolution. Hubs which are heavily connected components in a graph may be identified and targeted to 'knock out' a system. In a typical interaction-based modelling of metabolic pathways, connections between the various proteins and metabolites in a system are obtained. When further analysed, specific hubs emerge to be more connected. These hubs may serve as interesting targets as they have the potential to affect several other connections in the system. The advantage of interaction-based modelling is that the amount of data required is relatively less and it is possible to generate interaction networks from existing databases. There is a need for more such derived databases, which would be of immense use in applications such as drug discovery.

Promise of Systems Biology

Systems biology finds application in several fields, including metabolic engineering and drug discovery. It has an immense potential to improve our fundamental understanding of biological systems. Biology has itself immensely benefited from building on the study of 'model' organisms such as Arabidopsis thaliana, Drosophila melanogaster, C. elegans and Escherichia coli. Systems approaches have been successfully applied for the study of model organisms such as Escherichia coli, where the metabolic capabilities have been predicted in silico and verified experimentally. Systems-level studies of organisms such as S. cerevisiae are expected to significantly impact the study of more complex organisms such as humans.

An excellent application of systems biology in metabolic engineering, with commercial potential, has been illustrated by Stephanopoulos and co-workers, for improving lysine production. Stephanopoulos and co-workers have also reported a genome-wide FBA of Escherichia coli to discover putative genes impacting network properties and cellular phenotype, for reengineering lycopene synthesis. Metabolic fluxes were calculated such as to optimise growth, followed by scanning the genome for single and multiple gene knockouts that yield improved product yield while maintaining acceptable overall growth rate. For lycopene biosynthesis in Escherichia coli, such targets were identified and subsequently tested experimentally by constructing the corresponding single, double and triple gene knockouts. A triple knockout construct ($\Delta gdhA\Delta aceA\Delta fdhF$) was identified, which exhibited a 37% increase over an engineered, high producing parental strain.

Another field where excellent progress has been made is in the modelling of the heart as a virtual organ, at various levels. Models of different cell types in the heart have led to the creation of the first virtual organ, which is being used in drug discovery and testing and in simulating the action of devices such as cardiac defibrillators. The culmination of systems modelling lies in the modelling of complete systems, accounting for all component reactions, the localisation of these components and their interactions. The interaction between these organelles or compartments and the interface with the physical world, in terms of external temperature, pH and other effects becomes more relevant in highest levels of biological hierarchy. Computational models of human physiology come into play both to relate to whole animal models used in traditional pharmacology and more importantly, to build integrated data-driven models that can be refined to mimic the human physiology more closely.

The IUPS Physiome project is a project that is aimed at describing the human organism quantitatively, to understand key elements of physiology and pathophysiology. The salient features of the project are the databasing of physiological, pharmacological and pathological information on humans and other organisms and integration through computational modelling. The models span a wide range, from diagrammatic schema suggesting relationships among system components, to fully quantitative computational models describing the behaviour of physiological systems and response of an organism to environmental change. Each mathematical model is an internally self-consistent summaryofavailable information and thereby defines a working hypothesis about how a system operates. Predictions from such models are subject to tests, with new results leading to new models. The goal is to understand the behaviour of complex biological systems through a step-by-step process of building upon and refining existing knowledge.

Efforts are underway to extend these concepts further to virtual patients. Entelos' has developed models of human physiology that supplement animal model systems. For example, Entelos' Diabetes PhysioLab has more than 60 virtual patients, each one representing a hypothesis of the pathophysiology of diabetes, constrained by the pathway networks and consistent with validation experiments. Such models have the potential for performing patient profiling, classifying patient types and even to tailor-design treatment regimes, with a long-term goal of making personalised medicine, a reality.

The possibility of drug discovery based on systems biology is exciting – it holds promise for the discovery of more efficacious drugs with fewer adverse effects. Often, adverse drug reactions might emerge on account of the binding of the drug to proteins other than the intended targets. By considering larger systems and accounting for such possibilities, it is possible that such problems may be identified by in silico analyses. It is envisaged that the complete understanding of a system in terms of all the components present and their complex interaction network would assist in discovering the ideal drug, which has high specificity and effectiveness.

Biochemical Systems Theory

Biochemical systems theory is a mathematical modelling framework for biochemical systems, based on ordinary differential equations (ODE), in which biochemical processes are represented using power-law expansions in the variables of the system.

This framework, which became known as Biochemical Systems Theory, has been developed since the 1960s by Michael Savageau, Eberhard Voit and others for the systems analysis of biochemical processes. According to Cornish-Bowden (2007) they "regarded this as a general theory of metabolic control, which includes both metabolic control analysis and flux-oriented theory as special cases".

Representation

The dynamics of a species is represented by a differential equation with the structure:

$$\frac{dX_i}{dt} = \sum_j \mu_{ij} \cdot \gamma_j \prod_k X_k^{f_{jk}}$$

where X_i represents one of the n_d variables of the model (metabolite concentrations, protein concentrations or levels of gene expression). j represents the n_f biochemical processes affecting the dynamics of the species. On the other hand, μ_{ij} (stoichiometric coefficient), γ_j (rate constants) and f_{jk} (kinetic orders) are two different kinds of parameters defining the dynamics of the system.

The principal difference of power-law models with respect to other ODE models used in biochemical systems is that the kinetic orders can be non-integer numbers. A kinetic order can have even negative value when inhibition is modeled. In this way, power-law models have a higher flexibility to reproduce the non-linearity of biochemical systems.

Models using power-law expansions have been used during the last 35 years to model and analyze several kinds of biochemical systems including metabolic networks, genetic networks and recently in cell signalling.

Biological Network Inference

Biological network inference is the process of making inferences and predictions about biological networks and a network is a set of nodes and a set of directed or undirected edges between the nodes. Many types of biological networks exist, including transcriptional, signalling and metabolic. Few such networks are known in anything approaching their complete structure, even in the simplest bacteria. Still less is known on the parameters governing the behavior of such networks over time, how the networks at different levels in a cell interact, and how to predict the complete state description of a eukaryotic cell or bacterial organism at a given point in the future. Systems biology, in this sense, is still in its infancy.

There is great interest in network medicine for the modelling biological systems.

methods using high-throughput data for inference of regulatory networks rely on searching for patterns of partial correlation or conditional probabilities that indicate causal influence. Such patterns of partial correlations found in the high-throughput data, possibly combined with other supplemental data on the genes or proteins in the proposed networks, or combined with other information on the organism, form the basis upon which such algorithms work. Such algorithms can be of use in inferring the topology of any network where the change in state of one node can affect the state of other nodes.

Transcriptional Regulatory Networks

Genes are the nodes and the edges are directed. A gene serves as the source of a direct regulatory edge to a target gene by producing an RNA or protein molecule that functions as a transcriptional activator or inhibitor of the target gene. If the gene is an activator, then it is the source of a positive regulatory connection; if an inhibitor, then it is the source of a negative regulatory connection. Computational algorithms take as primary input data measurements of mRNA expression levels of the genes under consideration for inclusion in the network, returning an estimate of the network topology. Such algorithms are typically based on linearity, independence or normality assumptions, which must be verified on a case-by-case basis. Clustering or some form of statistical classification is typically employed to perform an initial organization of the high-throughput mRNA expression values derived from microarray experiments, in particular to select sets of genes as candidates for network nodes. The question then arises: how can the clustering or classification results be connected to the underlying biology? Such results can be useful for pattern classification – for example, to classify subtypes of cancer, or to predict differential responses to a drug (pharmacogenomics). But to understand the relationships between the genes, that is, to more precisely define the influence of each gene on the others, the scientist typically attempts to reconstruct the transcriptional regulatory network. This can be done by data integration in dynamic models supported by background literature, or information in public databases, combined with the clustering results. The modelling can be done by a Boolean network, by Ordinary differential equations or Linear regression models, e.g. Least-angle regression, by Bayesian network or based on Information theory approaches. For instance it can be done by the application of a correlation-based inference algorithm,an approach which is having increased success as the size of the available microarray sets keeps increasing.

Signal Transduction

Signal transduction networks (very important in the biology of cancer). Proteins are the nodes and directed edges represent interaction in which the biochemical conformation of the child is modified by the action of the parent (e.g. mediated by phosphorylation, ubiquitylation, methylation, etc.). Primary input into the inference algorithm would be data from a set of experiments measuring protein activation/inactivation (e.g., phosphorylation/dephosphorylation) across a set of proteins. Inference for such signalling networks is complicated by the fact that total concentrations of signalling proteins will fluctuate over time due to transcriptional and translational regulation. Such variation can lead to statistical confounding. Accordingly, more sophisticated statistical techniques must be applied to analyse such datasets.

Metabolic

Metabolite networks. Metabolites are the nodes and the edges are directed. Primary input into an algorithm would be data from a set of experiments measuring metabolite levels.

Protein-protein Interaction

Protein-protein interaction networks are also under very active study. However, reconstruction of these networks does not use correlation-based inference in the sense discussed for the networks already described (interaction does not necessarily imply a change in protein state).

BioPAX

BioPAX (Biological Pathway Exchange) is a RDF/OWL-based standard language to represent biological pathways at the molecular and cellular level. Its major use is to facilitate the exchange of pathway data. Pathway data captures our understanding of biological processes, but its rapid growth necessitates development of databases and computational tools to aid interpretation. However, the current fragmentation of pathway information across many databases with incompatible formats presents barriers to its effective use. BioPAX solves this problem by making pathway data substantially easier to collect, index, interpret and share. BioPAX can represent metabolic and signaling pathways, molecular and genetic interactions and gene regulation networks. BioPAX was created through a community process. Through BioPAX, millions of interactions organized into thousands of pathways across many organisms, from a growing number of sources, are available. Thus, large amounts of pathway data are available in a computable form to support visualization, analysis and biological discovery.

It is supported by a variety of online databases (e.g. Reactome) and tools. The latest released version is BioPAX Level 3. There is also an effort to create a version of BioPAX as part of OBO.

Governance and Development

The next version of BioPAX, Level 4, is being developed by a community of researchers.

Development is coordinated by board of editors and facilitated by various BioPAX work groups.

Systems Biology Pathway Exchange (SBPAX) is an extension for Level 3 and proposal for Level 4 to add quantitative data and systems biology terms (such as Systems Biology Ontology). SBPAX export has been implemented by the pathway databases Signaling Gateway Molecule Pages and the SABIO-Reaction Kinetics Database. SBPAX import has been implemented by the cellular modelling framework Virtual Cell.

Other proposals for Level 4 include improved support for Semantic Web, validation and visualization.

Software

Software supporting BioPAX include:

- Paxtools, a Java API for handling BioPAX files.

- Systems Biology Linker (Sybil), an application for visualizing BioPAX and converting BioPAX to SBML, as part of the Virtual Cell.

- ChiBE (Chisio BioPAX Editor), an application for visualizing and editing BioPAX.

- BioPAX Validator - syntax and semantic rules and best practices.

- Cytoscape includes a BioPAX reader and other extensions, such as Pathway-Commons plugin and CyPath2 app.

- BiNoM, a cytoscape plugin for network analysis, with functions to import and export BioPAX level 3 files.

- BioPAX-pattern, a Java API for defining and searching graph patterns in Bio-PAX files.

Cellular Model

Creating a cellular model has been a particularly challenging task of systems biology and mathematical biology. It involves developing efficient algorithms, data structures, visualization and communication tools to orchestrate the integration of large quantities of biological data with the goal of computer modelling.

It is also directly associated with bioinformatics, computational biology and Artificial life. It involves the use of computer simulations of the many cellular subsystems such as the networks of metabolites and enzymes which comprise metabolism, signal transduction pathways and gene regulatory networks to both analyze and visualize the complex connections of these cellular processes.

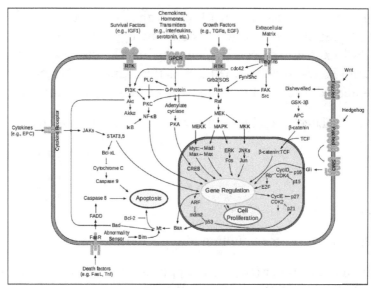

Part of the cell cycle.

The complex network of biochemical reaction/transport processes and their spatial organization make the development of a predictive model of a living cell a grand challenge for the 21st century.

The eukaryotic cell cycle is very complex and is one of the most studied topics, since its misregulation leads to cancers. It is possibly a good example of a mathematical model as it deals with simple calculus but gives valid results. Two research groups have produced several models of the cell cycle simulating several organisms. They have recently produced a generic eukaryotic cell cycle model which can represent a particular eukaryote depending on the values of the parameters, demonstrating that the idiosyncrasies of the individual cell cycles are due to different protein concentrations and affinities, while the underlying mechanisms are conserved.

By means of a system of ordinary differential equations these models show the change in time (dynamical system) of the protein inside a single typical cell; this type of model is called a deterministic process (whereas a model describing a statistical distribution of protein concentrations in a population of cells is called a stochastic process).

To obtain these equations an iterative series of steps must be done: first the several models and observations are combined to form a consensus diagram and the appropriate kinetic laws are chosen to write the differential equations, such as rate kinetics for stoichiometric reactions, Michaelis-Menten kinetics for enzyme substrate reactions and Goldbeter–Koshland kinetics for ultrasensitive transcription factors, afterwards the parameters of the equations (rate constants, enzyme efficiency coefficients and Michaelis constants) must be fitted to match observations; when they cannot be fitted the kinetic equation is revised and when that is not possible the wiring diagram is modified. The parameters are fitted and validated using observations of both wild type and mutants, such as protein half-life and cell size.

In order to fit the parameters the differential equations need to be studied. This can be done either by simulation or by analysis.

In a simulation, given a starting vector (list of the values of the variables), the progression of the system is calculated by solving the equations at each time-frame in small increments.

In analysis, the properties of the equations are used to investigate the behavior of the system depending of the values of the parameters and variables. A system of differential equations can be represented as a vector field, where each vector described the change (in concentration of two or more protein) determining where and how fast the trajectory (simulation) is heading. Vector fields can have several special points: a stable point, called a sink, that attracts in all directions (forcing the concentrations to be at a certain value), an unstable point, either a source or a saddle point which repels (forcing the concentrations to change away from a certain value), and a limit cycle, a closed trajectory towards which several trajectories spiral towards (making the concentrations oscillate).

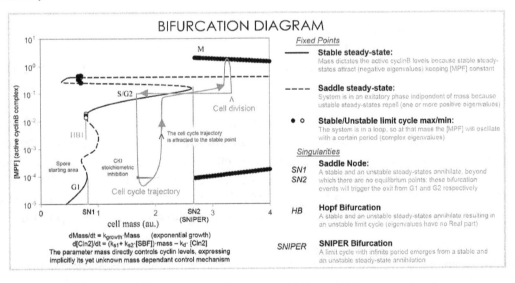

A better representation which can handle the large number of variables and parameters is called a bifurcation diagram (bifurcation theory): the presence of these special steady-state points at certain values of a parameter (e.g. mass) is represented by a point and once the parameter passes a certain value, a qualitative change occurs, called a bifurcation, in which the nature of the space changes, with profound consequences for the protein concentrations: the cell cycle has phases (partially corresponding to G1 and G2) in which mass, via a stable point, controls cyclin levels, and phases (S and M phases) in which the concentrations change independently, but once the phase has changed at a bifurcation event (cell cycle checkpoint), the system cannot go back to the previous levels since at the current mass the vector field is profoundly different and the mass cannot be reversed back through the bifurcation event, making a checkpoint irreversible. In particular the S and M checkpoints are regulated by means of special bifurcations called a Hopf bifurcation and an infinite period bifurcation.

Molecular Level Simulations

Cell Collective is a modelling software that enables one to house dynamical biological data, build computational models, stimulate, break and recreate models. The development is led by Tomas Helikar, a researcher within the field of computational biology. It is designed for biologists, students learning about computational biology, teachers focused on teaching life sciences, and researchers within the field of life science. The complexities of math and computer science are built into the backend and one can learn about the methods used for modelling biological species, but complex math equations, algorithms, programming are not required and hence won't impede model building.

The mathematical framework behind Cell Collective is based on a common qualitative (discrete) modelling technique where the regulatory mechanism of each node is described with a logical function.

Model validation The model was constructed using local (e.g., protein–protein interaction) information from the primary literature. In other words, during the construction phase of the model, there was no attempt to determine the local interactions based on any other larger phenotypes or phenomena. However, after the model was completed, verification of the accuracy of the model involved testing it for the ability to reproduce complex input–output phenomena that have been observed in the laboratory. To do this, the T-cell model was simulated under a multitude of cellular conditions and analyzed in terms of input–output dose–response curves to determine whether the model behaves as expected, including various downstream effects as a result of activation of the TCR, G-protein-coupled receptor, cytokine, and integrin pathways. The E-Cell Project aims "to make precise whole cell simulation at the molecular level possible".

CytoSolve - developed by V. A. Shiva Ayyadurai and C. Forbes Dewey Jr. of Department of Biological Engineering at the Massachusetts Institute of Technology - provided a method to model the whole cell by dynamically integrating multiple molecular pathway models.

In the July 2012 issue of Cell, a team led by Markus Covert at Stanford published the most complete computational model of a cell to date. The model of the roughly 500-gene Mycoplasma genitalium contains 28 algorithmically-independent components incorporating work from over 900 sources. It accounts for interactions of the complete genome, transcriptome, proteome, and metabolome of the organism, marking a significant advancement for the field.

Most attempts at modelling cell cycle processes have focused on the broad, complicated molecular interactions of many different chemicals, including several cyclin and
cyclin-dependent kinase molecules as they correspond to the S, M, G1 and G2 phases
of the cell cycle. Virginia Tech and Institute de Génétique et Développement de Rennes
produced a simplified model of the cell cycle using only one cyclin/CDK interaction.
This model showed the ability to control totally functional cell division through regulation and manipulation only the one interaction, and even allowed researchers to skip
phases through varying the concentration of CDK. This model could help understand
how the relatively simple interactions of one chemical translate to a cellular level model
of cell division.

Cancer Systems Biology

Cancer systems biology (CSB) recognizes that many individual disciplines and data
types can be usefully brought to bear, alone or in combination, to systematically study
cancer. The diversity of interactions among cancer systems biologists, who come from
fields such as cancer biology, biochemistry, bioinformatics, engineering, mathematics,
physics, and computer science, can lead to novel approaches to the fundamental challenges within the field of cancer research. The inaugural Systems Approaches to Cancer
Biology Conference highlighted the important biological insights gained through these
synergistic interactions and discussed the unique challenges faced by multidisciplinary
investigators. The meeting was organized and purposefully populated by mostly early
career tenure-track and junior investigators in training, offering a unique perspective
on the emerging field of cancer systems biology.

Central to the meeting was the question of what exactly constitutes CSB, especially in
comparison to quantitative or computational work within other fields. Through the diversity of approaches discussed, it became clear that the field is not defined by a particular set of methods, nor simply by the application of computational methods to cancer
data. Rather, the field is defined by a recognition that cancer is a dynamic, multifacto-
rial, and complex process that must be understood using both experimental methods
and analytical approaches that bridge traditional disciplinary boundaries to directly
address these concomitant challenges.

Embracing Cancer's Complexity

In his opening remarks to the meeting, Douglas Lauffenburger made the observation
that CSB is a field for those who actively embrace the complexity of biology. A central
component of this complexity, the heterogeneity of cancer within and across patients,
is undeniably a barrier to accurate diagnosis and treatment. CSB is uniquely poised to
address this heterogeneity through application of computational analyses that glean
insights from preclinical and clinical datasets. For example, Andrea Bild presented on

the striking temporal evolution of tumor heterogeneity measured by whole-genome sequencing in an individual breast cancer patient during the course of their various treatment regimens. Her study underscored the necessity of understanding subclonal evolution within a single patient and how this might influence treatment options and decisions. In a related longitudinal genomic and transcriptomic analysis of patients with glioblastoma, Jiguang Wang reported that upon treatment, many patients experience a loss of the dominant driver mutation but gain many novel mutations at relapse that change their disease subtype. Wendy Fantl showed that intra- and intertumoral heterogeneity is also reflected at the protein level and that increased tumor cell diversity measured with mass cytometry (CyTOF) is related to aggressive disease in ovarian cancer. As this and other single-cell studies are finding, the persistence of intratumor heterogeneity makes it important to develop analytical and experimental tools that can predict the best treatment options. John Paul Shen demonstrated that yeast can be used as a model system for identifying synthetic lethalities between inactivated tumor suppressor genes and genes that encode druggable proteins. Laura Heiser compared -omics data from a panel of breast cancer cell lines against publicly available molecular profiling data from primary tumors in The Cancer Genome Atlas to identify conserved pathways and gene sets recurrently aberrant in different breast cancer subtypes. She described how the cell lines recapitulate major subtypes of breast cancer and can be used to identify distinct therapeutic vulnerabilities across subsets of the cell lines. Coupling the knowledge gained from profiling tumor heterogeneity with an arsenal of computationally predicted treatment options may lead to the realization of precision cancer treatments.

CSB is driving numerous technological developments to better study the complex and dynamic nature of cancer. Frank Stegmeier (KSQ Therapeutics) compared large-scale shRNA-mediated knockdown to CRISPR-CAS9 knockout technology, highlighting the benefits and drawbacks of both approaches. CRISPR-based knockout screens identified more synthetic lethal genes compared with RNAi across a panel of cancer cell lines, implying that the identification of cellular dependencies may require full gene inactivation. On a related topic, Kevin Janes presented an elegant mathematical model illustrating that the network perturbation effects of gene knockdown versus chemical inhibition of protein activity encoded by the same gene can be vastly different. The difference in effect depended intimately on the network context of the molecule and was nonlinearly related to the extent of gene knockdown. New experimental systems were described by Yvonne Chen, who described the systems-level design and synthetic biology implementation of an 'OR-gate' T-cell receptor intended to target heterogeneous tumor populations and prevent drug resistance caused by tumor cell antigen loss, and Shelly Peyton, who presented an in vitro biomaterial platform that enabled systematic comparison of various microenvironments as sites for potential metastases. These novel experimental approaches will fuel the collection of robust and reproducible data sets that can then be coupled with computational analysis to provide an essential step forward toward systems-level understanding of the complex tumor ecosystem.

Computational tools can aid in understanding the complexity of cancer by integrating new datasets with prior knowledge. Ben Raphael described the HotNet2 algorithm, which integrates cancer mutational data with known protein interactions. His group's analysis demonstrated that while there are only a relatively small number of bona fide cancer driver mutations, many lower incidence mutations cluster within signaling pathways that may provide mechanistic insight to their role in progression. Indeed, the phenotypic consequence of most detectable mutations is unknown. To this end, Pau Creixell (MIT) suggested that in the case of protein kinases, our understanding of individual cancers might be aided by characterizing the specific functional consequences of somatic mutations. By analyzing the exomes and phospho proteomes of ovarian cancer cell lines using the ReKINect computational platform, he demonstrated that individual kinase mutations in cancer variously affect the activity and specificity of important mutated kinases. Taken together, the Raphael and Creixell studies suggested that integrating protein-level data with mutational information can be a powerful approach but that caution must be taken when assuming the consequence of a mutation with respect to protein activity. For example, in both studies, mutations were identified that were neither recurrent nor simply activating/inactivating, yet were functional through their network effects.

Reproducibility and Data Sharing

In some cases, the scale and complexity of systems-level studies make reproducibility a challenge, especially when connecting preclinical and clinical research. Executing reproducible research requires the ability to recapitulate data analysis and laboratory protocols. The development of software protocols has provided the means to automatically document analyses for purposes of reproducibility. For example, Ben Raphael showcased his network algorithms by providing direct links to the source code, available on GitHub, and making all data available on Synapse. Trey Ideker described NDEx, a new resource to facilitate the sharing of networks derived from biologic data to make these studies more reproducible. Data sharing is an essential part of recapitulating and building on prior work and thus is a critical aspect of reproducible research. Building new models from existing data can additionally lead to novel findings, as showcased in the meeting by Stacey Finley who presented a mathematical model to predict levels of angiogenic factors during tumor treatment, and Jorge Zanudo who presented a mathematical model to predict activated signaling pathways during the epithelial-to-mesenchymal transition in cancer. Each of these models relied on parameters from open data in publications that span years of research, scientific disciplines, and experimental systems. Many of the present works took advantage of open-access datasets such as ICGC or TCGA as well as more modestly sized datasets collected through collaborations or gleaned from the literature tailored to their studies. With this in mind, closing keynote speaker Gordon Mills dubbed the conference community the "Society for Data Parasites" in support of data sharing as a means to accelerate the study of cancer.

Clinical Translation and Collaborative Science

During his opening comments, Douglas Lauffenburger pointed out that the results of CSB must ultimately improve patient care. Toward this goal, the Systems Approaches to Cancer Biology meeting included a number of studies with a strong translational focus. Galit Lahav, the opening keynote speaker, showed how oscillating behavior in p53, a key tumor suppressor, can give rise to dynamic transcriptional and phenotypic behavior at the single-cell level that is often masked in bulk-population analyses. This has directly led to recommendations for timing of treatments involving DNA-damaging therapies such as cisplatin and radiation. Jiyang Yu (Pfizer) used an shRNA screen to identify HDAC6 as a potential target for inflammatory breast cancer. HDAC6 is not itself an oncogene in IBC, but Yu identified it as a key regulator of other genes involved in IBC proliferation. Mohammed Shahrok Espahani described cancer personalized profiling by deep sequencing (CAPP-seq), a method for targeted sequencing of circulating tumor DNA (ctDNA) that may enable "liquid biopsies" to track cancer progression. Raghu Kalluri showed that exosomes in fact can contain DNA and can provide ctDNA with reduced contamination from nontumor cells. The systems approaches taken in these studies yield clinical impact that go beyond what traditional studies based on single genomic mutations or amplification events can uncover.

Progress in translational research often depends on collecting multiple types of molecular data from the same tumor samples to enable comprehensive, systems-level studies. Early efforts to understand breast cancer at a systems level applied hierarchical clustering methods to gene expression data to identify clinically relevant subtypes. Anne-Lise Børresen-Dale described her team's efforts to extend this work, which went beyond clustering of transcriptomic data to also include other types of molecular data and to provide additional biologic insights about these breast cancer subtypes. Interestingly, this analysis identified different subtypes, depending on the measurement (e.g. mRNA levels, somatic mutations, etc.) used in the analysis. This observation that subtype clusters are not uniquely defined was further supported by Kevin Brennan who found that DNA methylation profiles segregate head and neck squamous cell carcinoma by etiologic factors.

To collect, analyze, and interpret multidimensional datasets, multi-institutional collaborations are often crucial. Over the past several decades, Børresen-Dale has helped assemble a large group of international collaborators to derive insights about the interplay among genomic, transcriptomic, proteomic, and metabolomic features in breast cancer. For example, they examined the transcriptional consequences of somatic mutations and found that tumor cells express these mutations more actively than stromal cells and that this relationship depends on estrogen receptor status. As noted by Gordon Mills, greater collaboration across institutions and between academia and industry should help accelerate clinical translation of CSB studies.

References

- Gérard, Claude; Tyson, John J.; Coudreuse, Damien; Novák, Béla (2015-02-06). "Cell Cycle Control by a Minimal Cdk Network". Plos Comput Biol. 11 (2): e1004056. Doi:10.1371/journal. pcbi.1004056. PMC 4319789. PMID 25658582

- Tieri P, Farina L, Petti M, Astolfi L, Paci P, Castiglione F (2018). "Network Inference and Reconstruction in Bioinformatics". Encyclopedia of Bioinformatics and Computational Biology. 2: 805–813. Doi:10.1016/B978-0-12-809633-8.20290-2

- Helikar T, Kowal B, Madrahimov A, Shrestha M, Pedersen J, Limbu K, et al. Bio-Logic Builder: a nontechnical tool for building dynamical, qualitative models. Plos One (2012) 7(10):e46417.10.1371/journal.pone.0046417

- Dinasarapu A.R; Saunders B; Ozerlat I; Azam K; Subramaniam S (2010). "Signaling Gateway Molecule Pages – a data model perspective". Bioinformatics. 27 (12): 1736–1738. Doi:10.1093/bioinformatics/btr190. PMC 3106186. PMID 21505029

- Banf, Michael; Rhee, Seung Y. (January 2017). "Computational inference of gene regulatory networks: Approaches, limitations and opportunities". Biochimica et Biophysica Acta (BBA) - Gene Regulatory Mechanisms. 1860(1): 41–52. Doi:10.1016/j.bbagrm.2016.09.003. ISSN 1874-9399

PERMISSIONS

All chapters in this book are published with permission under the Creative Commons Attribution Share Alike License or equivalent. Every chapter published in this book has been scrutinized by our experts. Their significance has been extensively debated. The topics covered herein carry significant information for a comprehensive understanding. They may even be implemented as practical applications or may be referred to as a beginning point for further studies.

We would like to thank the editorial team for lending their expertise to make the book truly unique. They have played a crucial role in the development of this book. Without their invaluable contributions this book wouldn't have been possible. They have made vital efforts to compile up to date information on the varied aspects of this subject to make this book a valuable addition to the collection of many professionals and students.

This book was conceptualized with the vision of imparting up-to-date and integrated information in this field. To ensure the same, a matchless editorial board was set up. Every individual on the board went through rigorous rounds of assessment to prove their worth. After which they invested a large part of their time researching and compiling the most relevant data for our readers.

The editorial board has been involved in producing this book since its inception. They have spent rigorous hours researching and exploring the diverse topics which have resulted in the successful publishing of this book. They have passed on their knowledge of decades through this book. To expedite this challenging task, the publisher supported the team at every step. A small team of assistant editors was also appointed to further simplify the editing procedure and attain best results for the readers.

Apart from the editorial board, the designing team has also invested a significant amount of their time in understanding the subject and creating the most relevant covers. They scrutinized every image to scout for the most suitable representation of the subject and create an appropriate cover for the book.

The publishing team has been an ardent support to the editorial, designing and production team. Their endless efforts to recruit the best for this project, has resulted in the accomplishment of this book. They are a veteran in the field of academics and their pool of knowledge is as vast as their experience in printing. Their expertise and guidance has proved useful at every step. Their uncompromising quality standards have made this book an exceptional effort. Their encouragement from time to time has been an inspiration for everyone.

The publisher and the editorial board hope that this book will prove to be a valuable piece of knowledge for students, practitioners and scholars across the globe.

INDEX

Printed in the USA
CPSIA information can be obtained
at www.ICGtesting.com
JSHW052018301024
72690JS00004B/113

9 781641 165587